Experiencing Human Resource Management

Experiencing Human Resource Management

edited by
Christopher Mabey
Denise Skinner
Timothy Clark

SAGE Publications
London • Thousand Oaks • New Delhi

First published 1998
Reprinted 1999

SAGE Publications Ltd
6 Bonhill Street
London EC2A 4PU

SAGE Publications Inc
2455 Teller Road
Thousand Oaks, California 91320

SAGE Publications India Pvt Ltd
32, M-Block Market
Greater Kailash – I
New Delhi 110 048

British Library Cataloguing in Publication Data

A catalogue record for this book is
available from the British Library

ISBN 0 7619 5116 4
ISBN 0 7619 5117 2 (pbk)

Library of Congress catalog record card number 97-062126

Typeset by M Rules
Printed in Great Britain by Biddles Ltd, www.Biddles.co.uk

Contents

List of editors and contributors vii
List of figures ix
List of tables x
Acknowledgements xi
Foreword by John Monks xiii

PART I INTRODUCTION

1 Experiencing HRM: the importance of the inside story 1
 Timothy Clark, Christopher Mabey and Denise Skinner

2 The morality of HRM 14
 Karen Legge

PART II QUALITY AND CULTURE CHANGE PROGRAMMES

3 Empowerment through quality management: employee
 accounts from inside a bank, a hotel and two factories 33
 Chris Rees

4 Total quality management: shop floor perspectives 54
 Linda Glover and Deborah Fitzgerald-Moore

5 Changing corporate culture: paradoxes and tensions
 in a local authority 73
 Graeme Martin, Phil Beaumont and Harry Staines

PART III THE PERCEIVED IMPACT OF HRM ON
PERFORMANCE AND PRODUCTIVITY

6 Training and development at an agrochemical plant 97
 Jason Heyes

7 View from the bridge and life on deck:
 contrasts and contradictions in performance-related pay 113
 Aisling Kelly and Kathy Monks

Contents

8 Culture change within a regional business network 129
   Julia Connell and Suzanne Ryan

PART IV HRM PROVIDING CHOICES AND OPPORTUNITIES

9 Strategic integration and industrial relations in greenfield
   sites 150
   Patrick Gunnigle and Michael Morley

10 From public sector employees to portfolio workers:
   pioneers of new careers? 169
   Mary Mallon

11 Diversity climates and gendered cultures: a cross sector
   analysis 187
   Paul Iles, Elisabeth Wilson and Deborah Hicks-Clarke

12 A trail of clues for graduate trainees 205
   Diane Preston and Cathy Hart

13 Inside or outside HRM? Lateral learning in two voluntary
   sector organizations 218
   Rona S. Beattie and Marilyn McDougall

PART V CONCLUSION

14 Getting the story straight 237
   Christopher Mabey, Timothy Clark and Denise Skinner

Index 245

Editors and Contributors

Editors

Christopher Mabey, Senior Lecturer and Head of Centre for Human Resource and Change Management at the Open University Business School

Denise Skinner, Senior Lecturer at Nene College of Higher Education; formerly Research Assistant, Open University Business School

Timothy Clark, Reader in Management, King's College, University of London; formerly Research Fellow in International Management at Open University Business School

Contributors

Rona S. Beattie, Lecturer in Human Resource Development at Glasgow Caledonian University

Phil Beaumont, Professor of Human Resource Management, Glasgow Business School, University of Glasgow

Julia Connell, Lecturer, Employment Studies Group, Department of Management, University of Newcastle, Australia

Linda Glover, Senior Lecturer in Human Resource Management, Leicester Business School, De Montfort University

Deborah Fitzgerald-Moore, Senior Lecturer in the Management School of Tourism and Hospitality Studies, Leeds Metropolitan University

Patrick Gunnigle, Professor of Business Studies and Director of the Employment Relations Research Unit, University of Limerick

Cathy Hart, Lecturer in Retailing and Operations Management, Loughborough University Business School

Jason Heyes, Lecturer in Industrial Relations, Leeds University Business School

Deborah Hicks-Clarke, PhD student at Liverpool Business School, researching climates for diversity

Paul Iles, Littlewoods Professor of Human Resource Development and Head of the Liverpool Centre for HRD at the Liverpool Business School, Liverpool John Moores University

Aisling Kelly, Researcher at Dublin City University Business School

Karen Legge, Professor, Department of Behaviour in Organizations, The Management School, Lancaster University

Mary Mallon, Researcher in Human Resource Management at Sheffield Hallam University

Graeme Martin, Director of the Dundee Business School, University of Abertay Dundee

Marilyn McDougall, Director of the Forum for Innovation and Enterprise at Glasgow Caledonian University

Kathy Monks, Senior Lecturer in HRM at Dublin City University Business School

Michael Morley, Lecturer in Human Resource Management and Industrial Relations, University of Limerick

Diane Preston, Lecturer in Human Resource Management, Open University Business School

Chris Rees, Lecturer, School of Human Resource Management, Kingston University

Suzanne Ryan, Lecturer, Employment Studies Group, Department of Management, University of Newcastle, Australia

Harry Staines, Senior Lecturer in Statistics, School of Information, University of Abertay Dundee

Elisabeth Wilson, Senior Lecturer in HRM at the Liverpool Business School, currently pursuing a PhD on gendered cultures

List of figures

Figure 2.1   Ford's ethnically mixed workforce of 1991 lost its
             colour when white faces were superimposed on
             black bodies for a new brochure   17
Figure 4.1   Factors influencing shop floor perceptions of TQM   69
Figure 13.1 Typology of peer mentoring relationships   222
Figure 13.2 Factors influencing peer mentoring   233

List of tables

Table 2.1   Sisson's model of rhetoric and reality in HRM   20
Table 4.1   TQM implementation within the case study plants   60
Table 5.1   The council's mission and values statement   80
Table 5.2   Assessment of the change programme: some key
            findings for the workforce as a whole   84
Table 5.3   Variation in responses within the workforce   85
Table 5.4   A comparison of the Housing Department survey results   86
Table 6.1   Pay relativities at Reaction's Agro plant   104
Table 7.1   First-ranked objectives of the scheme   119
Table 7.2   Drawbacks with the scheme ranked in order of
            importance   120
Table 7.3   Links between performance and pay   122
Table 7.4   Matrix correlation of individual effort and achievement   124
Table 8.1   Perceived change in workplace culture and non-culture
            dimensions in the previous 12-month period   138
Table 8.2   Significant differences between management and non-
            management towards culture and non-culture workplace
            dimensions   139
Table 9.1   Description of variables used to construct composite
            indicator of strategic integration in industrial relations   153
Table 9.2   Impact of industrial relations considerations on location
            decision by ownership   156
Table 9.3   Ownership and formal strategy development   157
Table 9.4   Impact of industrial relations considerations on business
            policy decisions by ownership   159
Table 9.5   Role of the personnel/industrial relations function by
            ownership   160
Table 9.6   Explaining strategic integration in industrial relations   162
Table 9.7   Levels of strategic integration in greenfield companies   164
Table 9.8   Composite strategic integration measure and constituent
            indicators   165
Table 13.1 Benefits of peer mentoring   231

Acknowledgements

Since its formation the Centre for Human Resource and Change Management at the Open University Business School has pursued the receiving end of HRM as a focal research agenda. The members of the Centre share a common concern to uncover the reality of change programmes and employee practices that go under the name of HRM. Our view is that the seldom heard voice of the recipients, those who cope with the practical consequences of HR initiatives and strategies on a daily basis, represents the reality of HRM as perceived by the majority of the workforce and as such should form a significant contribution to the ongoing debates.

To further raise the profile of this neglected yet crucial area we held a conference in April 1996 to provide a forum for those who were interested in, or who had undertaken, empirical work exploring the experience of the individual (at whatever level) on the receiving end of HR initiatives. We had an overwhelming response to the call for papers, suggesting that we had indeed struck a rich vein of interest. The chapters in this volume are taken from the 72 papers that the refereeing panel chose to be presented at the conference.

From all those who attended the conference and made it such a success, we would like to pick out a few for special thanks. We asked Professor Karen Legge to give the opening address, to 'light the blue touch-paper' for the conference as it were. This she did exceedingly well in our view, and for this reason we have chosen her paper to launch this book. In addition to the academic papers we were also pleased to have the input and support of a number of leading practitioners: Graham Mole, Director of HRD at Willis Caroon PLC, shared with us his perspective from the position of an HR policy-maker; Geoff Armstrong and John Monks participated in lively plenary sessions at pivotal points during the two days; and John Edmonds (General Secretary of the GMB) rounded things off with a robust and provocative union view of HR nostrums. We were also indebted to many academic colleagues from the Open University and other universities who ably chaired sessions in the four parallel tracks. Finally, but by no means least, we would like to thank Barbara Sinclair who excelled as conference administrator.

Christopher Mabey
Denise Skinner
Timothy Clark

Foreword

John Monks, TUC General Secretary

The modern business world is one in which there is constant pressure to achieve ever higher standards of performance. We are told that in the global market there is no place for complacency. In services as well as manufacturing the search is on to get more for less. As a result, in many workplaces the stress factor has gone through the roof. A whole new lexicon has been developed for what used to be called the sack. 'Downsizing' and 'restructuring' are just a couple of the terms which employees and their representatives have come to dread as employers seek to improve performance by reducing staff costs.

Yet alongside the competitive imperative we have seen the development of a management philosophy which can be summed up in the phrase 'our people are our greatest asset'. Human resource management is one of the practical manifestations of that philosophy. It is a wide-ranging if not particularly elegant phrase and its advocates would argue that HRM provides a way of marrying maximum output to maximum job satisfaction.

There is a mountain of literature showing how it can be done. From a trade union point of view the issues are both contentious and complex. Unions have a range of experiences and their general response to human resource management has depended very much on the circumstances in which the new management techniques have been introduced. Some employers have used the rhetoric of HRM to conceal a deliberate anti-union policy. They have sought to replace collective machinery with an individualized industrial relations. In our experience, far from enhancing the individual's involvement, the result is to leave employees less involved and less well informed. In the wrong hands HRM becomes both a sharp weapon to prise workers apart from their union, and a blunt instrument to bully employees.

On the other hand there are positive experiences of HRM techniques used by management, employees and their trade union representatives working together to create more positive arrangements which recognize each other's interests and which acknowledge a shared commitment to quality work, the importance of skills, and the need for change to be achieved by agreement. The TUC's study of HRM, conducted in 1994, concluded that more work was needed to ensure that the rhetoric of HRM matched the practice.

This collection takes that process a step further forward. The contributions look at HRM not from the perspective of the employer or potential employer, seeking ways of dealing with the human resource side of management, but rather from the perspective of the recipient – and even in some cases the victims – of HRM.

The case studies are wide and varied. They cover large and small companies, the public sector and the private sector too. They are not confined to the British experience either. Together they comprise a fascinating picture of HRM in practice, from which Christopher Mabey and his colleagues have been able to draw some perceptive conclusions.

These are changing times in British industrial relations. The Labour government, elected in May 1997, offers an approach based on partnership rather than conflict. We are promised, among other things, legislation introducing a minimum wage and before too long a law which stops employers refusing to recognize a union even where it enjoys the support of a majority of employees. These measures should alter the industrial relations climate for the better. Human resource management techniques can play a part in such developments. If they are to do so then there is a need to understand the techniques as they have been and are being applied in practice. These essays should help that process of understanding and will be of value to practitioners, employers and union representatives as well as to those whose interest in HRM is more academic.

Part I

INTRODUCTION

1

Experiencing HRM:
The Importance of the Inside Story

Timothy Clark, Christopher Mabey and Denise Skinner

As contemporary organizations attempt to become more competitive by responding to rapid discontinuities in their environments they are increasingly likely to be embarking on programmes of profound organizational change. In seeking to orchestrate such change, organizations have not been without offers of assistance. The last two decades have been littered with a steady stream of apparently highly attractive suggestions for remodelling businesses which cluster under the general banner of human resource management (HRM). These have included quality circles, theory Z, delayering, total quality management (TQM), corporate culture, excellence, lean production, business process re-engineering (BPR), the learning organization, and so forth. But what has been the experience of those who have been on the receiving end of these HR inspired initiatives? This book aims to provide some answers to this question.

Our purpose in this chapter is to set the scene for the rest of the book by arguing the importance of examining HRM from the perspective of those on the 'receiving end'. We begin by outlining a number of reasons for the lack of focus on the inside story in HRM, locating these primarily in the managerialist orientation of HRM. Following this we outline the case for the inside view of HRM. Finally, we detail the structure of the book.

The managerialist orientation of HRM

There are some literatures which give a great deal of prominence to the individual perspective. One thinks of such 'classic' studies as Whyte's *Street Corner Society* (1955), Festinger et al.'s *When Prophecy Fails* (1956) and Roy's study of the machine shop (1954) which all helped to usher in a genre of insider stories to their respective discourses. Then, of course, we have whole disciplines, such as social anthropology, which are predicated upon the ethnographic account gleaned from those on the 'inside'. Also in the field of industrial relations, whilst there has been a recent tendency towards large-scale surveys (e.g. WIRS, see Millard et al., 1993), there is still a strong tradition of ethnographic and other intensive methods which elevate the voice of the individual employee (see McCarthy, 1994). Sadly, analysis of HRM from the viewpoint of those on the receiving end has to date been the exception rather than the rule in the HR literature.[1] As Karen Legge points out in Chapter 2, there has been a tendency in the HRM literature to focus on reporting the voice of management – the initiators and implementers of change. In this chapter we outline a number of possible reasons for this managerialist orientation in HRM.

Managers as readers of popular management books

Many HRM initiatives have their origins in the popular management books produced by a small group of influential writers who are consultants, managers, and/or business academics (sometimes combinations of all three). These writers include Tom Peters, James Champy, Stephen Covey, Michael Hammer, Rosabeth Moss Kanter, Peter Senge and the like. Few people within organizations will not be currently experiencing the consequences of some programme of organizational change which derives from the prescriptions of this small number of popular management writers. Burrell has labelled these books 'Heathrow management theory' since they are 'management books available at most airport book shops which are attractive to businessmen and women as supposed aids to their executive performance' (1989: 307).

Popular management books sell in their millions and often reach the best-seller lists. For example Peters and Waterman's *In Search of Excellence* (1982) sold 122,000 copies in the first two months of publication. Within one year it had sold more copies than any other book except the *Living Bible* in 1972 and 1973, and has sold more than 5 million copies world-wide. Stephen Covey's book *Seven Habits* (1989) spent four years on the *New York Times* best-seller list and has sold more than 6 million copies world-wide. Hammer and Champy's book *Reengineering the Corporation* (1993) has sold over 2 million copies to date and is currently perhaps the most influential management book in the world. Their influence cannot be underestimated for, as Clegg and Palmer (1996: 6) point out, most people's understanding of the nature of modern organizational life comes from reading these books. They have therefore had enormous impact on the managerial audience.

These books offer new forms of organization, working practices, attitudes and relationships for new times – or, as Peters refers to them, 'crazy new times'. Indeed, a distinctive feature of the ideas disseminated in these books is a forceful denunciation of previous principles of organization, management and structure. They suggest that traditional organizational systems and processes are ill-suited and so are irrelevant to contemporary competitive conditions. For example, Peters writes: 'We must move beyond change and embrace nothing less than the literal abandonment of the conventions that brought us to this point. Eradicate "change" from your vocabulary. Substitute "abandonment" or "revolution" instead' (1994: 3). In a similar vein Hammer and Champy write: 'Reengineering is the search for new models of organizing work. Tradition counts for nothing. Reengineering is the new beginning' (1993: 3). Critical to many of these ideas therefore is the argument that traditional forms of organization and management have reached their limits and are inappropriate for current conditions.[2]

However, by encouraging managers to abandon the traditional and embrace new forms of organization and management they create not only the new organization but also the individual who will work effectively and successfully within it. Indeed, Clark and Salaman (1997) argue that part of the reason for the enormous success and impact of this literature is related to the fact that it appeals directly to managers not simply because it defines the 'new' ideal form of organization, but because it enhances managers' confidence in performing their role by defining the qualities necessary for leadership success (i.e. how to be an effective senior manager). They suggest that management theories purveyed through popular management books help managers to make sense of themselves by providing them with purpose and hope, and by defining for them who they are, why they exist, why they are important and how they can succeed. As Alvesson argues, part of the appeal of these texts is that 'the questions formulated and answered, the perspective taken, the sectional interests supported etc. are grounded in a world view, a set of beliefs and values, which indicate that the top managers of corporations and other organizations are a highly important group' (1990: 217). Hence, popular management theory is redolent with values that appeal fundamentally to managers.

Offering attractive conceptions of the role of managers is not something unique to modern popular management writing. It has always been so. Early management writers – such as Bedaux, Brech, Fayol, Follett, Mayo, Taylor, and Urwick – not only articulated conceptions of the organization but also defined the character and attributes of the manager. For example, Bendix in his classic book notes that 'all ideologies of management have in common the effort to interpret the exercise of authority in a favourable light', and, in a prescient remark, continues: 'To do this, the exercise of authority is . . . justified with the assertion that the few possess qualities of excellence which enable them to realise the interests of many' (1956: 13). Today this is the role of popular management books. They define the managerial – or leadership – qualities necessary for effective implementation of the management role in the contemporary organization: 'Their tales are of miraculous strategic virtuosity, of heroic organisational turn-rounds, of battles with organisational monsters (poor quality, poor service levels, huge inventories, etc.); about the necessary virtues for organizational success and how these virtues may be gained. Above all they are of the heroes/ines who make success possible – the new manager' (Clark and Salaman, 1997). This emphasis on management and the managerial role means that much of popular management theory, and the change initiatives it inspires, supports an ideology of managerialism.

Strategic integration and HRM

Strategic integration is central to HRM. As is common with the development of any new discipline area a large proportion of the early literature on HRM was concerned with establishing its distinctiveness relative to previous approaches to the employment relationship, primarily personnel administration/management. Numerous reviews of the normative literature (see, for example, Clark, 1996; Legge, 1995; Mabey and Salaman, 1995; Storey, 1992) suggest that one of the key differences between HRM and personnel administration/management is the link between organizational strategy and human resource strategies. Beaumont, for example, argues that 'The key messages . . . in the human resource management literature are a strategic focus, the need for human resource policies and practices to be consistent with overall business strategy, and the need for individual components of a human resource package to reinforce each other' (1992: 25). The origins of this can be found in Fombrun et al.'s *Strategic Human Resource Management* (1984). In this the authors developed the notion of strategic HRM which entailed the interconnection of business strategies, organizational structures and HRM. The authors argued in a classic statement that 'The critical management task is to align the formal structure and human resource systems so that they drive the strategic objectives of the organisation' (1984: 37). This suggests that central to HRM is the notion that organizational effectiveness is dependent upon the 'tight fit', or integration, between HR strategies and organizational strategies. The basic argument is reasonably straightforward (although by no means easy to achieve in practice). It posits that competitive advantage will accrue to those organizations best able to exploit environmental opportunities and avoid or survive threats; and that the strategic management of human resources will assist organizations in this by encouraging and generating appropriate sorts of behaviours, attitudes and competencies from employees. Hence, the efforts of the HR function are directed at developing coherent, planned and monitored policies on all aspects of the organization which influence or structure employee behaviour such that these generate behaviours which support the achievement of organizational strategies. As Miller puts it: 'HRM cannot be conceptualised as a stand-alone corporate issue. Strategically it must flow from and be dependent upon the organization's (market orientated) corporate strategy' (1987: 348).

If integration is central to the nature and achievement of HRM then it is likely to become an, or even *the*, empirical focus of academic researchers. One implication of this focus is that HRM becomes concerned with examining those who determine and implement strategy – senior management. If this is the case, is it any surprise that the dominant epistemological approach in HRM is positivism with its realistic ontology and its concern to explain and 'predict what happens in the social world by searching for regularities and causal relationships between its constituent elements' (Legge, 1995: 308)? Much of HRM research thus becomes a search for what is going on 'out there' by answering such questions as: is HRM as a strategic and coherent model being implemented? What is the popularity and prevalence of different HRM practices? What factors can account for these outcomes? These are after all questions to which managers want answers. What managers want more than anything is certainty tied to prescription. A positivist approach is best able to provide this.

The link between researchers' priorities and HRM

Following on from the previous point, another reason for the preponderance of the management perspective in HRM is the way that the priorities, concerns and agendas of researchers are inextricably tied to those of HRM itself. The emergence of HRM must have been viewed as a very welcome development by many hard-pressed academics. It has enabled some academic departments and subject areas which were on the decline or becoming marginalized to gain a new lease of life by cloaking themselves in the aura of HRM. Academics have responded by developing all the paraphernalia necessary to support an emerging discipline: repackaged courses; new lectureships and professorial posts in HRM; and new academic journals.

However, in enthusiastically embracing HRM, academics have had to cut their cloth accordingly. In particular, radical critiques of HRM argue that it is essentially managerialist. That is, it supports the activity and actions of management and as a consequence can be seen to be a powerful and new form of managerial rhetoric. Seen in this way its power lies not in its impact on corporate or individual performance so much as in its capacity to reflect current societal values and political priorities, and to represent managerial conceptions of organization and of intra-organizational relationships. It can thus be seen as a new form of managerial control – not simply control through managerial practices and organization structures, but control of the ways in which conceiving, understanding and knowing organizations, organizational dynamics, and critically organizational members, are conducted and framed. For example, Clark (1996) on the basis of a review of the HRM literature in seven European countries concludes that managers have achieved greater autonomy over employee relations matters and as a result have begun to operate in a less restricted environment, albeit within a framework often determined jointly with employees' representatives (for example, German works councils). Clark argues that in this situation managers have sought to utilize a language which conceptualizes and legitimizes a 'new reality' in which they are once again supreme. Purcell (1993: 515) has remarked that this represents a rediscovery of the management prerogative. It appears that, for all the differences in culture and socio-economic context, managers in these seven countries have sought to make use of a new language which reinforces their agenda by reclothing the traditional concerns of management – the achievement of productivity and profitability via command and control – through reconceptualizing management, organization and employee. This, in turn, makes changes to the management of the employment relationship more acceptable since they are in harmony with wider societal values. Such developments are perhaps associated with a revival of the 'manager's right to manage'.

The nature of funding for academic research

Finally, the managerial focus of HRM is also supported by a number of external factors of which the most important is the nature of funding for academic research. To be successful funding bodies increasingly demand that applications demonstrate their relevance to appropriate user groups. This can be achieved in a number of different ways, for example by attracting matching funding, by gaining access, by establishing 'advisory panels', by attracting letters of support and so forth. In other words, funding bodies require some kind of proof of support from either those on whom one wishes to conduct research or the eventual users of the research outcomes. Since HRM has a managerial orientation these are inevitably managers. It therefore becomes very difficult to break this vicious circle since a researcher's (indirect) sponsors, participants and users tend to be from the same group.

On a purely practical note, gaining access to the managers of an organization for research purposes is usually far more straightforward than achieving access to the majority of the rest of the workforce – although there are no guarantees that the managers approached will participate. In most organizations the names of individual managers, particularly at senior levels, are readily available in corporate publications (e.g. the annual report and accounts), thus enabling researchers to use directed postal questionnaires and telephone surveys to gather large amounts of data. Many senior managers are also members of professional associations, such as the Institute of Personnel Development, which publish the names, positions and addresses of their members. The same is not true for the shop floor where access is usually dependent upon management co-operation, and requires the involvement of people who, unlike academics and HR directors, have no vested interest in exploring HR issues and who may perceive little personal benefit accruing from the research.

Why the inside story?

A key first reason for examining the 'receiving end' of HRM relates to the agenda for the study of HRM in the 1990s. As Hendry and Pettigrew note, 'Treatments of HRM need to be more sensitive to developments in corporate practice . . . and to discriminate between those practices which sustain HRM and those which negate it. Better descriptions of structures and strategy making in complex organisations . . . and frameworks for understanding them are an essential underpinning for analysing HRM' (1990: 35). In our view the second part of this agenda has been better addressed by subsequent HR literature than the first part. The discrimination between practices which sustain HRM can surely only take place with reference to the first-hand accounts of employees themselves. It is they, after all, who are expected to enthusiastically engage with and fully participate in the HR strategies promulgated by senior management in their organizations. And it is largely upon them that such strategies stand or fall, are seen to endure and succeed or wither and fail.

Towards the end of his review of *New Perspectives in Human Resource Management* Storey called for 'a more systematic study than has been attempted so far, on the way in which employment practices have impacted upon people who are deemed to be the recipients of the array of "messages" and initiatives [of HRM] . . . Too much of the present literature is limited to descriptions of formal systems (e.g. the impressive interlacing of multiple communication devices; or the outline of a new training programme). At best this tends to be supplemented with anecdote' (1989: 180–1). There are several reasons why, in the study of HRM phenomena, this shift of emphasis to the individual is to be encouraged.

Individuals as consumers of change

First, individuals are, as Storey points out, the primary recipients and 'consumers' of the initiatives that cluster under the banner of HRM. It would be difficult to forget this. Alongside the voices of senior managers making noble claims for the intentions and outcomes of their HR strategies, we have the conference sessions of consultants recounting the successes of their recent HR interventions, the handbooks of internal change agents describing the virtues of their unique skills and techniques, and the writings of academics occasionally chiming in with all of this, but more often debunking it. Surely, amidst this cacophony of HR remedies, recipes and rejoinders there is a place for hearing another voice: that of those on the receiving end of all this activity.

The individual as prime arbiter

Secondly, given some of the central tenets of HRM it is surprising how little listening is devoted to the rank and file inside organizations. Guest, for example, since introducing his model of HRM (1987) with subsequent enhancements (1992: 128–9), has remained optimistic that a given combination of HR policy levers will, when supported by appropriate leadership, culture and strategy in the organization, lead to certain attractive HR and organizational outcomes. Individual commitment, he concludes, 'can be enhanced through careful policies of recruitment, selection and socialisation and through job design. Together these can help to create a fit between a person's expectations and the realities of organisational life' (1992: 131). Others are less sanguine about this possibility. For example, a review by Ezzamel et al. of a number of practices associated with 'enlightened' HRM, including team working, empowerment and culture change, leads them to the view that 'HRM cannot free itself either from its own internal contradictions or, more fatefully, from the contradictory tensions that bedevil an employment relationship in which there is an endemic conflict, as well as a coincidence, of values and priorities between employers and employed' (1996: 78). But whichever view one takes, the individual remains a key, if not the prime, arbiter.

The location of the adjustment burden

A third and even more compelling reason why the individual's perspective of HRM needs to be privileged is that this is exactly where the adjustment burden is typically placed. This may not be immediately apparent, well publicized, or even tacitly understood by the players concerned. Writing about equal opportunity and positive action programmes, Austin and Shapiro note that: 'the basic premise which underpins these policies is that specific employee groups require some additional training and development to ease their integration into the workforce, or "catch up" with "normal employees" . . . individuals are expected to suppress their differences and to assimilate into the prevailing organisational culture' (1996: 64). The same idea of the individual gradually finding herself 'out of line' and deeming it necessary (because the alternatives are not practical or comfortable?) to accommodate to other corporate inspired HR initiatives permeates the literature on stress management workshops (Newton, 1995), culture change programmes (Ogbonna and Wilkinson, 1992) and total quality management (Wilkinson and Willmott, 1995).

The mute individual

Fourthly, individuals deserve attention if for no other reason than that they are the central, non-passive, co-creating actors in the conceiving, implementing and reconstructing of HR strategies. But owing to the effects of the very HR initiative in which they are participating, they are often unable or unwilling to give voice to their real reactions, emotions and evaluations. This may be because they are simply not aware of (or willing to admit) how their particular frames of reference and personal agendas are shaping their interpretation of events. Pettigrew and Whipp note, for instance, that 'one of the defining features of the [organization change] process, in so far as managerial action is concerned, is ambiguity. Seldom is there an easily isolated logic to strategic change. Instead that process may derive its force from an amalgam of economic, personal and political imperatives. Their interaction through time requires that those responsible for managing that process make continual assessments, repeated choices and continual adjustments' (1992: 31). Those on the receiving end of such changes may be equally inarticulate concerning their reactions but for entirely different reasons, and it may be that the changes they are experiencing also render them incapable of action. As Weick has noted: 'shy people find it difficult to take action, alienated people find it difficult to sustain action and depressed people find it difficult to do both . . . The confusion of those who remain [after downsizing] stems not so much from their "survivor guilt" as from their inability to act' (1995: 174).

The individual as consumer and focus of HR initiatives

A final reason for emphasizing those on the receiving end of HRM is that individuals are the primary recipients and 'consumers' of the initiatives that cluster under the banner of HRM. They are the target audience and the people whose relationship with the organization is being modified. Most of the programmes of organizational change referred to above contain a specific image of an organizational ideal which is claimed to be particularly well suited to the environmental conditions which pertain(ed) at the time. In general this organizational ideal is premised on such notions of flexibility, continual change, entrepreneurialism, decentralization, devolution of decision-making and so on. What is being advocated is a move away from Fordism and bureaucracy towards delayered, flatter, more responsive organizations in which the customer is king.

Less obviously, in producing the modern organization HRM initiatives also produce or 'make up' the subjects (i.e. the people) who work in them. Change programmes do not simply reinvent the organization; they also, and perhaps more importantly, reinvent the nature of employees, their attitudes and behaviours, and their relationship with the organization. New forms of organization require new types of employee. Consequently, many HR initiatives are addressed, at least in the first instance, not to the functioning and structuring of organizations but to the individuals who work within them. Keenoy and Anthony acknowledge this when they write that 'Once it was deemed sufficient to redesign the organisation so as to make it fit human capacity and understanding: now it is better to redesign human understanding to fit the organisation's purposes' (1992: 239). Furthermore, Wood (1989) argues that the reason many of the recent programmes of organizational change appeal to and are popular with managers is the new forms of work-based identities they seek to engender within organizational members. The attractiveness of such initiatives is as much, if not more, to do with the way in which they seek to 'form identities' as with the value of the management techniques or organizational forms they propose.

The focus on the individual therefore merits attention since a critical feature of many recent HR initiatives is the way in which they seek to extend management control not through external regulation by bureaucratic control but by the internalization of a new set of values 'so that, in principle, their uniquely human powers of judgement and discretion are directed unequivocally towards working methods that will deliver capital accumulation' (Willmott, 1993: 519). In other words they seek to install systems of control within the organization which are focused on individuals disciplining themselves by coming to know which attitudes and behaviours are, and are not, acceptable. Thus, employees come to judge themselves in terms of the values of the organization and so come to want what managers want them to aspire to, those things which are designed into the organization and disseminated via its cultural values. Control is thus built into the subjectivity of the individual employee with the consequence that employees can safely be autonomous because they will 'discipline themselves with feelings of anxiety, shame and guilt that are aroused when they sense or judge themselves to impugn or fall short of the hallowed values of the corporation' (1993: 523). Since many HRM initiatives have as their central focus the individual, the unit of analysis should also be the individual.

Conclusion

In this chapter we have presented a number of arguments which suggest that the inside view should become more prominent if we are to gain a fuller understanding of the HRM phenomenon. We have suggested that the voice of those at the receiving end has tended to be under-represented in the HRM literature. Whether owing to the priorities inherent within HRM (i.e. its focus on strategic integration), to the difficulties in obtaining access or to the structure of funding for academic research, all too often we hear the voice of those who promoted or initiated the change (i.e. management) to the exclusion of those on the receiving end of the change programme. Yet the inside view of HRM is critical when one considers that individuals are the primary recipients and 'consumers' of the various initiatives which cluster under the HRM banner. Indeed, more often than not the focus for HR initiatives is not an organization's structures but the individuals who work within them. Increasingly the characteristics and skills of employees are being remoulded to meet the demands of the new organizational ideal. It is therefore at the individual level where the adjustment burden is at its greatest and where our research should increasingly be focused. This book is an attempt to 'kick start' this process.

There are a number of different ways of structuring your reading of the subsequent chapters. This is aided by the fact that the book is divided into five parts.

The second part is concerned with organization-wide HR strategies which, in each of the three accounts, represent attempts by senior management to significantly shift individual attitudes and team-level or organizational culture; two of the chapters do this under the quality management banner. Collectively these 'shop floor' accounts helpfully move the debate on from polarized views concerning hard versus soft HRM, and exploitative versus emancipatory working processes, by demonstrating a range of not altogether predictable reactions registered by those at the 'sharp end'. Nevertheless, outcomes are heavily constrained by short timescales, the personal agendas of senior stakeholders and – in some cases – the interference of external environmental events, all of which had an important influence on the trust relations upon which the HR strategies were premised.

The third part is entitled 'The Perceived Impact of HRM on Performance and Productivity'. Here, each of the chapters explores the impact of an ostensibly isolated HR initiative: in one case it is training, in another it is performance-related pay and in a third it is the pooling of competencies via strategic alliances. What emerges, however, are two important lessons concerning the evaluation of HRM. The first is the inevitably systemic way in which an HR intervention in one subsystem of the organization sets in motion attitudinal and commercial ripples across the affected organization and/or network of which it is part. The second, and related, is the noticeable dissonance between how the occupational groups involved assessed the success or failure of the same HR initiative.

The five chapters in the fourth part take a further series of HR policies and processes in order to examine more fully the notion of choice and opportunity. In some cases this is analysed at a macro level, as in the chapter which suggests greenfield sites afford companies considerable strategic discretion when establishing employment relations arrangements, and the chapter on gendered cultures which proposes the potential business and professional benefits of HR strategies which actively encourage diversity in the workplace. In other cases the focus is upon the psychological contract between individual and organization, and how induction, socialization, learning and career management can be negotiated most astutely for all parties concerned.

Another way of structuring your reading is to examine the contents of each chapter in terms of a series of questions. Three that we have chosen to seek answers to (although they are by no means the only ones) in the Conclusion are: Is HRM delivering on its promises? Are the changes in workplace policies and practices truly strategic in nature? Who is benefiting from changes occurring in the name of HRM?

Some readers will have a practitioner focus and may want to use this volume to assess the value of a particular HR practice; the choice of chapters has, to some extent, been made to facilitate this by encompassing treatment of as wide a range of HR initiatives as possible. Also, we have deliberately given authors space to review relevant literatures and explain their methodologies fairly fully (both relative luxuries in a book of this nature) in order to help students access quickly key readings and relevant research designs for their own empirical work.

Finally, Legge's chapter in the first part may provide a useful touchstone for the rest of the volume in that she asks how we judge the impact, value and contribution of HR interventions. When viewed through the eyes of those running or owning organizations the yardsticks of success come readily to hand: economic viability, quality of service, return on net assets, political defensibility and so on. But what criteria do we use to tap the strength of feeling, the sense of justice or injustice, the perceptions of gain and loss as articulated by those (typically, but not exclusively) in the lower reaches of the organizations concerned? At the end of the day we cannot escape the need for some kind of ethical framework, because the political success of HRM is a function of the distribution of power within and around an organization, and as such is at root a moral issue.

Notes

1 Some examples of studies which do emphasize the 'inside story' of HRM include the work of Storey (e.g. 1992; 1996) and a trickle of studies that have explored discrete HR episodes, such as applicant perspectives on selection procedures (Gilliland, 1995); the effect of early induction and career development processes on graduates (Mabey et al., 1996); employee perceptions and experience of trade unions (Gallie et al., 1996); the perceived fairness of the means to decide pay rises (Folger and Konovsky, 1989); individual reactions to succession planning and career development initiatives (Mabey and Iles, 1993); a longitudinal analysis of the impact of an employee involvement programme (Guest et al., 1993); feedback on performance followed by setting goals (Tziner and Latham, 1989); an analysis of attempts to shift the psychological contract (Sparrow, 1996); insider interpretations of culture change programmes (Hope and Hendry, 1995); and middle managers' perceptions of strategic HR change interventions (Skinner and Mabey, 1997).

2 In this respect popular management theory shares a number of characteristics with the 'classic' social theories of Marx, Durkheim, Weber, Simmel and Freud. Using a rhetorical analysis Davis (1986) suggests that these texts are persuasive because they: (1) identify a novel factor which affects many aspects of modern life; (2) contrast modern society with previous societies unaffected by this factor to highlight the uniqueness and importance of the factor; (3) demonstrate how this factor has subverted aspects of life that people value; (4) play up the fears of their audience by pointing out the pernicious spread of this factor; and (5) show the way forward by suggesting ways to control or at least live with this factor.

References

Alvesson, M. (1990) 'On the popularity of organizational culture', *Acta Sociologica*, 33: 31–49.

Austin, S. and Shapiro, G. (1996) 'Equality-driven employee involvement', *Journal of General Management*, 21 (4): 62–76.

Beaumont, P.B. (1992) 'The US human resource management literature: a review', in G. Salaman (ed.), *Human Resources Strategies*. London: Sage. pp. 20–37.

Bendix, R. (1956) *Work and Authority in Industry*. New York: Wiley.

Burrell, G. (1989) 'The absent centre: the neglect of philosophy in Anglo-American management theory', *Human Systems Management*, 8: 307–12.

Clark, T. (1996) *European Human Resource Management*. Oxford: Blackwell.

Clark, T. and Salaman, G. (1997) 'Telling tales: management gurus' narratives and the construction of managerial identity', *Journal of Management Studies*, 32 (2).

Clegg, S.R. and Palmer, G. (1996) 'Introduction: producing management knowledge', in S.R. Clegg and G. Palmer (eds), *The Politics of Management Knowledge*. London: Sage.

Covey, S.R. (1989) *The Seven Habits of Highly Effective People: Powerful Lessons in Personal Change*. New York: Simon and Schuster.

Davis, M.S. (1986) '"That's classic!": the phenomenology and rhetoric of successful social theories', *Philosophy of the Social Sciences*, 16: 285–301.

Ezzamel, M., Lilley, S., Wilkinson, A. and Willmott, H. (1996) 'Practices and practicalities in human resource management', *Human Resource Management Journal*, 6 (1): 63–80.

Festinger, L., Riecken, H.W. and Schacter, S. (1956) *When Prophecy Fails: a Social and Psychological Study of a Modern Group that Predicted the Destruction of the World*. New York: Harper and Row.

Folger, R. and Konovsky, M.A. (1989) 'Effects of procedural and distributive justice on reactions to pay raise decisions', *Academy of Management Journal*, 32 (1): 115–30.

Fombrun, C.J., Tichy, N.M. and Devanna, M.A. (1984) *Strategic Human Resource Management*. New York: Wiley.

Gallie, G., Penn, R. and Rose, M. (1996) *Trade Unions in Recession*. Oxford: Oxford University Press.

Gilliland, S.W. (1995) 'Fairness from the applicant's perspective: reactions to employee selection procedures', *International Journal of Selection and Assessment*, 3 (1): 11–19.

Guest, D.J. (1987) 'Human resource management and industrial relations', *Journal of Management Studies*, 24: 503–21.

Guest, D.J. (1992) 'Employment commitment and control', in J.F. Hartley and G.M. Stephenson (eds), *Employment Relations*. Oxford: Blackwell.

Guest, D.J., Peccei, R. and Thomas, A. (1993) 'The impact of employee involvement on organisational commitment and "them" and "us" attitudes', *Industrial Relations Journal*, 24 (3): 191–200.

Hammer, M. and Champy, J. (1993) *Reengineering the Corporation: a Manifesto for Business Revolution*. London: Nicholas Brealey.

Hendry, C. and Pettigrew, A. (1990) 'Human resource management: an agenda for the 1990s', *International Journal of Human Resource Management*, 1: 17–44.

Hope, V. and Hendry, J. (1995) 'Corporate culture change – is it relevant for the organisations of the 1990s?', *Human Resource Management Journal*, 5 (4): 67–73.

Keenoy, T. and Anthony, P. (1992) 'HRM: metaphor and morality', in P. Blyton and P. Turnbull (eds), *Reassessing Human Resource Management*. London: Sage, pp. 233–55.

Legge, K. (1995) *Human Resource Management: Rhetorics and Realities*. London: Macmillan.

McCarthy, W. (1994) 'Of hats and cattle: or the limits of macro-survey research in industrial relations', *British Journal of Relations*, 25: 315–22.

Mabey, C. and Iles, P.A. (1993) 'The strategic integration of assessment and development practices: succession planning and new manager development', *Human Resource Management Journal*, 3 (4): 16–34.

Mabey, C. and Salaman, G. (1995) *Strategic Human Resource Management*. Oxford: Blackwell.

Mabey, C., Clark, T. and Daniels, K. (1996) 'A six year longitudinal study of graduate expectations: the implications for company recruitment and selection strategies', *International Journal of Selection and Assessment*, 4 (3): 139–50.

Miller, P. (1987) 'Strategic industrial relations and human resource management: distinction, definition and recognition', *Journal of Management Studies*, 24 (4): 347–61.

Millward, W., Stephens, M., Smart, D. and Hawes, W. (1993) *Workplace Industrial Relations in Transition*. Aldershot: Dartmouth.

Newton, T. (1995) *Managing Stress: Emotion and Power at Work*. London: Sage.

Ogbonna, E. and Wilkinson, B. (1992) 'Corporate strategy and corporate culture: the view from the check-out', *Personnel Review*, 19 (4): 9–15.

Peters, T. (1994) *The Tom Peters Seminar: Crazy Times Call for Crazy Organizations*. London: Macmillan.

Peters, T. and Waterman R. (1982) *In Search of Excellence*. New York: Harper and Row.

Pettigrew, A. and Whipp, R. (1992) *Managing Change for Critical Success*. Oxford: Blackwell.

Purcell, J. (1993) 'The challenge of human resource management for industrial relations research and practice', *International Journal of Human Resource Management*, 4 (3): 511–27.

Roy, D. (1954) 'Efficiency and the "fix": informal inter-group relations in a piecework machine shop', *American Journal of Sociology*, 60: 255–66.

Skinner, D. and Mabey, C. (1997) 'Managers' perceptions of HR change', *Personnel Review*, forthcoming.

Sparrow, P. (1996) Transitions in the psychological contract: some evidence from the banking sector, *Human Resource Management Journal*, 6 (4): 75–92.

Storey, J. (1989) *New Perspectives in Human Resource Management*. London: Routledge.

Storey, J. (1992) *Developments in the Management of Human Resources*. Oxford: Blackwell.

Storey, J. (1996) *Blackwell Cases in Human Resource and Change Management*. Oxford: Blackwell.

Tziner, A. and Latham, G.P. (1989) 'The effects of appraisal instrument, feedback and goal-setting on worker satisfaction and commitment', *Journal of Organisational Behaviour*, 10: 145–53.

Weick, K.A. (1995) *Sensemaking in Organizations*. London: Sage.

Whyte, W.F. (1955) *Street Corner Society: the Social Structure of an Indian Slum*. Chicago: University of Chicago Press.

Wilkinson, B. and Willmott, H. (eds) (1995) *Making Quality Critical*. London: Routledge.

Willmott, H. (1993) 'Strength is ignorance; slavery is freedom: culture in modern organizations', *Journal of Management Studies*, 30: 515–52.

Wood, S. (1989) 'New wave management', *Work, Employment and Society*, 3: 379–402.

2

The Morality of HRM

Karen Legge

When reading accounts of human resource management (HRM) practice in the UK and North America, it is noticeable the extent to which the data are (literally) the voices of management. To take a few examples. John Storey's classic research study of mainstream UK organizations involved interviews with 'a vertical slice of mainly line managers . . . drawn from corporate level, through MDs of various businesses, works managers and so on down through the operational structure to first line management' (1992: 19). Similarly, the second Warwick company-level survey (Marginson et al., 1993: 2–3) involved a questionnaire administered via interviews with a senior executive responsible for personnel and industrial relations matters, and one responsible for finance at 812 UK corporate offices. Again, Wood (1995; 1996) and Wood and Albanese's (1995) recent research on high-commitment management in manufacturing plants chose as respondents 'a senior member of the personnel department or, where one did not exist . . . the senior person in the plant responsible for personnel who was normally a production manager' (1995: 58), even though the avowed intention was to gain 'information on production workers, respondents being told that we were interested in direct or indirect, skilled or unskilled, workers, "groups, which in the past, have been called hourly paid or manual workers"'. Guest and Peccei's postal questionnaires to NHS provider trusts were sent to 'the most senior personnel specialist and the deputy general manager/deputy chief executive in each unit' (1994: 225). Not surprisingly, given the positivistic, quantitative research preferences of most North American academics, postal questionnaires to senior management are generally the order of the day. Huselid (1995), for example, directed his postal questionnaires at the 'senior HR professional in each firm'. Even WIRS 3 (Millward et al., 1992: 3), which *did* administer its questionnaires via interview to worker representatives as well as management (again 'the senior person at the establishment dealing with industrial relations and personnel matters and a financial manager'), has a preponderance of management responses (2550 as opposed to 1466 from worker representatives).

The reasons for this bias are not hard to find. If a postal questionnaire is being used, sheer problems of identification and potential response rate (bad enough at the best of times: Wood only achieved 16 per cent from his *managers*) tend to rule out non-managerial respondents. Even if the questionnaire is being administered via interviews, problems of access to the shop or office floor can loom large. But leaving aside these practical difficulties, there have been good reasons for focusing on managerial respondents. Much early research on HRM inevitably sought answers to basic questions such as what initiatives management were undertaking; to what extent these initiatives had a 'strategic' character; and whether the combination of initiatives added up to a qualitative shift in the approach to the management of employees (see, for example, Storey, 1992). Such questions clearly address managerial concerns and management is the obvious and first port of call for information. Secondly, though, the spirit of the times – management as hero in the enterprise culture – directed attention towards management and away from the rest of the workplace (unless redefined as self-managing). Indeed, managers as heroes have written their own accounts of HRM (Wickens, 1987; 1995). With unemployment high and unions on the retreat, with managerial prerogative in the ascendant and labour quiescent, interest in shop and office floor life declined to some extent. And, indeed, as Storey (1992: 215) explicitly acknowledges, anyone interested in the impact of so-called HRM initiatives would look first to middle and junior managers as these groups were the *first* recipients or 'objects of change', given the slower percolation to the shop floor.

Suffice to say here that while the management accounts of HRM initiatives range from the messianic to the equivocal, not to say sceptical, the shop floor accounts are generally even more guarded. This is not to say that the voice of non-managerial employees has been entirely muted. Case study research from the avowedly Marxist to the pluralist in orientation has surfaced the shop floor experience, though the usual problems of generalization remain (e.g. Garrahan and Stewart, 1992; Sewell and Wilkinson, 1992a; 1992b; Geary, 1992). At best they appear to reflect disappointed expectations (e.g. Wilkinson et al., 1992) and, at worst, a realization of labour intensification (e.g. Garrahan and Stewart, 1992). The negative messages, of course, may reflect the labour process leanings of the researchers involved. It is true that, particularly on television documentary programmes, employees can be found proclaiming the transformation of work though team building and empowerment. I remember a report on BBC2 'Newsnight' about B&Q employees, engaging in morning exercises and experiencing pep talks, who proclaimed the virtues of teamworking and customer service and the pleasures of working in such an uplifting environment – for £3.50 per hour. I guess I wasn't the only one to find the words 'false consciousness' and 'docile bodies' automatically springing to my lips (indeed, there was an ex-employee who felt the same). Yet I also felt such sentiments were patronizing.

This book invites us to consider the 'inside story' of HRM, to consider whether 'the current nostrums of HRM work, and what is the experience of those at the receiving end'. Only empirical research can answer such questions. But what frameworks or perspectives might we use to guide such research and evaluate the empirical data we already have? This is the issue I wish to address. First, though, let me share a recent image of the experience of employment in the 1990s.

Let's take Ford. John Storey (1992) and Ken Starkey and Alan McKinlay (1993) have written of the changes at Ford, notably the employee involvement programme. The change package, entitled 'Mission Values and Guiding Principles', contains such statements as:

- *Customers are the focus of everything we do*   Our work must be done with our customers in mind, providing better products and services than our competition.
- *Employee involvement is our way of life*   We are a team. We must treat each other with trust and respect.
- *Integrity is never compromised*   The conduct of our Company world wide must be pursued in a manner that is socially responsible and commands respect for its integrity and for its positive contribution to society. Our doors are open to men and women alike without discrimination and without regard to ethnic origin or personal beliefs. (cited in Storey, 1992: 57)

All this is good 'soft' model HRM stuff. How then do we account for the embarrassing incident in February 1996, when Ford admitted to an 'error' involving their advertising agency whereby five black/Asian workers appeared in promotional material as white people (see Figure 2.1). Following an unofficial three-hour stoppage (reportedly costing £2.8 million) Ford apologized and paid the four remaining employees (one had left since the original 1991 promotional material had been drawn up) £1500 each.

There are various ways of looking at this incident. At first sight it is reassuringly familiar. Ford has not changed, standardization still rules, but it's 'any colour as long as they're not black' (*The Times*, 19 February 1996). At second sight it clearly contravenes 'new' Ford's aspirations to treat employees with respect and violates assertions of mutual trust. It completely contradicts Ford's proclamation of treating people 'without regard to ethnic origin'. Further, it is clear that the employees involved found this a hurtful and humiliating experience. As one of them said (*The Guardian*, 19 February 1996): 'They wanted me in the picture when they wanted to show the mix of ethnic groups in Ford's workplace, but suddenly I wasn't good enough.' The employee, Douglas Sinclair, with Ford for 30 years, did not appreciate being transformed from being black, bearded and with perfect eyesight into a clean shaven white man with glasses, or being called 'two face' by 'humorous' workmates. Patricia Marquis, aged 30, was not keen on suddenly ageing 20 years and turning white: 'I felt humiliated and angry. I wanted an explanation.'

And, of course, there is an explanation. The advertising agency had altered the photograph for use in marketing promotions in Poland, where it was believed black faces would not be as acceptable as white. Hence, while the action taken by the advertising agency condones a market's perceived racial prejudice (and hence contradicts 'integrity is never compromised'), paradoxically it supports 'customers are the focus of everything we do.' The familiar contradiction between HRM's 'external' and 'internal' fit surfaces again. Nevertheless, it could be argued that Ford's efforts in retrieving the situation

Figure 2.1 *Ford's ethnically mixed workforce of 1991 (above) lost its colour when white faces were superimposed on black bodies for a new brochure*

(public apology, compensation payments, public assertion of equal opportunities policy) are either a reassertion of 'soft' model HRM's mutuality principles or a pragmatic attempt to avert an all-out strike – or that there are elements of both positions.

The experience of HRM

Before I turn to the framework or perspectives we might use to guide research on the experience of HRM and evaluate the empirical data we already have, it might be useful just to summarize some of the conclusions I drew (Legge, 1995) from analysing the published empirical data on HRM implementation in the late 1980s and early 1990s (I recognize that some of these conclusions may be a bit dated now and I will indicate where I think so). Following Guest's (1987) model I looked for evidence of the extent to which HRM policies and practices achieved integration with business strategy and internal consistency, commitment, flexibility and quality. This is a bit old-fashioned. Today's approach (Purcell, 1996; Guest, 1996; Huselid, 1995; Wood, 1995; 1996) seems to be to consider HRM in terms of best practice: 'high-performance work practices' (Huselid, 1995) or 'high-commitment management' (Wood, 1995; 1996). Admittedly these reflect the values of Guest's (1987) normative model, and have been summarized by Purcell (1996: 4) as comprising:

- careful recruitment and selection (with emphasis on traits and competency)
- extensive use of systems of communication
- teamworking with flexible job design
- emphasis on training and learning
- involvement in decision-making with responsibility
- performance appraisal with tight links to contingent pay.

And certainly Huselid found some evidence that such 'high-performance work practices' are associated with positive outcomes, such as (low) employee turnover and productivity and short- and long-term measures of corporate financial performance. Similarly Guest and Hoque (1994) found that, on greenfield sites, using above the median level of HRM practices, when combined with a strategic HRM approach, appeared to result in superior HRM outcomes (commitment, employee quality, aspects of flexibility), if not superior productivity or product quality.

One may, of course, be sceptical about the direction of causality in such cross-sectional studies. One may question the universal appropriateness of such policies if cost effectiveness as a route to market share and profitability is the goal. One may even wonder if the outcomes are a one-off effect of a change process – a sort of Hawthorne effect. Certainly John Purcell (1996) has these doubts. But, it is possible that if such policies are applied in the spirit of mutuality this interpretation of the findings might be right.

My analysis of the research findings of the 1980s and early 1990s presents a more downbeat view. In brief, I found:

1   There were some increases in numerical flexibility that largely reflected sectoral changes in the private sector and government policy in the public sector. The increases in functional flexibility that occurred seemed more to do with job enlargement, where management were seeking a reduction of porosity, intensification of effort and a reassertion of managerial prerogative rather than any widespread multi-skilling. As for financial flexibility – performance-related pay – there are queries as to its degree of implementation and effectiveness.

2   Where a flexible response to product market competition is most readily and obviously seen is in widely reported cases of delayering and downsizing. This has resulted from the contraction of the manufacturing base in the early 1980s; the impact of privatization and 'market disciplines'/regulatory control, not to mention cash limits, on erstwhile public sector industries and services; and the partly IT but also deregulation and merger inspired rationalization of financial services in the 1990s. This has gone hand in hand with increased temporal flexibility (zero hours) etc. and a reported increase in managerial working hours for those lucky enough to hang on to employment (Vielba, 1995).

3   Turning to team building, employee empowerment and involvement – yes, there is evidence that all three are formally taking place, especially the last. What in practice these mean depends very much on the prevailing organizational culture and market environment (Marchington et al., 1994). Certainly the messianic accounts by managerialist writers and the positive experiences reported by employees (on TV), for example at Rover, may be juxtaposed against the more critical accounts of writers in the labour process tradition who, in place of the 'tripod of success' of 'flexibility, quality and teamwork', identify a 'tripod of subjugation' of 'management by stress', 'management through blame' and 'management through compliance' (cf. Wickens, 1987; Garrahan and Stewart, 1992; Delbridge and Turnbull, 1992). You pays your money and takes your pick.

4   There is evidence too of cultural management programmes – such as the oft-cited programmes at BA – designed to secure employee commitment to the values embodied in the company mission statement, notably to quality, whether in product or customer service. Whether such programmes secure attitudinal commitment or, in the context of continuingly high residual unemployment and job insecurity, generate what has been termed 'resigned behavioural compliance' (Ogbonna and Wilkinson, 1990) is a matter of debate. As Ron Todd said in 1983, 'we've got 3 million on the dole, and another 23 million scared to death.' Either way, it is extremely difficult to demonstrate a link between commitment/behavioural compliance and performance.

5   Finally, 'the internal contradictions of HRM are no secret': there are tensions (paradoxically) between commitment and flexibility, individualism

Table 2.1   *Sisson's model of rhetoric and reality in HRM*

Rhetoric	Reality
Customer first	Market forces supreme
Total quality management	Doing more with less
Lean production	Mean production
Flexibility	Management 'can do' what it wants
Core and periphery	Reducing the organization's commitments
Devolution/delayering	Reducing the number of middle managers
Downsizing/rightsizing	Redundancy
New working patterns	Part-time instead of full-time jobs
Empowerment	Making someone else take the risk and responsibility
Training and development	Manipulation
Employability	No employment security
Recognizing contribution of the individual	Undermining the trade union and collective bargaining
Teamworking	Reducing the individual's discretion

Source: Sisson, 1994: 5

and teamworking, personal empowerment and the pressures for standardization and control embodied in a range of HRM associated and interrelated initiatives such as TQM, JIT, customer sovereignty and corporate cultural management.

What we have here, I guess, are all the tensions expressed in Storey's (1987) distinction between the soft 'developmental humanism' and the hard 'utilitarian instrumentalism' models of HRM. Or, put somewhat differently, are we seeing, as Sisson (1994) suggests, how the soft rhetoric of the 'HRM organization' may be used to meet the reality of the hard face of managerial prerogative in the service of capitalism/competitive advantage (see Table 2.1)?

Taking it all together, what are the implications of these findings for the recipients of HRM? My best guess is that if you are a core knowledge worker with skills which are scarce and highly in demand, life may be good – empowerment, high rewards and some element of job security (if at the cost of a workaholic lifestyle). For the bulk of the workforce, though, things are not so rosy. Not only are part-time and fixed-term contract jobs growing at the expense of full-time permanent jobs, but all jobs are increasingly insecure. Further, there is indisputable evidence that labour intensification is increasing all round (see Legge, 1988; Metcalf, 1988; 1989; Nolan and Marginson, 1990; Guest, 1990; Edwards and Whitston, 1991). But how do employees experience such employment?

Evaluating the experience of HRM

The perspective I wish to bring to the experience of HRM is one derived from business ethics. In very general terms I would suggest that the experience of

HRM is more likely (but not necessarily) to be viewed positively if its underlying principles are ethical. This sounds like a statement of the obvious. It is less obvious if we consider that, depending on the ethical position adopted, a given set of HRM policies and practices may be viewed in very different lights.

Business ethics is about reflection on the nature and place of morality in business (for some general discussions of business ethics, see Beauchamp and Bowie, 1988; Donaldson, 1989; Donaldson and Werhane, 1993; de George, 1990). As this seems to limit the focus to profit-seeking organizations, I prefer to think in terms of organizational ethics. Key concepts when we think in terms of organizational ethics might include right, obligation, justice, fairness, good, virtue, responsibility, trust and so on. Such concepts are implicit in any evaluation of our socio-economic order. Just as capitalism highlights such 'goods' as freedom, autonomy, efficiency and sees 'justice' in terms of equality of opportunity, so the Marxist critique would point to the injustice of exploitation, alienation and the protection of the interests of the few at the expense of social justice for the many. Capitalism rests on the premise that a transaction is fair if both parties engage without coercion and with adequate and appropriate knowledge of relevant aspects of the transaction. Marxism would question this assumed lack of coercion and equality of knowledge in a social system of structural inequalities. All organization rests on an assumption of some level of trust, but we sometimes forget the extent to which our assumptions about the management of employment relationships have ethical foundations. The concepts that I have mentioned are embedded in three normative ethical theories in terms of which we can evaluate HRM policies and practices. These are deontological, utilitarian and stakeholder theories. So, first, let us briefly outline their respective basic tenets.

Deontological theories maintain that the concept of duty is, in some respects, independent of the concept of good and that some actions are right or wrong for reasons other than their consequences. Kantian ethics fall into this category. Kant argues that what makes an action right or wrong is not the sum of its consequences but the fact that it conforms to moral law. Moral laws of duty demand that people act not only in accordance with duty but for the sake of duty. It is not good enough to perform a morally correct action, because this could stem from self-interested motives that have nothing to do with morality. Rather an action is moral if it conforms to moral law that is based not in intuition, conscience or utility, but in pure reason. We can determine moral law by analysing the nature of reason itself and what it means to be a rational being. Reason has three major characteristics: consistency (hence moral actions must not contradict one another); universality (because reason is the same for all, what is rational for me is rational for everyone else); and *a priori* derivation (it is not based on experience, hence the morality of an action does not depend on its consequences). A person acts morally if the sole motive for an action is the recognition of moral duty based on a valid rule.

In sharp contrast to a deontological position is *utilitarianism*. Utilitarianism claims that the morality of actions is to be judged by their consequences. An action is moral if, when compared with any alternative action, it produces the greatest amount of good (or the least possible balance of bad consequences), for the greatest number of people directly or indirectly affected by that action. The 'good' may be variously conceptualized as 'pleasure', 'happiness' or 'intrinsic value'. The maximization of the good calls for efficiency. It also allows that people might be treated as a means to an end, if the end is the maximization of the good (or minimization of the bad) for the greatest number.

Finally, we have the *stakeholder* theories of justice. These have a rather different emphasis from the deontological and utilitarian theories, in that the emphasis is less on the 'good' than on the 'right' (i.e. the just distribution of the 'good'). Popular versions of stakeholder theory (e.g. Evan and Freeman, 1988) assert that organizations have stakeholders, that is, groups and individuals who potentially benefit from or are harmed by an organization's actions. Stakeholders of an organization might comprise, for example, not just shareholders (owners), but management, other employees, customers, suppliers, and the local community. The stakes of each group are reciprocal, since each can affect the others in terms of harms and benefits as well as rights and duties. This principle of reciprocity leads to two further principles:

- The organization should be managed for the benefit of its stakeholders: its customers, suppliers, owners, employees and local communities. The rights of these groups must be ensured and, further, the groups must participate, in some sense, in decisions that substantially affect their welfare.
- Management bears a fiduciary relationship to stakeholders and to the organization as an abstract entity. It must act in the interests of the stakeholders as their agent, and it must act in the interests of the organization to ensure the survival of the firm, safeguarding the long-term stakes of each group.

'Participate in decisions that substantially affect their welfare' has resonances of Rawls's 'egalitarian theory of justice'. Rawls (1971) argues that we should look for a conception of justice that nullifies the accidents of natural endowment and the contingencies of social circumstances as counters in the quest for political and economic advantage. His approach is, in a sense, Kantian in that he attempts to derive principles of distributive justice that should be acceptable to all rational people and, hence, universal. In order to find such principles, Rawls suggests we perform a thought experiment. Suppose all people are behind a 'veil of ignorance', where we know we are rational beings and that we value our own good, but we do not know if we are male or female, rich or poor, talented or untalented, able-bodied or suffering disability, white or black – and so on. What principles would we call just or fair if we did not know what place we would have in society (read 'organization')? In such circumstances, Rawls argues, people would agree two principles of justice:

1   Each person is to have an equal right to the most extensive basic liberty compatible with similar liberty for others.

2   Social and economic inequalities are to be arranged so that they are both
    (a) reasonably expected to be to everyone's advantage and (b) attached to
    positions and offices open to all.

Now obviously there are some difficulties with all these theories. It is often
said that deontologists covertly appeal to utilitarian consequences in order to
demonstrate the rightness of actions, particularly when there is a clash of
moral rules. Utilitarianism has to cope with the problem of lack of knowledge
of all consequences, of weighing together different kinds of good and evil and
of the issue of unjust consequences. Stakeholder analysis has the problem of
short- versus long-term justice and the dangers of pseudo-participation.
Rawls's second principle can be attacked as being too strong (as long as equal
opportunities exist, why should rewards have to take account of producing
benefit for the least advantaged groups in society?) or too weak (in that it
would allow the very, very rich to get very much richer as long as the very,
very poor got a little less poor). But, leaving these on one side, I want to take
the central tenets of each theory and evaluate HRM policies and practices in
their light. For the purposes of this chapter, I see the central tenets, very
much simplified, as follows:

Deontology   Treat people with respect and as ends in their own right, not
solely as means to others' ends. Any moral rule (such as 'A fair day's work for
a fair day's pay') must be capable of being consistently universalized, must
respect the dignity of persons, and must be acceptable to rational beings.
Any action performed out of self-interest is not moral.

Utilitarianism   The greatest good to the greatest number allows people to be
treated as means to ends, if it is to the advantage of the majority. Actions
should be judged in terms of their consequences.

Stakeholder/Rawlsian theory   The good must be distributed with mutual
consultation and so that no organizational stakeholders are complete losers
while others are clear winners. Management must place a priority on the
long-term interests of stakeholders and the survival of the organization.

The ethics of HRM policy and practice

How ethical is HRM? This very much depends on the theory of ethics you
adopt.
    The deontological position at first sight resonates with the values embed-
ded in 'soft' model HRM. For a start, it is consistent with HRM's emphasis
on individualism and responsible autonomy. Take Walton's (1985) classic
statement of mutuality in HRM:

> The new HRM model is composed of policies that promote mutuality – mutual
> goals, mutual influence, mutual respect, mutual rewards, mutual responsibility.

This also asserts respect for human beings and is consistent with the idea of responsible autonomy for rational beings. In theory, I guess, it could be universalized. However, there is a potential problem. Walton (1985) goes on to say:

> The theory is that policies of mutuality will elicit commitment, which in turn will yield both better economic performance and greater human development.

Even in this most 'utopian' model (Purcell, 1996: 130) treating people with respect is justified in terms of 'better economic performance' and hence, in part, people are being used as means to an end, contradicting a basic principle of Kantian ethics. However, it might be argued that all is not lost. According to some commentators (Beauchamp and Bowie, 1988: 38) Kant does not prohibit the use of persons categorically and without qualification. He argues only that we must not treat another person exclusively as a means to our own ends. What must be avoided is to disregard someone's personhood by exploiting or otherwise using them without regard to their own interests, needs and conscientious concerns. If 'soft' model HRM genuinely promotes 'greater human development' for *all* employees, it could be argued that, if so implemented, it would pass muster in terms of the deontologists.

The problem is, how often does this occur? If we follow the core–periphery ideas about organizational design and the employment contract, for example, can we be sure that employees on non-standard contracts are being treated with equal regard as those in the core? Possibly, when terms and conditions are equalized pro rata and the non-standard contract is freely chosen.[1] However, much anecdotal evidence would suggest this is not the case. Under the heading 'School-leavers' pay down 20%', *The Independent* (5 March 1996: 6) reported a study by the Low Pay Unit on data from the careers service and Job Centres in Greater Manchester. It was claimed that nearly half the 16-year-olds who leave school are paid less than £1.50 per hour and that their average wage has dropped in real terms by one-fifth in five years. However, the anecdote that caught my eye was the story of a 16-year-old who was paid £30 for a 40-hour week in a garage. When he inquired about compensation for losing the tip of a finger at work, apparently he was told that he was a 'subcontractor'. Obviously, this is an example of what Guest (1995: 125) calls a 'black hole' firm, rather than an adherent to 'soft' model HRM, but note the HRM-type language of the flexible firm. The author of the report, Gabrielle Cox, says: 'It is bad enough for adult workers to face exploitation, but a society which allows its young people to be treated in this way must question its sense of values.'

But, another difficulty remains. For an action to be moral it must be consistently universalized. But what happens if there is a clash between the actions that two second-order moral rules command? What if 'I must respect the interests of my employees' clashes with 'I must respect the interests of my shareholders'? Either we must allow for an exception to resolve the conflicting interests, or we must decide which course of action takes priority in terms of *prima facie* obligations. The problem with the latter, as hinted earlier, is that in prioritizing *prima facie* obligations we tend to resort to evaluating consequences (if in terms of respect for people) and hence are incorporating utilitarian reasoning.

The deontologist's notion that, for a rule (and consequent action) to be moral, it must be capable of being consistently universalized, may be acceptable if a 'best practice' (Purcell, 1996) model of HRM is adopted.[2] However, if integration with business strategy points to a contingent rather than absolutist approach (Legge, 1989; Purcell, 1996), the universalization of any moral rule (for example, respect for the employee, from which might derive injunctions about employee development and training, job security, fair rewards and so on) becomes suspect in both theory and practice. The contradictions embedded in HRM are illustrative of the Kantian dilemma that second-order moral rules can clash and that resolution can often only be achieved by a back-door admission of utilitarianism.

So, in terms of deontological ethics there is a question mark over HRM. There is no problem if respect for the individual is universally and consistently applied as a moral good irrespective of consequences; not so, if otherwise. By these injunctions empowerment, for example, must genuinely be about increasing employees' autonomy, choices and development as a good in itself, not, as Sisson has it, 'making someone else take the risk and responsibility' (1994: 15). While 'soft' model HRM, on the most generous interpretation, may just qualify as ethical from the deontologist's standpoint, 'hard' model HRM, which treats the human resource as something to be used like any other factor in production (or, in Marxist terms, to be 'exploited'), is definitely immoral.

Happily, utilitarianism sends a far more reassuring message. Irrespective about what downsizing and labour intensification imply for respect for individuals as ends in themselves, utilitarianism is the route to justifying such activities. It is perfectly ethical to use people as means to an end, if this is for the greatest good of the majority. Leaving aside the practical difficulty of quantifying different forms of goodness (and evil), here is the moral justification for choosing whatever strategies would appear to deliver competitive advantage. The argument would be that competitive advantage ensures organizational survival and organizational survival protects employees' jobs, quite apart from maintaining employment in suppliers, satisfying consumer needs and so on. Hence, using people to achieve competitive advantage is quite acceptable as long as it does deliver positive consequences to the majority of – dare I say it – stakeholders. So 'tough love' in all its forms is morally justifiable: employees may be compelled to work harder and more flexibly for 'their own good', or they may be made redundant for the greater good. Injustices, in terms of *prima facie* obligations (for example, to 'do as you would be done by'), are justified if the consequences of such actions are to the benefit of the majority. And it could well be argued that such a logic has prevailed in the years of the enterprise culture and the advent of HRM in all its forms. The standard of living of the majority in employment has increased markedly over the last 16 years. Even in the depths of recession in manufacturing industry in the early 1980s, with high levels of inflation and inexorably rising unemployment, real earnings for the majority in work rose steadily. With falling unemployment in the mid to late 1980s, combined with rising house prices but otherwise fairly low inflation, the experience of the majority was of 'feeling good' with 'loadsa money'. This diminished in the 1990s because not only did the real standard of living of those in employment remain static or marginally decline (pay increases below the rate of inflation, negative equity), but employees who had been and always saw themselves as part of the bene-fiting majority (white collar and managerial employees in large bureaucracies) now became victims of downsizing, delayering, labour intensification and other manifestations of 'tough love'. But such actions, as far as utilitarianism is concerned, are perfectly ethical if the balance of good consequences out-weighs the negative. The problems technically of making such an assessment, as already suggested, are enormous. But, very loosely speaking, if as a result of such actions the majority remain in employment, this employment is more secure and capable of generating enhanced benefit to its recipients (than if the action had not been taken), only a minority suffer, and their suffering does not outweigh the benefits to the majority, then the action is ethical.

But what of this minority? If a deontologist would not accept their fate, those engaging in stakeholder analysis would also raise critical questions. Stakeholder analysis, asserting the Kantian principle that stakeholders should be treated with respect and not just as means to an end, would be concerned that some employees might lose out in order that the interests of other stake-holders are protected. Thus, if you accept Garrahan and Stewart's (1992) and Delbridge and Turnbull's (1992) critical accounts of JIT and TQM, employees are called upon to experience a measure of labour intensification in the interests of customers (enhanced quality and customer responsiveness) and shareholders (greater competitive advantage leading ultimately to capital growth and/or profit). However, by this logic, shareholders themselves may be required to forgo the maximum amount of dividend payment, in the interests of investment in job-creating new plant and in long-term development activ-ities such as training. In practice, though, management are provided with a loophole, through their obligation to act 'to ensure the survival of the orga-nization, safeguarding the long-term stakes of each group'. Almost any action (redundancy, wage cutting, freezing of recruitment and training expenditure, seeking cheaper suppliers, cutting dividends) could be justified in terms of the short-term survival of the organization, irrespective of the damage to the present incumbents of the stakeholder position. All that is required for the action to be moral is that the groups involved must participate in deci-sions that affect their welfare. And here we are back to the Marxist criticism of capitalist 'free' transactions, that structural inequalities do not allow an equal participation in such decision-making. How meaningful is employee consent to decisions that adversely affect them, if they perceive little choice ('3 million unemployed, 23 million scared to death', to echo Ron Todd again) or if, via HRM-type cultural management, their awareness of their real interests is obscured (cf. Lukes, 1974)? Further, stakeholder analysis, in its very com-mitment to safeguarding 'the long-term stakes of each group', affords little protection to individual members of each group in the face of present (possibly adverse) action in the interests of organizational survival. As a shareholder, I might have to forgo dividends in order that the organization can invest for future survival and profitability, for the good of future shareholders. Hence shareholders as a *group* are not damaged, even if I as an individual shareholder (who might walk under a bus tomorrow) have lost out.

Rawls's ethical stance might be seen as pointing to the golden mean of 'do as you would be done by': certainly such a maxim would seem consistent with the implications of the 'veil of ignorance' and the idea that inequalities should only be tolerated if reasonably expected to be to everyone's (including those who are least advantaged) benefit. Is the core–periphery distinction, or performance-related pay, or any other form of differentiation to which differential benefits are attached, clearly to everyone's advantage? Certainly a case can be made that all organization rests on differentiation. Concepts of fairness may accord too with differential benefits for differentiated work. The importance of fairness in relation to satisfaction and motivation and, hence, contribution may be argued. The problem is the quantitative issue. How much extra should be given to scarce skills, high levels of contribution, even if it is recognized that such differentiation benefits all? Certainly, Cedric Brown's vast salary increase at British Gas, at a time when showroom staff were confronting at best real pay cuts and at worst redundancy, could hardly be said to be ethical in terms of Rawlsian principles (particularly given the declining levels of performance of British Gas *vis-à-vis* its range of stakeholders, on virtually every performance measure you would care to take). Is it ethical to justify high levels of pay and job security for core staff on the grounds that they are crucial to the achievement of competitive advantage and organizational survival, when paying very low wages to staff in the periphery? And to do this by arguing that the core staff in the long term are guaranteeing the jobs of the staff in the periphery, and therefore someone must subsidize core-staff wages in the long-term interests of all?

Conclusions

I have raised the issue of ethics in employment relationships as I think that people's experience of HRM policies and practices is likely to be both directly and indirectly influenced by the sorts of ethical concerns outlined here. Directly in the sense that, if ethical values are embodied in HR policies, at least some recipients are likely to have a positive experience of employment. Indirectly in that, if the experience is not positive, but is informed by values that intend to deliver goods to a majority, at least some justification may be offered for unpalatable actions, which may (or may not) make negative outcomes easier to swallow.

If deontological ethics inform HRM, there is a good chance of Walton's mutuality model of HRM seeing the light of day and, if so, of employees experiencing HRM positively. This is highly unlikely. At best, in my view, such a model may be implemented by organizations in knowledge-based industries seeking high-value-added contribution, but even here the motive is likely to reflect self-interest, regarding employees as a means to an end. This, of course, is perfectly acceptable in terms of utilitarianism. The majority of employees can enjoy the benefits of softish HRM at the core and in the first periphery, and a quite reasonable justification can be given for the rightness of actions that result in unfortunate consequences for the minority. This is fine as long as such consequences only touch a minority. When most of us are on non-standard, temporary, fixed-term contracts, facing high employment insecurity and ever-increasing labour intensification, the fact that a minority have salaries like telephone numbers becomes unacceptable. Utilitarianism obviously only provides a moral justification if actions taken in its name *do* produce benefits for the majority that outweigh the costs to the minority. As already discussed, the ethics of stakeholder analysis, while looking persuasive at first sight, contain potential escape clauses that can render them little more than well-meaning rhetoric in practice (hence, no doubt, the appeal to well-meaning politicians). The recognition of the customer's stake is certainly in tune with the ideas of flexibility and responsiveness that underlie most models of HRM. Perhaps it is helpful too in according employees a dual identity: 'You may not like what is happening to you as an employee, but you'll appreciate the outcomes as a customer.' Finally, Rawlsian ethics, though formally Kantian in its attempt to derive *a priori* principles of distributive justice that are acceptable to all rational persons, in practice comes over as a form of utilitarianism. In a world of scarce resources this is likely to mean that, as employees are used as a means to an end, there will be some that lose out. For these people 'soft' model HRM may be an irrelevancy, while 'hard' model HRM is likely to be an uncomfortable experience.

Notes

1 This has been referred to as 'supply side' factors in terms of employment choice as, for example, when people actually seek part-time in preference to full-time work (Hunter et al., 1993).
2 Such as 'high-performance work practices' or 'high-commitment management'. Indeed Wood explicitly states: 'The implication of this research is that high commitment management is universally applicable' (1995: 57).

References

Beauchamp, T.L. and Bowie, N. E. (1988) *Ethical Theory and Business* (3rd edn). Englewood Cliffs, NJ: Prentice-Hall.
De George, R. T. (1990) *Business Ethics* (3rd edn). New York: Macmillan.
Delbridge, R. and Turnbull, P. (1992) 'Human resource maximization: the management of labour under just-in-time manufacturing systems', in P. Blyton and P. Turnbull (eds), *Reassessing Human Resource Management*. London: Sage. pp. 56–73.
Donaldson, J. (1989) *Key Issues in Business Ethics*. London: Academic Press.
Donaldson, T. and Werhane, P. H. (eds) (1993) *Ethical Issues in Business: a Philosophical Approach* (4th edn). Englewood Cliffs, NJ: Prentice-Hall.

Edwards, P. K. and Whitston, C. (1991) 'Workers are working harder: effort and shopfloor relations in the 1980s', *British Journal of Industrial Relations,* 29 (4): 593–601.

Evan, W.M. and Freeman, R. E. (1988) 'A stakeholder theory of the modern corporation: Kantian capitalism', in T. Beauchamp and N. Bowie (eds), *Ethical Theory and Business* (3rd edn). Englewood Cliffs, NJ: Prentice-Hall. pp. 97–106.

Garrahan, P. and Stewart, P. (1992) *The Nissan Enigma: Flexibility at Work in a Local Economy.* London: Mansell.

Geary, J. (1992) 'Employment flexibility and human resource management', *Work, Employment and Society,* 6 (2): 251–70.

Guest, D.E. (1987) 'Human resource management and industrial relations', *Journal of Management Studies,* 24 (5): 503–21.

Guest, D.E. (1990) 'Have British workers been working harder in Thatcher's Britain? A reconsideration of the concept of effort', *British Journal of Industrial Relations,* 28 (3): 293–312.

Guest, D.E. (1995) 'Human resource management, industrial relations and trade unions', in J. Storey (ed.), *Human Resource Management: a Critical Text.* London: Routledge.

Guest, D.E. (1996) 'Human resource management, fit and performance'. Paper presented to the ESRC Seminar Series on Contribution of HR Strategy to Business Performance, Cranfield, 1 February.

Guest, D.E. and Hoque, K. (1994) 'The good, the bad and the ugly: human resource management in new non-union establishments', *Human Resource Management Journal,* 5 (1): 1–14.

Guest, D.E. and Peccei, R. (1994) 'The nature and cause of effective human resource management', *British Journal of Industrial Relations,* 32 (2): 219–42.

Hunter, L., McGregor, A., MacInnes, J. and Sproull, A. (1993) 'The "flexible firm": strategy and segmentation', *British Journal of Industrial Relations,* 31 (3): 383–407.

Huselid, M. (1995) 'The impact of human resource management practices on turnover, productivity and corporate financial performance', *Academy of Management Journal,* 38 (3): 635–72.

Legge, K. (1988) *Personnel Management in Recession and Recovery: a Comparative Analysis of What the Surveys Say. Personnel Review,* 17 (2), monograph issue.

Legge, K. (1989) 'Human resource management: a critical analysis', in J. Storey (ed.), *New Perspectives on Human Resource Management.* London: Routledge. pp. 19–40.

Legge, K. (1995) *Human Resource Management: the Rhetorics, the Realities.* Basingstoke: Macmillan.

Lukes, S. (1974) *Power: a Radical View.* London: Macmillan.

Marchington, M., Wilkinson, A., Ackers, P. and Goodman, J. (1994) 'Understanding the meaning of participation: views from the workplace', *Human Relations,* 47 (8): 867–94.

Marginson, P., Armstrong, P., Edwards, P. and Purcell, J. with Hubbard, N. (1993) 'The control of industrial relations in large companies: an initial analysis of the second company level industrial relations survey'. Warwick Papers in Industrial Relations 45, IRRU, School of Industrial and Business Studies, University of Warwick, December.

Metcalf, D. (1988) 'Trade unions and economic performance: the British evidence'. Discussion Paper 320, LSE Centre for Labour Economies, London.

Metcalf, D. (1989) 'Water notes dry up: the impact of Donovan reform proposals and Thatcherism at work on labour productivity in British manufacturing industry', *British Journal of Industrial Relations,* 27 (1): 1–31.

Millward, N., Stevens, M., Smart, D. and Hawes, W.R. (1992) *Workplace Industrial Relations in Transition.* ED/ESRC/PSI/ACAS Surveys. Aldershot: Dartmouth.

Nolan, P. and Marginson, P. (1990) 'Skating on thin ice? David Metcalf on trade unions and productivity', *British Journal of Industrial Relations,* 18 (2): 225–47.

Ogbonna, E. and Wilkinson, B. (1990) 'Corporate strategy and corporate culture: the view from the checkout', *Personnel Review,* 19 (4): 9–15.

Purcell, J. (1996) 'Human resource bundles of best practice: a utopian cul-de-sac?' Paper presented to the ESRC Seminar Series on Contribution of HR Strategy to Business Performance, Cranfield, 1 February.

Rawls, J. (1971) *A Theory of Justice,* Cambridge, MA: Harvard University Press.

Sewell, G. and Wilkinson, B. (1992a). 'Empowerment or emasculation? Shopfloor surveillance in a total quality organisation', in P. Blyton and P. Turnbull (eds), *Reassessing Human Resource Management*. London: Sage. pp. 97–115.

Sewell, G. and Wilkinson, B. (1992b) '"Someone to watch over me": surveillance, discipline and the just-in-time labour process', *Sociology*, 26 (2): 271–89.

Sisson, K. (1994) 'Personnel management: paradigms, practice and prospects', in K. Sisson (ed.), *Personnel Management* (2nd edn). Oxford: Blackwell. pp. 3–50.

Starkey, K. and McKinlay, A. (1993) *Strategy and the Human Resource*. Oxford: Blackwell.

Storey, J. (1987) 'Developments in the management of human resources: an interim report'. Warwick Papers in Industrial Relations 17, IRRU, School of Industrial and Business Studies, University of Warwick, November.

Storey, J. (1992) *Developments in the Management of Human Resources*. Oxford: Blackwell.

Vielba, C. A. (1995) 'Managers' working hours'. Paper presented to the British Academy of Management Annual Conference, Sheffield University Management School, 11–13 September.

Walton, R.E. (1985) 'Towards a strategy of eliciting employee commitment based on policies of mutuality', in R.E. Walton and P.R. Lawrence (eds) *Human Resource Management, Trends and Challenges*. Boston: Harvard Business School Press. pp. 35–65.

Wickens, P. (1987) *The Road to Nissan*. London: Macmillan.

Wickens, P. (1995) *The Ascendant Organisation*. London: Macmillan.

Wilkinson, A., Marchington, M., Goodman, J. and Ackers, P. (1992) 'Total quality management and employee involvement', *Human Resource Management Journal*, 2 (4): 1–20.

Wood, S. (1995) 'The four pillars of HRM: are they connected?', *Human Resource Management Journal*, 5 (5): 48–58.

Wood, S. (1996) 'High commitment management and payment systems', *Journal of Management Studies*, 33 (1): 53–78.

Wood, S. and Albanese, M.T. (1995) 'Can we speak of high commitment management on the shop floor?', *Journal of Management Studies*, 32 (2): 215–47.

Part II

QUALITY AND CULTURE CHANGE PROGRAMMES

The debate concerning the supposed emancipation of operatives and shop floor employees resulting from those HR initiatives that cluster under the banner of quality and culture change programmes has been raging for some years. The argument can be characterized as devolution versus deskilling, empowerment versus intensification, commitment versus compliance, discretion versus surveillance, flattening structures versus bolstering bureaucracy and so on. For the most part practitioners and consultants are zealots while academics remain sceptical, but the empirical evidence used to support their respective cases is invariably strained through an ideological filter. For this reason the next three chapters are especially welcome, both for rehearsing this debate and for going on to determine grass-roots perceptions in a variety of organizations.

The chapter by Rees analyses employee perceptions of quality management strategies implemented in four case organizations. The author is careful to point out that QM does not represent a unified paradigm, nor are the principles of QM universally applicable. In an even-handed review of the literature, Rees picks out four distinct models of QM: optimistic, exploitative, contingency and reorganization of control. The results of his study, drawing primarily upon questionnaire data from a representative sample of lower-grade employees in each organization, lend support to the last of these models. He concludes that for these staff, QM clearly has both positive and negative consequences, and that despite the evident increase in work pressure associated with quality principles, such principles are nevertheless embraced by most employees as benefiting them and the wider organization. For Rees this coexistence of such paradoxical sentiments is unsurprising, reflecting as it does the fundamental contradiction at the heart of capitalist employment relations.

Just as competitive pressure was said to be a trigger for the launch of the quality programmes in Rees's study, the same was true of the two case organizations researched by Glover and Fitzgerald-Moore, a car components manufacturer and a heavy engineering company. Indeed commercial constraints led to an early end to the first study and a redundancy programme overshadowed the second. In order to ascertain the shop floor perspective they conducted individual and group interviews, supported by observation and questionnaire data. Once again they found a mixture of perceived benefits and tensions associated with QM, although the shop floor views in the engineering plant were predominantly negative. Their study is carefully located in the relevant literatures, with reference to the origins of the quality 'movement'. This is useful because, as the authors note, different conceptions of QM carry quite different expectations as to outcomes, some modest and pragmatic and others far more ambitious and far-reaching. Staff will tend to judge the success or otherwise of such HR initiatives against the 'promises' made at their outset. Thus it may not be labour intensification, peer pressure or surveillance that disillusions so much as the frustration that 'TQM had been perceived as being capable of delivering benefits but had not done so.' Raised expectations and the hope of greater trust in relations with senior management do not materialize.

The importance of identifying the criteria by which HR interventions are to be evaluated is also emphasized in the chapter by Martin, Beaumont and Staines in which they assess the impact of a culture change programme in a Scottish local authority. The programme comprised a range of HR policy and practice initiatives including delayering, business planning, training and team briefing. The research team assessed this by carrying out an employee audit, in part replication of two benchmark surveys that had been carried out previously, and by focus group discussions with employees in one particular department. The high expectations of senior management that widespread attitude change would ensue were largely unfulfilled. The authors relate this to a persistent weakness in culture change writing and practice, namely the assumption that an integrative organizational paradigm exists and/or can be attained. They also point to the inevitable tension between the aspirations, on the part of organizational leaders, for a strong corporate culture on the one hand, and 'the low-trust assumptions embedded in the fundamentally unchanged hierarchical nature of bureaucratic organizations' on the other. Once again, as with the more focused attempts to shift shop floor behaviour and attitudes reported in the other QM studies, control is not removed but rather reorganized.

3

Empowerment through Quality Management: Employee Accounts from inside a Bank, a Hotel and two Factories

Chris Rees

Quality management (QM) is unquestionably one of the leading management fashions of the 1990s. QM programmes derive from a growing belief during the 1980s that commercial success comes not simply from low-cost competitiveness but from high and reliable quality. The aim is to foster the commitment of employees across the organization to quality in terms of product and service delivery, and to create a culture of 'continuous improvement'.

The subject of QM has generated a substantial body of literature. Much of this literature is highly prescriptive, concentrating on the constituent elements of the QM approach and the reasons it is deemed advantageous for employers. Far less attention has been paid to the question of how such strategies are perceived by employees, or to the nature and extent of the employee participation which is inherent in the QM philosophy. This chapter contributes to a redressing of the balance in the QM literature, by focusing on the complexities of QM in practice, and by attempting to illuminate the real extent of employee participation and involvement in quality improvement initiatives.

The chapter presents findings from four case study companies. The views of managers at two of these companies have already been reported elsewhere. These managers were generally keen to stress how QM has allowed employees 'to express their views more openly and take greater personal responsibility for their work. At the same time they acknowledge the clear trends towards the closer monitoring and tighter control of that work' (Rees, 1995: 108). This chapter seeks to describe whether and to what extent this complex picture is reflected in the attitudes of *employees* across the four organizations. It argues for a conception of QM which is theoretically in the 'middle range', in so far as it views QM as essentially a form of management control whilst recognizing the real benefits which it can provide for some employees. The chapter argues that in each of the four case study companies, 'empowerment' is one of the major defining features of the QM strategy, but that although this is based upon giving greater autonomy and discretion to employees over their immediate work environment, QM also invariably entails a simultaneous increase in managerial control.

The quality management literature

In this section the major approaches to the subject of quality management are reviewed by looking at the various ways in which the implications of QM for employees have been addressed. This will allow the theoretical position of the study to be more clearly specified, before details are given of the four case study companies.

As already noted, the bulk of the literature on QM is highly prescriptive, and tends to assume that employees will simply welcome QM. This approach is best exemplified in the work of the so-called management 'gurus' (cf. Crosby, 1984; Ishikawa, 1985; Deming, 1986; Juran, 1988), and in Britain by Oakland (1993). However, the limitations of the prescriptive approach are by now well established. For instance, it is common within this literature for solutions to the technical issues of designing appropriate quality procedures to be fully specified, whilst the employee co-operation that QM may require is taken for granted. There is usually very little discussion of the practical problems that managers may experience in attempting to apply the techniques, and little or no information about how QM is perceived by employees. Moreover, the principles of QM are generally assumed to be universally applicable, and it is also assumed that all organizations will necessarily benefit from the introduction of QM.

Although the prescriptive literature on QM may be of limited value, there has in recent years arisen a large body of more analytical work which takes a far more critical perspective on the nature and implications of quality initiatives, and it is this literature with which the current study is primarily engaged. It has developed out of the field of industrial sociology as well as more mainstream industrial relations and HRM debates, and can be broadly categorized into four distinct approaches: (i) the optimistic model; (ii) the exploitation model; (iii) the contingency model; and (iv) the reorganization of control model.

Optimistic models

The optimistic argument is essentially that QM and other similar forms of work reorganization entail an increase in workers' skills and result in genuine employee 'empowerment'. For example, some writers within the labour process tradition have argued that QM production methods do indeed reunite conceptual and manual tasks, and are therefore largely progressive in their implications for employees. This view is often predicated on the notion of a clear-cut qualitative break from a previous era of Fordist mass production and Taylorist management practices, to a new so-called 'post-Fordist' era of technical innovation, reskilling and high-trust teamworking. In this context,

QM is seen as benefiting employees, in so far as it allows for job enlargement, multi-skilling and enhanced responsibility for quality control at the point of production or service delivery (for the roots of this approach: see Piore and Sabel, 1984; Abernathy et al., 1983; Tolliday and Zeitlin, 1986).

The limitations of this argument have been well rehearsed. For example, Elger (1990) has shown how buzz-words like 'flexible specialization', 'functional flexibility' and 'Japanization' may serve to highlight potentially significant changes, but they still obscure the shifting and contradictory nature of the social relations involved. Much of Pollert's work has questioned the whole model of transformation through flexible specialization (see Pollert, 1991).

An optimistic view of the implications of QM for employees is perhaps more likely to be found within the more mainstream HRM literature. Here, for instance, Cruise O'Brien (1995) discusses the potential for QM to increase the commitment of employees to performance improvement, whilst Hill (1991a; 1991b) has concluded that QM has the potential to institutionalize employee participation on a permanent basis. As we will see, this view has also been subjected to a good deal of criticism, much of it from a 'contingency' perspective.

Exploitation models

In marked contrast to the optimistic approach is the argument that QM necessarily results in the increasing subordination of employees in return for little or no extra reward. Rather than conceiving of a radical shift to 'post-Fordism', the majority of recent work within the labour process tradition has emphasized the essential continuity within recent changes, highlighting the continuing 'degradation of work' through the deskilling effects of new technology, and the reproduction of established patterns of work organization. In this context, QM is seen as simply the latest in a long line of work intensification techniques, albeit a more sophisticated one than traditional Taylorism (for the roots of this approach see Braverman, 1974; Sayer, 1986; Tomaney, 1990).

A typical example of this approach is that of Delbridge and Turnbull (1992). They describe task-based teamworking as a form of 'management through compliance', whereby organizing workers into teams and making these teams accountable for their own performance allows firms operating a just-in-time (JIT) production system to impose a 'customer ethos' on the workforce, and harness the peer pressure of fellow team members to ensure compliance to company objectives. Total quality control (TQC) is similarly characterized as 'management through blame', with the use of quality charts and statistical process control (SPC) tending to structure experimentation and therefore in fact reduce workers' freedom to make process changes, whilst at the same time acting as a system of surveillance and monitoring to ensure compliance. And JIT is defined as 'management by stress', since it is underwritten by the notion of 'continuous improvement', whereby all elements of waste are systematically and progressively eliminated, thus implying a continual intensification of the work routine.

Similarly, in a study of a Japanese-owned electronics plant, Sewell and Wilkinson (1992) use Foucault's (1977) concept of the 'panopticon' to describe the surveillance and control capacities of the quality monitoring system. This includes the use of 'traffic lights' above each worker, which act as a constant reminder of individual performance whilst also relaying this information to the wider audience of the team. The system allows management to solve the 'quality–quantity dilemma' by establishing a dynamic balance between production volume and production quality, whereby 'the extent of the amber zone (one to four errors) has been set . . . to represent a level of performance where the number of errors are acceptable but which also creates a climate where all members are constantly made aware of the need to make improvements' (1992: 108). There does appear to be a growing number of critical case studies that suggest a clear contrast between what Sewell and Wilkinson call the 'rhetoric of empowerment, trust and mutual dependency . . . [and] the shop-floor reality of pervasive regimes of constant electronic and peer group scrutiny' (1992: 98; see also McArdle et al., 1995; Parker and Slaughter, 1993; Tuckman, 1995).

However, just as the 'optimistic/empowerment' perspective tends to underestimate the complexities of contemporary work restructuring, so this 'exploitation/intensification' argument similarly fails to adequately address the complexities of QM, or to recognize its essentially indeterminate nature in terms of its effects on employee autonomy and involvement. Take, for example, the case study by McArdle et al. (1995) of 'PCB Electronics'. They clearly document employees in the company as perceiving the move to QM as leading to a better way of working and higher job satisfaction, and yet conclude quite categorically that 'although employees at the plant *appear* to gain more satisfaction from the job enlargement process . . . TQM has introduced management by stress . . . into the plant and forced workers to indulge in their own work intensification' (1995: 170, my italics).

The study on which this chapter is based (Rees, 1996c) also found a good deal of evidence which shows a generally favourable attitude to QM on the part of employees. However, this evidence is not dismissed as 'false consciousness', but is considered to be as valid as other evidence which shows the more negative implications for employees which QM can have. The literature on QM implying work intensification must not be neglected, and studies such as those quoted above have usefully criticized the more optimistic accounts. But many such analyses tend to take an equally one-sided view. As such, it is necessary to adopt a more subtle position which can account for the complexities involved, and to utilize what Storey and Sisson have called 'theories of the "middle range"' (1989: 177).

Contingency models

One approach which appears to do exactly this is exemplified in the work of Adrian Wilkinson (Wilkinson et al., 1992; Wilkinson and Witcher, 1991). The essential argument is that QM could in principle bring significant benefits to both management and employees, but that when introduced it invariably fails to live up to the initial promise. In practice many companies pay only lip service to the idea of quality, there is often resistance from middle managers, and short-term demands often interfere with longer-term goals.

Other writers have also highlighted the contingent aspects of QM, such as the problematic nature of attempting to foster commitment to quality principles through the use of HRM techniques. Take, for example, the use of quality circles, which hold out the promise of improving communications and winning the active commitment of employees to quality improvements. Research has shown that quality circles are often established as a parallel or dualistic structure which coexists outside the existing organizational hierarchy, and as such are doomed to fail in the face of middle management recalcitrance and inadequate reward systems (Hill, 1991b; Schuler and Harris, 1992; Wilkinson, 1994).

More problematical still for management may be attempts to generate employee commitment to QM through the use of HRM-style appraisal and payment strategies. There is an implicit contradiction between collectivism and individualism in attempts to develop a collective identity around teamwork at the same time as discriminating between individual employees' contributions through performance-related pay (Legge, 1995), and employees themselves will recognize a payment strategy that pulls in different directions. Even where performance-related pay is not used, performance appraisals may be perceived as arbitrary and subjective. As for the use of job evaluation as a basis for a more simplified grading structure, this too can lead to a great deal of disquiet over the manner in which jobs are measured and evaluated. So, in this particular area, 'the HRM dimension to management's compensation strategies – appraisal, performance-related pay and job evaluation – [may itself be] . . . the locus for much of employees' dissatisfaction and not the level of compensation *per se*' (Geary, 1992: 50).

Attempts to foster commitment to QM through the use of HRM techniques are clearly far from straightforward, and as such it may be necessary for employers adopting quality principles to pay far more attention to the promotion of an appropriate organizational culture. Here too, however, the problems are well documented. It is now widely accepted that in many organizations QM programmes are initially received with some enthusiasm by employees, but that this soon wanes and disillusionment quickly follows. Seddon (1989) has claimed that this is due to management's preoccupation with the 'harder' QM considerations such as costs and production performance, and their relative neglect of the 'softer' aspects such as employee commitment and customer perceptions. Wilkinson makes a similar point when he argues that

> there may well be tensions between the production-oriented 'hard' aspects of TQM which tend to emphasise working within prescribed procedures and the 'soft' aspects which emphasise employee involvement and commitment. Management [often] give insufficient attention to examining the underlying values and resulting behaviour of employees, with the result that there is a failure to achieve the 'cultural change' necessary if TQM is to be successfully implemented. (1992: 326)

Oliver and Wilkinson (1992) have similarly noted that many British employers do not fully appreciate the high dependency relationships implicit in the use of hard QM, and generally have failed to synchronize their personnel and labour relations carefully to manufacturing strategy.

Wilkins (1984) has argued that successful QM companies are able to develop a management ideology and an organizational culture in such a way that employees simply adopt the new philosophy as if it were communicated directly by the senior managers who originally articulated it. Others are far less optimistic. Ogbonna (1992), for instance, has questioned the extent to which the ideology of QM is capable of penetrating deep-seated attitudes. More to the point, he questions the extent to which QM organizations are really concerned about genuine cultural change. Put simply, it may not matter to management whether or not employee behaviour is based on internalized values, as long as it is the right behaviour (see also Sturdy, 1994).

In contrast to extreme applications of the optimistic and exploitation models, research adopting a contingency perspective highlights the need to resist the easy conclusion that the implications of QM for employees are necessarily either all good or all bad. Rather, the reality is often a mixture of extended employee involvement together with tighter management control. As Wilkinson et al. conclude from their own case study research,

> TQM might be seen as an attempt by management to control employees through internal discipline and self-control. However [in both case studies] the workforce appeared to be reasonably enthusiastic about the TQM programme . . . As a form of involvement, TQM may appear to offer immediate, tangible benefits to employees in a way that traditional forms of participation perhaps do not. (1991: 30)

Reorganization of control models

Finally, a fourth distinct analytical perspective on QM can be identified. It has something in common with the labour process tradition, in that the nature of production and the organization of work tasks are considered to be crucial factors in determining the boundaries of employee autonomy and discretion. However, it stops short of concluding that the implications of QM for employees tend invariably to be negative. Rather, QM is here seen as 'one among a series of changes, which also embrace new technology and new payment systems, which re-organise the shop-floor so that in some respects commitment is enhanced while in others control is also tightened' (Collinson et al., 1997).

This position also shares much common ground with the contingency model, stressing as it does that many of the practices associated with QM have had ambiguous effects so far as employees are concerned. There is now a range of case study literature which addresses the 'optimistic/empowerment' and the 'exploitation/intensification' theses and concludes that neither of these contradictory interpretations is wholly accurate. Rather, as Glover and Fitzgerald-Moore say in Chapter 4 in this volume, QM tends to give greater autonomy to those at the lower end of the organizational hierarchy at the same time as providing for tighter management control (see also Bratton, 1992;

Dawson and Webb, 1989; Geary, 1993; 1994; Rees, 1996a; 1996b; Webb, 1995). Perhaps the clearest exposition of this view is to be found in the work of John Geary. Discussing the nature of direct task participation, he concludes that

> although management may grant employees considerable freedom to be self-managing, it is a practice which has not diluted managerial control over the labour process: it has rather been redefined and exercised in a different form. It would seem that management has at once become both enabling and restraining. (1994: 650)

This chapter goes on to describe and explain findings which show the various ways in which these twin dimensions of QM are reflected in the views of employees at four different organizations.

An analysis of four case study companies

The reorganization of control which QM implies is not easily observed and quantified, and as a result the full implications of QM for employee involvement can only be adequately addressed through detailed case study research. Four companies were studied. Two of these are in the manufacturing sector ('Auto Components' and 'Office Tech') and two are in the private services sector ('New Bank' and 'Hotel Co.'). Two main approaches were used in order to probe the nature of each QM strategy and its implications for employees in four organizations. Firstly, in each case a series of lengthy semi-structured interviews were conducted with members of management at all levels in the organization. It is important not to restrict attention to those directly involved with the QM programme, and so the views of a wide range of managers on the relevance of QM and its place within business policy more generally were sought. Secondly, detailed structured questionnaires were administered to a representative sample of lower-grade employees at each of the organizations (in the two manufacturing companies this meant shop floor production workers and operatives; in New Bank, clerical grades; and in Hotel Co. those below assistant manager level) and it is primarily from these questionnaire data that the current chapter draws.

The rationale behind this two-pronged approach was that it allowed the study to go beyond the broad policy statements of senior management to consider the impact of QM on employees. The focus of the employee survey can be summarized in terms of three key sets of questions as follows.

Management communication   Have employees perceived an increase in top-down communication since the QM programme was introduced? If so, which communication methods do they find most useful? Do employees consider these forms of communication to have increased trust between themselves and management? Are management perceived as being more 'open' in their style?

Employee empowerment   Do employees feel that they have greater autonomy and discretion over problem-solving and decision-making? How much influence do employees believe that they have over quality improvement? Do they feel they can have the most influence through formal involvement groups and quality circles, or through more informal means?

Effort levels and work intensification   Do employees feel that they are working harder since QM was introduced? If so, in what ways? Are employees more aware of monitoring and surveillance of their work? If so, what form does this take? Does it cause employees to feel under pressure or stress? If so, is this sufficient to detract from any perceived benefits of QM?

A comparison of QM strategies in the four companies

This section summarizes very briefly the nature of the QM strategy at each of the four case study companies, highlighting how each strategy ties in with the 'hard/soft' conception of QM outlined previously.

Manufacturing: Automotive Components

Auto Components is a British company operating on a brownfield site in the East Midlands. It manufactures a range of specialist parts for motor car engines, concentrating in particular on valve guides and valve seat inserts. It has around 200 employees, and the vast majority of shop floor workers are members of the Amalgamated Engineering and Electrical Union.

The quality strategy at Auto Components began with a heavy emphasis on the quality of the product and on the hard aspects of QM, and it can be traced to the introduction of statistical process control in the mid 1980s. From the initial impetus of SPC the company then decided to move towards modern manufacturing methods, and made a heavy capital investment (of around £2.5 million) in new plant. This new plant was located in a new factory on the site, where a section of the workforce has been trained in quality control techniques and now operates in task-based teams with full functional flexibility. The company sees the technology that has been introduced as lending itself to a particular form of production organization, namely cellular manufacturing, and as providing benefits in terms of greater efficiency and productivity.

Having begun with a clear emphasis on the hard production aspects of QM, Auto Components has more recently progressively moved to introduce the softer aspects. An integrated package of employee communication and involvement measures has been established, with a heavy emphasis on training and on methods of involving employees more in quality improvement activities. Taken together, the company refers to its overall QM strategy as 'continuous ongoing improvement' (COI). Formal quality circle teams (called 'COI groups') are a key aspect of the quality strategy, and shop floor workers are also encouraged to take greater personal responsibility for the quality of their work.

Competitive pressures and rising customer expectations are clearly identified as the major reasons for the introduction of the QM programme. After a turbulent decade in the 1980s, Auto Components is now in a healthy position. It has won three QI awards from Ford as well as the Queen's Award for Export, and in 1993 was Chrysler Supplier of the Year throughout Europe. Management believe they have a comprehensive QM programme in place which will lead to further quality improvements and thence in turn to a still better market position.

Manufacturing: Office Technology

Office Tech has a very different history and background from Auto Components, and this has heavily influenced the course that QM has taken. It is a wholly owned British subsidiary of a Japanese parent company, and was established on a greenfield site in the West Midlands in 1986. At this site the company is primarily involved in the manufacture of photocopying machines. It has around 350 employees, and is non-union.

Office Tech has had a strong quality ethos from the day it was established, with the emphasis very much on product quality. Managers throughout the company define quality in terms of providing the customer with a reliable product, and consistency in product quality is achieved through a wide range of quantifiable production techniques and standards. Like Auto Components, a key element of the QM strategy is the idea of making continuous improvements to the product, and this is embodied in the Japanese principle of *kaizen*, which refers to making improvements through small incremental steps. At Office Tech it is not just production workers who work to such principles. Management also try to ensure that their own decision-making procedures follow an identifiable format which leads to a continual increase in the efficiency of management activities. This is embodied in the 'plan do check action' (PDCA) cycle, whereby department heads submit activity plans containing quantifiable targets to the Managing Director on a regular six-monthly basis.

As regards quality assurance, Office Tech works to the principle of 'zero defects', so that if one defect is found the whole batch has to be rechecked. This principle is used on incoming parts, on the production line, and on finished goods. Coupled with the *kaizen* principle of continuous improvement, the company believes that this represents a stringent quality standard.

The vast majority of production workers at Office Tech man individual workstations on a linear assembly line. There is no cellular manufacturing in this main production area, and thus the scope for functional flexibility between jobs is limited for the majority of employees. The company has experimented with quality circles, and has recently made more rigorous attempts to increase the flow of communication from management to shop floor operatives. It has also begun to encourage employees more frequently to put forward their own suggestions and ideas for quality improvements. In general, however, progress on the softer aspects of QM remains slow, and the company's overall QM strategy is defined in large part by the use of hard quantifiable techniques for ensuring consistency in product quality.

Private services: Banking

New Bank is a major financial services institution, employing around 40,000 people across a network of retail banking branches and business centres throughout Britain. In the late 1980s, with competition developing rapidly within the financial services market, the company perceived the need to compete more on quality and to improve the level of customer service. Although the company is not formally committed to the banner headline of total quality management, its stated corporate mission is to become 'first choice' for customers and staff, and in so doing the quality of customer service is recognized as of paramount importance. The main driving force behind the introduction of QM at New Bank was the perceived need to gain competitive advantage in a market place where the products on offer are fundamentally the same.

The QM strategy at New Bank began with an emphasis on the softer elements, instilling in employees the importance of customer service, and 'empowering' them to take greater personal responsibility for the quality of service provision. In the mid 1980s a 'smile campaign' was initiated, one of the first signs of recognition of the importance of customer service. The company quickly followed this up with the introduction of quality circle groups into branches. These were called 'quality service action teams', a formalized approach designed to encourage ideas from employees about ways of improving customer service. Aside from problem-solving teams, New Bank has also introduced a wide range of methods for communicating with employees. These include notice boards, staff circulars, newsletters, management briefings, and an increasing use of video communications.

In general, the QM strategy at New Bank differs from that at Auto Components and Office Tech in that it is focused primarily around the softer aspects of customer service and employee 'empowerment'. However, there has recently been an identifiable shift in emphasis away from the purely qualitative aspects of QM and towards attempts at measuring and quantifying customer service initiatives. One example of this is the introduction of so-called 'mystery shoppers' into branches. Detailed reports are compiled following these visits, providing branch managers with quantifiable data on levels of staff courtesy and efficiency of service. More generally, the company is making more stringent attempts to elicit and monitor customer feedback, such as through the use of customer questionnaires, which are used to compile an overall 'customer satisfaction index' giving scores for individual branches and offices.

Private services: Hotel Group

Hotel Co. is one of the leading hotel groups in Britain, with 15 hotels situated throughout the UK. Staff numbers range from around 130 in the 11 full-service hotels to around 30 in the 4 smaller limited-facility establishments. In the early 1980s the company perceived that it could only gain competitive advantage through its service standards surpassing those of other hotels, and the

QM strategy at Hotel Co. is thus similar to that at New Bank in being centred around improvements in customer service.

Hotel Co. launched its first 'customer care' programme in 1984, based on impressing upon staff in front line positions the importance of providing good customer service. However, the principal defining feature at the beginning of the company's QM strategy was the introduction at the same time of a comprehensive quality circle initiative, with every hotel in the group required to set up problem-solving teams. From this initial heavy emphasis on quality circles, the company has since moved to a more integrated QM strategy. Two years were spent planning and developing a thoroughgoing TQM programme, largely under the personal guidance of the Managing Director. The programme includes not just an emphasis on employee involvement in problem-solving through formal quality circle meetings, but also a central focus on 'empowering' staff to take greater personal responsibility for the service provided in the hotels.

Again in a similar fashion to New Bank, Hotel Co. is now beginning to put more emphasis on measuring and monitoring the nature and effectiveness of this empowerment. A variety of measures of the effectiveness of QM initiatives are being introduced, and attempts are being made to utilize customer feedback to greater effect. Standardized procedures for dealing with customers have also been introduced. In giving the reasons for moving to a QM strategy, managers at Hotel Co. reflect the views of managers at the other three case study companies by stressing the role of competitive pressures. In particular they point to the need to gain a competitive edge through focusing on quality in a market place where the product on offer to the customer is essentially identical.

Employee perceptions of QM

This section provides a broad summary of some of the key issues arising from the employee questionnaire returns. Rather than presenting quantitative data, a number of central themes are briefly highlighted. The findings from the four case studies show a mixed reaction among employees to the three sets of key questions outlined previously, a complex range of responses which are fully explicable only in terms of the specific organizational context of each company. However, a broad pattern emerges in which it is possible to highlight clearly both positive and negative implications of QM for employees.

General attitudes to quality

Beginning with the evidence on the 'positive' side, a number of questions were asked of employees about their general attitude to the QM strategy at their own organization. Virtually all employees described the concept of quality as either 'very important' or the 'most important issue' in the company. Perhaps unsurprisingly, employees at the two manufacturing companies tended to define this in terms of quality of the product, whilst larger numbers at the two service sector companies referred to customer service. The largest proportion of employees at Hotel Co. described quality as relating to 'everything that the company does'. The TQM programme at Hotel Co. is certainly communicated to employees as covering all aspects of the operation of the business, and this message would seem to have got through.

Large numbers of employees across the four companies said they had been in favour of the QM strategy when it was first introduced. An open-ended question asked why this was, and the two most common replies were: (i) QM is generally 'the best way forward'; and (ii) it is 'necessary for competitive reasons' or for 'company survival'. These answers clearly demonstrate support for the rationale which managers have used to justify QM. Moreover, large numbers of employees (particularly at Auto Components and Hotel Co.) said they were now more supportive of QM. As for the reasons for this, the vast majority said they had 'seen the benefits' it had brought, or were now 'more aware of the reasons' for its introduction. Virtually all employees expected there to be further quality-related changes taking place, and large proportions said they supported these changes.

Communication and trust

A series of questions were asked about management communication and levels of trust. A large majority of employees at both Auto Components and Hotel Co. reported there to be either 'complete trust' or 'trust most of the time', whilst the numbers saying this at the other two companies were somewhat lower. Over one-third of employees (except at Office Tech) said that this trust had increased since the QM strategy was introduced. When asked the reasons for this, most said there was now a 'better atmosphere', there was 'more communication', and managers had a 'better attitude'. An exception to this was New Bank, where an almost equally large proportion reported exactly the opposite.

Overall, virtually all employees reported feeling either 'a fair amount' or 'a great deal' of loyalty towards the company (these figures were especially high at Auto Components and Hotel Co.). Employees across the four companies had clearly perceived a large increase in management communication since the QM strategy was introduced, and large numbers said this had significantly increased employees' trust in management (again, the numbers saying this were highest at Auto Components and Hotel Co.).

Task-based teamworking

Turning to employee attitudes towards task-based teamworking, there is an interesting difference between the responses of those working in the new factory at Auto Components (who now work in formal multi-skilled teams) and those working in the older factory on the more traditional linear production lines. Although all those in the older factory described themselves as working 'individually', other questions revealed a striking degree of 'team spirit' among them. This highlights the need in such surveys to ask further questions, rather than a simple 'yes/no' question about the existence or otherwise of teamworking. Certainly at these four case study companies, even where functional or task flexibility is not a recognized management policy or has not been found to be a central feature of the organization of work routines, employees will tend nevertheless to apply the term 'teamworking' to other more general forms of day-to-day co-operation between themselves and their work colleagues.

A large proportion of employees across the four companies said that other team members would 'always' help them out with problems, and a clear majority at each company reported the sense of teamwork within their particular group to be either 'fairly strong' or 'very strong'. Large numbers felt that this sense of teamwork had increased during the previous three years, and even larger numbers said that the responsibility of their team for organizing work had increased. Finally, a majority at each company said they had acquired new skills as a result of teamworking. Most at Auto Components referred to 'technical' skills, and at the other three companies to 'communication' or 'social' skills.

Problem-solving teamworking

A form of teamworking used more widely across the four companies is problem-solving teamworking, which usually takes the form of quality circles. Whilst task-based teamworking can be considered as an element of 'hard QM', in that it stems from the nature of the organization of production, problem-solving teams are policy development rather than task-based groups. They are considered to be an element of 'soft QM' in so far as they are set up by management for the explicit purpose of involving employees in decision-making, in an attempt to make greater use of their latent potential and encourage their commitment to managerial objectives.

By far the largest proportion of employees at each company reported that they 'always' attended problem-solving meetings. When asked why this was, the two most common replies were: (i) to be 'kept informed' or to 'know what is going on'; and (ii) because they allow 'involvement in discussing and solving problems'. When asked how much consideration they thought management gave to the ideas which come from these meetings, around two-thirds at each company said either 'a reasonable amount' or 'a great deal of serious consideration'. And when asked if they thought such groups were generally a good thing, virtually all employees replied 'yes'.

Influence over quality and problem-solving

Another set of questions probed employees' views about the more informal ways in which they may have some influence over quality. The vast majority of employees said that they frequently put forward informal suggestions, and most said that things did change as a result. As for the nature of these changes, an open-ended question elicited the following three most common answers: (i) 'work flow or workstation changes'; (ii) 'job-specific changes'; and (iii) 'minor technical changes'. This clearly shows that although employees do feel that they have an influence over quality, the scope of this influence is limited to a relatively narrow range of issues relating to their own immediate work situation.

A large majority of employees at each company said they felt that management were now more willing to listen to their suggestions than before QM was introduced, and around two-thirds believed managers gave either 'a reasonable amount' or 'a great deal of serious consideration' to such suggestions. A clear majority felt that their own influence over quality had either 'increased' or 'increased greatly'. The largest proportions at Auto Components and Hotel Co. put this down to their involvement in problem-solving teams, whilst those at Office Tech and New Bank were more likely to refer to having 'more responsibility' or 'more autonomy'. Finally, a large majority at each company said they felt that employees in general had either 'a fair amount' or 'a great deal of influence' over quality.

It is apparent from the responses of employees across this range of issues that their attitudes to the principles of QM were generally favourable, and there was a widespread acceptance of the importance of the concept of quality. Most perceived there to have been an increase in communication from management, and this was generally welcomed. Moreover, the vast majority felt that their level of influence over quality and involvement in problem-solving had increased, and there was considerable enthusiasm among employees for some of the specific quality improvement initiatives. Overall, the language of 'customer orientation' and 'continuous improvement' seemed to have cut quite deeply, and employees showed remarkably little scepticism about core QM ideas.

Effort levels

Having said all this, the data also revealed a clear downside to QM as far as employees were concerned. Primary among the 'negative' implications of QM is the fact that a majority of employees at each company said that they were now working harder than three years ago. When asked in an open-ended question why this was, a large proportion referred to there having been an 'increase in production' or in 'workload', whilst a number of others (particularly at New Bank) said that there were now 'fewer people doing more work', a clear indication of an intensification of work.

What is notable, however, is that when asked if they enjoyed working this hard, a large majority of employees replied 'yes'. As for the reasons, the largest proportion at Auto Components said that working hard 'passes the time' or 'makes the day go quicker', whilst those at the two service sector companies were more likely to refer to a sense of 'pride' and 'job satisfaction', or to finding hard work 'rewarding and challenging'. Not that harder work was by any means entirely welcomed. Two-thirds at Auto Components mentioned the 'boredom' and 'monotony' of their work, whilst large proportions at New Bank and Hotel Co. referred to the high workload as causing 'fatigue', 'tiredness' and 'stress'.

Monitoring and surveillance

Apart from increasing effort levels, another central contention of the 'exploitation/intensification' theorists is that QM strategies entail an increase in the monitoring and surveillance of work. The evidence here is less clear-cut, but it does lend some support to this view. A large proportion of employees at each company said they were aware of monitoring and surveillance either 'to a reasonable extent' or 'to a great extent' (although around one-third at each of the manufacturing companies said they were 'not aware at all'). Straightforward manager or supervisor 'over the shoulder presence' was commonly reported, with many referring to this as 'spying'. Almost half of employees at Office Tech referred to 'monitoring through performance appraisal', whilst a larger proportion at New Bank mentioned 'productivity statistics' or 'work measurement'. A clear majority of employees at each company felt that the level of this monitoring and surveillance had increased under the QM programme.

Discipline

Two questions were included in the questionnaire which asked employees about the specific issue of discipline, and the responses are revealing. Firstly, employees were asked an initial question about whether they thought management had become more or less strict since the introduction of the QM strategy. Whilst a clear majority at Office Tech said 'more strict', employees at the other three companies were in general equally as likely to say 'less strict' as 'more strict', with by far the largest proportions choosing to say there had been 'little or no change'. However, when then asked about whether there had been any change over certain specific issues, by far the largest proportion at each company said management were now 'more strict'. This was especially the case with regard to the issue of 'poor quality work'. A possible interpretation of these answers is that management had been successful in giving the impression to employees that they were now in general no more strict than before QM was introduced (as the answers to the first general question suggest), but that when employees were probed on particular issues, the practical reality of tighter discipline was revealed.

Stress and work pressure

Finally, a number of questions were asked about perceived levels of stress and work pressure. Firstly, employees were asked how frequently they felt under pressure from other members of their work team. The answers are mixed, with significant numbers saying they 'sometimes' or 'always' feel such pressure, but with generally larger numbers saying they 'rarely' or 'never' do. As for the nature of this pressure, the largest proportions at each company mentioned feeling a 'general pressure to work faster', with others saying that other team members sometimes 'make you look foolish if you make a mistake', and there is thus a 'fear of criticism' from within the team. This is evidence to support another central tenet of the 'exploitation model' of QM, namely that teamworking invariably leads to 'peer pressure'.

Employees were also asked if technology was a cause of pressure in any way. Again the responses are mixed. Of those who said they did feel such pressure, the majority said that technology tends to 'dictate the pace of work', or in a manufacturing environment 'set line speeds'. Finally, employees were asked how often they felt under pressure or stress at work, and the largest proportion at each company replied 'sometimes', with significant numbers replying 'often' or 'very often'.

Overall, although the questionnaire returns show employees across the four companies to have in many respects a favourable attitude towards QM, a series of questions on effort levels, discipline and stress revealed an atmosphere of considerable pressure. Most employees reported that they were now working harder than before the QM strategy was introduced. The monitoring of work performance was felt to be widespread and growing, targets were said to be stricter, and managers were said to be taking a tougher approach to discipline. Moreover, the majority of employees reported feeling under greater stress as a result of such changes.

Conclusion: explaining the 'paradox' of QM

It is apparent that the structure of authority at the four case study organizations was not radically changed by the QM initiatives, and managers and supervisors continued to exercise traditional powers. However, despite the fact that most employees were working harder, they did not appear to resent this. Indeed, most were satisfied to be working this hard. There was a recognition of the reality of competitive demands and of the rationale behind the QM strategy. Involvement in quality and in problem-solving was genuine, albeit tightly constrained by management control systems.

All of this points to the conclusion that what has occurred in each case is a *reorganization of control*. Although employees were given greater autonomy and discretion over their immediate work situation, QM also invariably entailed an increase in managerial control in other respects. QM thus allows for greater 'detailed control' for employees at the point of production or service delivery, whilst simultaneously providing management with increasing 'general control'.

A variety of different aspects of QM can be seen as contributing to increased managerial control: the routinization and standardization of production and work tasks; techniques for more closely monitoring and measuring work output and performance; increasingly tight discipline; pressures to conform to team or group expectations; and appraisal systems linking performance more closely to measurable indicators of product quality or customer satisfaction. So, just as there are a range of different factors which influence the nature of the QM strategy at each company, so too will there be variations in the precise means through which control is mediated.

Rather than attempting to explain these variations, the intention here is to describe what is *common* across the four companies, namely that for employees themselves QM clearly has both positive and negative consequences.

If we consider again the categorization of the literature presented earlier, we can see how some aspects of both the 'empowerment' and the 'intensification' perspectives are reflected in the findings. Considered as a whole, however, the results support neither the quality pundits, who assume that QM will necessarily transform organizations, nor those critics who see quality as simply a route to worker subordination. The former tend to neglect the constraints on quality programmes arising from job insecurity, stress and low morale, whilst the latter note these things but invariably assume that they are universal in their effects and that workers simply resent working harder. The findings presented here lend greatest support to the 'reorganization of control' model. As a result of his own case study research, Geary has noted 'the paradox [that] as workers were given more autonomy they were increasingly coming under tighter managerial control' (1994: 648). Although sympathetic to Geary's theoretical position, I would suggest that these twin dimensions of QM do not in the true sense represent a 'paradox', since they are in fact the inevitable outcome of any QM strategy. As such, it may be more fruitful to say that what they express is a fundamental contradiction at the heart of capitalist employment relations. As Hyman has observed of management strategy in general:

> The key to any credible treatment of strategy . . . is surely an emphasis on contradiction. Strategic choice exists, not because of the absence or weakness of structural determinations, but because these determinations are themselves contradictory . . . There is no 'one best way' of managing these contradictions, only different routes to partial failure . . . Employers require workers to be both dependable and disposable . . . Contradictory pressures within capitalism help explain the restless but fruitless search for managerial panaceas. (1987: 30, 43)

In broad terms, QM can perhaps best be seen as just the latest of these management panaceas to gain widespread influence (and one that is itself now being apparently superseded by other all-embracing concepts, such as 'business process re-engineering'). The contention here is that as a management strategy QM has proved as unsuccessful in overcoming fundamental contradictions as those which preceded it, but that this should not surprise us, since it is necessarily so. As Wilkinson and Willmott have more recently concluded,

> the 'quality revolution' can be seen as the most recent move in a developing process in which the organization of production is subordinated to the *contradictory logics of capitalist labour processes*. Means are now sought for securing an adequate return on capital in a situation where the basis of competition is quality and speed of innovation, not just price. To accommodate this shift, and thus to contribute to this change, quality initiatives are introduced that in many cases *expand employee discretion and eliminate sources of frustration as they extend and reinforce processes of management control*. (1995: 11, my italics)

Finally, it is worth briefly considering what the implications of this analysis are for management practice. Or, to put it more simply, to ask the question 'does QM work?' The results presented in this chapter certainly suggest that QM can be a partial success. Employees clearly did embrace quality principles, despite the evident increase in work pressure which they tended to bring with them. As other research involving the same author has concluded (Edwards et al., 1997; Rees et al., 1996), quality programmes can perhaps in this respect be seen as catalysts, bringing out a latent willingness to take responsibility and providing a focus and rationale for efforts at involvement.

Any assessment of the success or otherwise of QM essentially turns on what criteria are being used to measure it. Some argue that QM tends invariably to fail, in the sense that it does not lead to fundamental changes in employees' internal values, or to substantial increases in 'customer satisfaction' (Knights, 1995). However, what this chapter has sought to demonstrate is that focusing solely on whether QM has empowered employees and led to widespread quality improvements can lead to a polarized debate, with those who conclude that it has not secured these goals perhaps using an unduly harsh test of success. Seen instead as a relatively modest set of initiatives designed to encourage a sharper focus on customer service, QM can be said to have had a degree of success.

In other words, whether the conclusion is drawn that QM has succeeded or not depends on what management are considered to be attempting to achieve. For those managers interviewed at the four case study companies described here, 'quality' meant doing what they were doing more effectively and giving employees some say in the process. Despite the often messianic tone of the mission statement, anything more than this was not seriously on the agenda. To quote Hyman once again:

> Capital is . . . faced with essentially contradictory requirements: to limit the discretion which workers may apply against its interests; and to harness the willing application to profitable production of that discretion which cannot be eliminated . . . The notion of contradiction is again crucial: the function of labour control involves both the direction, surveillance and discipline of subordinates whose enthusiastic commitment to corporate objectives cannot be taken for granted; and the mobilisation of the discretion, initiative and diligence which coercive supervision, far from guaranteeing, is likely to destroy . . . Shifting fashions in labour management stem from this inherent contradiction: solutions to the problem of discipline aggravate the problem of consent, and vice versa. Accordingly, pragmatism may well be the most rational management principle. (1987: 40–2)

Considered in this way, QM may indeed be the latest fashion, but it is again no different to any previous management strategy which has aimed to generate the commitment of employees to corporate objectives. This chapter has sought to demonstrate that in considering the implications of any particular instance of QM, what one will find is a reorganization of control, whereby an organizationally specific mix of contingent factors leads to a particular balance between control and consent. Employees are likely to experience some genuine extension of discretion and autonomy, albeit relating only to the detail of their immediate work situation, whilst at the same time management will be able to consolidate their more general control. And the argument has been advanced that the best way of making sense of this shifting 'terrain of control' is by reference to the notion of contradiction. Moreover, I have indicated that although they may not conceive of the issue in the same terms, most managers are themselves not blind to the effects of these contradictions, and as a consequence pragmatism will indeed tend to be their most likely response.

References

Abernathy, W., Clark, K. and Kantrow, A. (1983) *Industrial Renaissance: Producing a Competitive Future for America*. New York: Basic Books.

Bratton, J. (1992) *Japanization at Work*. London: Macmillan.

Braverman, H. (1974) *Labor and Monopoly Capital: the Degradation of Work in the Twentieth Century*. London: Monthly Review Press.

Collinson, M., Rees, C. and Edwards, P.K. (1997) *Involving Employees in Total Quality Management: Employee Attitudes and Organizational Context in Unionised Environments*. London: Department of Trade and Industry.

Crosby, P. (1984) *Quality without Tears*. New York: McGraw-Hill.

Cruise O'Brien, R. (1995) 'Employee involvement in performance improvement: a consideration of tacit knowledge, commitment and trust', *Employee Relations*, 17 (3): 110–20.

Dawson, P. and Webb, J. (1989) 'New production arrangements: the totally flexible cage?', *Work, Employment and Society*, 3 (2): 221–38.

Delbridge, R. and Turnbull, P. (1992) 'Human resource maximisation: the management of labour under just-in-time manufacturing systems', in P. Blyton and P. Turnbull (eds), *Reassessing Human Resource Management*. London: Sage.

Deming, W. (1986) *Out of the Crisis*. Cambridge: Cambridge University Press.

Edwards, P.K., Collinson, M. and Rees, C. (1997) 'The determinants of employee responses to TWM: six case studies'. Unpublished paper.

Elger, T. (1990) 'Technical innovation and work re-organization in British manufacturing in the 1980s: continuity, intensification or transformation?', *Work, Employment and Society*, Special Issue, May: 67–102.

Foucault, M. (1977) *Discipline and Punish: the Birth of the Prison*. London: Allen Lane.

Geary, J.F. (1992) 'Pay, control and commitment: linking appraisal and reward', *Human Resource Management Journal*, 2 (4): 36–54.

Geary, J.F. (1993) 'Total quality management: a new form of labour management in Britain?' Paper presented at ISVET/ENI Conference on New Developments in British Industrial Relations, Rome, 29–30 April.

Geary, J.F. (1994) 'Task participation: enabled or constrained?', in K. Sisson (ed.), *Personnel Management: a Comprehensive Guide to Theory and Practice in Britain*. Oxford: Blackwell.

Hill, S. (1991a) 'How do you manage a flexible firm? The total quality model', *Work, Employment and Society*, 5 (3): 397–415.

Hill, S. (1991b) 'Why quality circles failed but total quality management might succeed', *British Journal of Industrial Relations*, 29 (4): 541–68.

Hyman, R. (1987) 'Strategy or structure? Capital, labour and control', *Work, Employment and Society*, 1 (1): 25–55.

Ishikawa, K. (1985) *What is Total Quality Control? The Japanese Way*. Englewood Cliffs, NJ: Prentice-Hall.

Juran, J. (1988) *Juran on Planning for Quality*. New York: Free Press.

Knights, D. (1995) 'Through the managerial looking glass: problematizing quality management and the new organisation'. Paper presented at Warwick Business School Seminar Series, 27 September.

Legge, K. (1995) *Human Resource Management: Rhetorics and Realities*. Basingstoke: Macmillan.

McArdle, L., Rowlinson, M., Procter, S., Hassard, J. and Forrester, P. (1995) 'Total quality management and participation: employee empowerment or the enhancement of exploitation?', in A. Wilkinson and H. Willmott (eds), *Making Quality Critical: New Perspectives on Organizational Change*. London: Routledge.

Oakland, J.S. (1993) *Total Quality Management: the Route to Improving Performance* (2nd edn). London: Butterworth Heinemann.

Ogbonna, E. (1992) 'Organisational culture and human resource management: dilemmas and contradictions', in P. Blyton and P. Turnbull (eds), *Reassessing Human Resource Management*. London: Sage

Oliver, N. and Wilkinson, B. (1992) *The Japanization of British Industry* (2nd edn). Oxford: Blackwell.

Parker, M. and Slaughter, J. (1993) 'Should the labour movement buy TQM?', *Journal of Organisational Change Management*, 6 (4): 43–56.

Piore, M. and Sabel, C. (1984) *The Second Industrial Divide: Possibilities for Prosperity*. New York: Basic Books.

Pollert, A. (ed.) (1991) *Farewell to Flexibility?* Oxford: Blackwell.

Rees, C. (1995) 'Quality management and HRM in the service industry: some case study evidence', *Employee Relations*, 17 (3): 99–109.

Rees, C. (1996a) 'Employee autonomy and management control in the quality organisation'. Paper presented at 14th Annual International Labour Process Conference, Aston University, 27–29 March.

Rees, C. (1996b) 'Employee perceptions of quality management: making sense of the paradox'. Paper presented at British Universities Industrial Relations Association Annual Conference, Bradford, 5–7 July.

Rees, C. (1996c) 'Employee involvement in quality management strategies: a case study based analysis'. Unpublished PhD thesis, University of Warwick.

Rees, C., Scarbrough, H. and Terry, M. (1996) 'The people management implications of leaner ways of working'. IPD Issues in People Management 15, Institute of Personnel and Development, London.

Sayer, A. (1986) 'New developments in manufacturing: the just-in-time system', *Capital and Class*, 30: 43–71.

Schuler, R. and Harris, D. (1992) *Managing Quality: the Primer for Middle Managers*. Reading, MA: Addison-Wesley.

Seddon, J. (1989) 'A passion for quality', *The TQM Magazine*, May: 153–7.

Sewell, G. and Wilkinson, B. (1992) 'Empowerment or emasculation? Shopfloor surveillance in a total quality organisation', in P. Blyton and P. Turnbull (eds), *Reassessing Human Resource Management*. London: Sage.

Storey, J. and Sisson, K. (1989) 'Looking to the future', in J. Storey (ed.), *New Perspectives on Human Resource Management*. London: Routledge.

Sturdy, A. (1994) 'Employee responses to customer orientation initiatives: smiling but not (always) meaning it'. Paper presented at 12th Annual International Labour Process Conference, Aston University, 23–25 March.

Tolliday, S. and Zeitlin, J. (eds.) (1986) *The Automobile Industry and its Workers: between Fordism and Flexibility*. Cambridge: Polity Press.

Tomaney, J. (1990) 'The reality of workplace flexibility', *Capital and Class*, 40: 29–60.

Tuckman, A. (1995) 'Ideology, quality and TQM', in A. Wilkinson and H. Willmott (eds), *Making Quality Critical: New Perspectives on Organizational Change*. London: Routledge.

Webb, J. (1995) 'Quality management and the management of quality', in A. Wilkinson and H. Willmott (eds), *Making Quality Critical: New Perspectives on Organisational Change*. London: Routledge.

Wilkins, A.L. (1984) 'The creation of company cultures', *Human Resource Management*, 23 (1): 41–60.

Wilkinson, A. (1992) 'The other side of quality: 'soft' issues and the human resource dimension', *Total Quality Management*, 3 (3): 323–9.

Wilkinson, A. (1994) 'Managing human resources for quality', in B.G. Dale (ed.), *Managing Quality* (2nd edn). Hemel Hempstead: Prentice-Hall.

Wilkinson, A., Allen, P. and Snape, E. (1991) 'TQM and the management of labour', *Employee Relations*, 13 (1): 24–31.

Wilkinson, A., Marchington, M., Goodman, J. and Ackers, P. (1992) 'Total quality management and employee involvement', *Human Resource Management Journal*, 2 (4): 1–20.

Wilkinson, A. and Willmott, H. (1995) 'Introduction', in A. Wilkinson and H. Willmott (eds), *Making Quality Critical: New Perspectives on Organizational Change*. London: Routledge.

Wilkinson, A. and Witcher, B. (1991) 'Fitness for use? Barriers to full TQM in the UK', *Management Decision*, 29 (8): 46–51.

4

Total Quality Management: Shop Floor Perspectives

Linda Glover and Deborah Fitzgerald-Moore

As companies have faced increasing competition, globalization and deep recession, it is of little surprise that issues of quality, adding value and minimizing cost are at the forefront of the corporate mind.

It is perhaps equally unsurprising that quality management initiatives such as total quality management (TQM) should appear so desirable. The protagonists of TQM promise a range of benefits including meeting customer requirements, producing zero defects, empowering employees, reducing waste and maximizing resources. Wilkinson and Marchington (1994) have argued that TQM represents 'the biggest single recent innovation in management'. QM strategies have been perceived as not only desirable but central to business survival.

Whilst there has been a plethora of articles in this area, there has been a dearth of discussion which explores shop floor experiences of TQM. Research in this area to date has tended to rely on quantitative approaches. This chapter is based on case study evidence which draws upon qualitative methodologies. The analysis is drawn from shop floor accounts of TQM. The chapter's aim is to portray the lived experience of total quality management as faithfully as possible.

Total quality management: historical context

Wilkinson and Willmott (1995a: 8) state that 'TQM has become the most celebrated and widely adopted form of quality management'; however, a coherent definition to which all adhere has been notoriously elusive. This has presented a number of issues for researchers in this area. Firstly, it can be very difficult to compare TQM initiatives either between different organizations, or within multi-site organizations as a result of different practitioner interpretations of TQM. The lack of coherent interpretation raises the importance of the researcher being sensitive to local contextual factors that affect the way that TQM is implemented within organizations.

Total quality management gained popularity in the United Kingdom from the 1980s onwards; however, the early writings of Deming on TQM can be traced back to the 1950s (Maiden, 1993). The early literature in this field was essentially prescriptive in nature, and promised a range of benefits to business should they engage in TQM. Whilst this literature has now been supplemented by a more critical authorship it is the prescriptive literature that is more likely to have influenced the actions of management. It is useful for the purposes of this chapter to return to some of the espoused principles of this literature in order to understand how the TQM concept has been sold to businesses. Practitioner interpretations impact upon the implementation of TQM within organizations. It also helps to give a framework for understanding the concepts that are subsequently 'sold' to shop floor workers.

Hill (1995) provides an overview of the key principles of TQM as defined by Deming (1986), Juran (1988) and Ishikawa (1985). He argues that one can draw out four core assumptions which are described as follows: firstly, that top management must drive TQM; secondly, that quality improvement occurs both vertically and horizontally within organizations; thirdly, that it is management's responsibility to continually review their organization's systems for quality; and finally, that an appropriate culture is a prerequisite of successful TQM. The last includes the development of positive attitudes to quality, more open communication and a shift from 'them and us' to a more unified culture which exists to further the needs of the organization.

Hill's review of the key principles demonstrates that TQM was originally developed as a management driven mechanism. Whilst it is concerned with changing cultures, the assumption made was that organizations would move towards a unitary framework. The unitaristic assumptions that underpin the various TQM models represent a major facet of TQM that is immediately open to criticism. Fox (1973) is amongst the early critics who have argued that unitarism is too simplistic a model and does not offer an adequate view of how organizations operate and of organizational conflict in particular. Wilkinson et al. have commented that 'assumptions underlying TQM are, of course unitarist, implying that employees are keen to participate in the pursuit of quality improvements with no immediate concern for extrinsic rewards' (1991: 31). One can appreciate the attractions of a 'conflict-free' model for successful business in the 1980s for practitioners. This period was characterized by the imperative for survival and this included the perceived need to move away from the 'British disease' of conflictual industrial relations which was seen to be undermining the performance of organizations (Collard, 1993; Semple, 1992; Roberts and Corcoran-Nantes, 1995).

The importance of human resource issues within TQM is now becoming more apparent (Wilkinson et al., 1991). In terms of definition, the HRM and TQM literature use the terms 'hard' and 'soft' in different ways, but an exploration of the implications of the implied approach to HRM within a TQM framework is an important one. Hard HRM relates to a utilitarian instrumentalist approach to the management of people, and soft HRM relates to a developmental humanist approach (Storey, 1987; Hendry and Pettigrew, 1990). Hard TQM relates to the quantitative aspects of TQM, for example statistical process control, and soft TQM relates to the need to develop a culture of customer responsiveness.

Wilkinson and Wilmott (1995a) have suggested that TQM has become associated with a soft approach to HRM; however, they are careful to remind us that the early quality theorists were essentially concentrating on developing systems that would produce quality products efficiently. This did not necessarily mean that the work experience would be improved as a consequence. They argue that many of the 'developmental humanist' assumptions, including empowerment and involvement, have been attached as a result of the influence of the popular management gurus such as Peters and Waterman (1982). This point is important. TQM is inevitably evaluated in relation to an individual's definition of it and in relation to the assumptions that they attribute to it. The lack of coherent definition has led to a multiplicity of interpretations, both at academic and at practitioner level (Pfeffer and Coote, 1991).

On a related issue, the early models of TQM were not synonymous with a move to full-blown industrial democracy. Marchington et al. have commented that 'Employee Involvement [including TQM] does not therefore imply a *de jure* sharing of authority or power with employees, although some forms of EI may provide new channels through which employee influence can be enhanced' (1994: 869). In the purest sense, it would be more likely that increased job-related participation would be encouraged by management, if it were seen as a mechanism that would result in solving quality-related problems. Whilst it is true to say that TQM programmes are likely to vary and one may find differing degrees of participation and involvement from company to company (Wood and Peccei, 1995), the brief review of some of the original principles of TQM highlights that it did not constitute a revolution in terms of altering the power balance in organizations. Therefore to search for, or expect to find, dramatically increased levels of power and authority on the shop floor is perhaps expecting more of TQM than it was initially envisaged to give.

Total quality management: a wolf in sheep's clothing?

As time has progressed, the prescriptive literature has been supplemented by what Rees (Chapter 3 in this volume) categorizes as the analytical models which include; the optimistic, exploitation, contingency and reorganization of control models. The debate has ranged from writers such as Hill who argue that TQM can potentially lead to a range of benefits for shop floor workers, including the institutionalization of participation, to the exploitation camp who believe that TQM inevitably leads to a range of negative consequences for shop floor workers (Sewell and Wilkinson, 1992). The critical perspectives have been vital in terms of offering alternative perspectives to the prescriptive camp, which has been woefully inadequate in exploring some of the cultural and organizational issues associated with moves to TQM.

Research has suggested that TQM programmes may tend to either explicitly or implicitly offer a range of benefits. The benefits may include the promise of increased job security, more involvement and participation, better working relationships and a more participative management style.

Some critics have looked at these so-called benefits sceptically, for example:

> It could be argued that by giving workers something to think about, management is taking away their freedom of thought and subordinating their subjectivity (Gramsci, 1971; Tuckman, 1995) . . . The willingness to accept TQM as the only way to work also obscures managerial action which has thus far prevented a response by employees. (McArdle et al., 1995: 166)

Hill (1995) suggests, however, that shop floor workers are not 'cultural dupes' that are easily seduced by TQM and that they are sensitive and critical to any perceived anomalies between their expectations of TQM and the 'reality' of their experience. In tandem with this, our research does not support the notion of 'false consciousness' as attributed by the exploitation literature. TQM seems to fire an expectation for high-trust relationships combined with a participative management style. Guimaraes has commented that through TQM management are 'expected to gain employees' trust, encourage problem solving and promote co-operation among departments' (1996: 20). Fulfilling such expectations can be problematic for a number of reasons. In many cases a change of management style is needed, from what may have been an auto-cratic past to a participative future. Wilkinson and Witcher (1991) highlighted a range of potential problems. They raise the issue that the elitist trappings of management such as a directors' dining suite, car parking and a social remoteness from shop floor workers may compound a resistance to change from within the management ranks. Individual managers may overtly or covertly resist attempts to dilute their power and privilege. If TQM is a man-agement driven mechanism, then herein lies one of the contradictions of TQM. Ogbonna and Wilkinson (1990) point to the possibility of 'resigned behavioural compliance' rather than changes in espoused values or basic assumptions. In terms of the discussion that follows, the important facet is how the shop floor perceived and interpreted management commitment to TQM, via an analysis of whether management behaviour matched their expectations of TQM. If the expectations are disappointed, they then lose 'faith' in the system.

One of the aims of a TQM programme may be to change the prevailing management/shop floor relationships, a move from 'them and us' to 'us'. Mullins (1993) has commented that changing the entrenched cultural norms of working relationships can be extremely problematic. TQM may also be seen as an attempt to bypass /marginalize the trade unions (Ackers et al., 1996). The new relationships may include individualistic forms of employee involve-ment, bolstered by job redesign and flatter organization structures. This chapter suggests that working relationships are viewed as a key indicator of the success of TQM by the shop floor; nevertheless we note in the ensuing dis-cussion that the operatives did not expect to see workplace unitarism.

The aspect of either implicitly or explicitly promised job security is partic-ularly relevant for the discussion of the findings that follow. Guimaraes

(1996) comments that a move to TQM is highly unlikely to offer the 'job for life'; however, what is important is that shop floor workers may perceive that it will. The implication is that if trust and co-operation (see Hill, 1991: 40) are built up with job security as an expectation, then these two prerequisites for 'success' would be easily shattered by the onset of a redundancy programme.

In summary, any analysis of the human resource issues associated with a move to TQM is fraught with a range of difficulties that stem from a lack of consistent definition and interpretation, which is at least partly related to the complexities associated with many of the terms. Our position is that TQM is essentially a management driven mechanism, but within certain parameters it may offer benefits for operatives. It will not, however, lead to a revolution in terms of redistributing power to the shop floor. Within organizations, 'soft TQM', which centres upon the need for culture change, involving such aspects as a suitable management style and increased participation, is most difficult to accurately articulate. One can describe many of the *techniques* associated with 'hard TQM' including statistical process control, Pareto analysis and so on. This is not to undermine the complexity of the human resource implications of hard TQM, but to point out that the core terminology is easier to describe. Articulating, visualizing and explaining in detail what 'culture' and 'culture change' *should* be associated with TQM, in a way that all can embrace, is fraught with difficulties. It can produce tensions at both shop floor and management levels and complexity in the research process.

The case study organizations

Empirical data from a car components manufacturing plant (Carplant) was collected and analysed in 1993. Research at a heavy engineering plant (EngPlant) began in 1995 and is ongoing. In each case study, both shop floor and management perceptions of TQM have been explored, but the focus for this chapter will be on the former. As the case organizations have requested that their identity not be disclosed, information about the businesses has been kept deliberately vague. The case study units were chosen for two main reasons; firstly, both companies had made a decision at corporate level to implement TQM; and secondly and most importantly, both companies were willing to give wide access to management, trade union and shop floor employees.

Qualitative techniques including individual/group interviews and observations were used to collect data within Carplant. The research at EngPlant included the use of the qualitative techniques described above, combined with a questionnaire-based attitude survey, the results of which are excluded pending further analysis. In both case studies, the interviews were structured in such a way as to encourage the interviewee(s) to lead discussion. Twenty-four interviews were carried out at the Carplant (including one group interview). Eighteen of the interviewees were from the shop floor. Approximately 50 per cent of the operatives interviewed were women which reflected the gender balance in the organization. Fifty-eight interviews (including five group interviews) have been carried out at EngPlant to date. Thirty-seven of the interviewees were from the shop floor. The interview data were semi-transcribed and the sentences were then labelled and categorized using grounded theory techniques (Strauss and Corbin, 1990).

The strength of the project has been the individual and group interviews with shop floor workers, giving them the opportunity to express their views in an area which has tended to rely on questionnaire techniques in the past. The qualitative approach allowed for the contextual sensitivity that purely quantitative approaches can lack (Marchington et al., 1994). The discussion of the findings demonstrates the importance of the contextual insight for this field of research.

The negotiation of wide access to employees and managers and the development of a trusting relationship between researcher and respondent were critical. In the case of EngPlant in particular, many of the shop floor workers registered concern that their comments could be transmitted to management. It is possible that this initial mistrust may have affected early results. However, as the project continues the insights should become richer as the employees' trust in the confidentiality of the research process increases.

The cases are presented not as direct comparisons but as each offering some different insights into shop floor perceptions of TQM. The discussion that follows will attempt to portray perceptions of the day-to-day experience of TQM on the shop floor. It uses the interviewees' words and aims to give as faithful an account as possible of their perspectives.

Background to the case study units

Both of the case study organizations employ approximately 400 staff and are part of large public limited companies, although the origins of each organization differ in nationality. Each plant is located in an area of high unemployment, created by the decline of local manufacturing and production activity over the 1980s. Both operations were viewed by the respective respondents as being crucial in terms of maintaining employment opportunities for the local community. Both have a history of autocratic management and adversarial management/trade-union relations. In particular Engplant was characterized by many interviewees as having been a 'no-go' industrial relations area throughout the 1970s and well into the 1980s. In 1991 the existing MD of Carplant was removed by head office, and a new MD, an HR Director and a Training and Development Manager were put in place. The development and implementation of TQM was approached differently by each organization and an overview of this is highlighted in Table 4.1.

Whilst there were some similarities in the way that the two cases implemented TQM, it is true to say that Carplant used a more holistic approach to implementation which included job redesign, the extensive use of TQM training (both on the job and via seminars), linking the payment system to quality and skill development, and the negotiation of TQ contracts with the trade

Table 4.1   *TQM implementation within the case study plants*

TQM programme	Carplant (1991)	EngPlant (1993)
Stated reason	Increased competition To emulate Japanese working practices	Increased competition Instructed by head office
Instigated by	Corporate-level management	Corporate-level management
Driven by	New Managing Director HR Director	General Manager TQ co-ordinator Quality steering
Designed	In-house	By management consultants

Introduced by	In-house TQM training by
	  CCMP management to all
	  employees
		In-house training by
		  management consultants
		Initially to management and
		  shop floor facilitators,
		  then cascaded to all
		  employees by facilitators

Trade union
  involvement
	Yes
	Negotiation of TQM
	  contracts
		No

Changes to working
  practices
	Move from production to
	  cell working
	Layout of factory redesigned
	Teamworking
		Minor changes, for
		  example the development
		  of process improvement
		  teams

Production oriented
  quantitative elements
  of TQM
	Tally charting
	Multiple attribute charts
	Pareto analysis
	Statistical process control
	Job redesign
	Production line to cell
	  manufacturing
		Tally charting
		Multiple attribute charts
		Pareto analysis
		Statistical process control
		Process improvement teams

Employee oriented
  elements of TQM
	Extensive follow-up
	  training for all aspects of
	  TQM
	Increased involvement:
	• team briefings
	• quality circles
	• suggestion schemes
	• teamworking
	Reward linked to quality and
	  staff development
	Appraisal linked to quality
	  and skills development
	Appraisal for management
	  linked to financial
	  performance indicators
		Limited follow-up training
		  for TQM
		Fragmented involvement in
		  some areas of the plant:
		• team briefings
		• suggestion schemes
		• quality circles
		No appraisal for operatives
		Appraisal for management
		  linked to financial
		  performance indicators

unions. The implementation was supported by a new participative style from the senior management team that were bought in to implement the system. Engplant in contrast tended to focus upon the hard aspects of TQM and did not make any significant changes to working arrangements. The senior management team remained unchanged. In 1994, shortly after the launch, 75 employees were made redundant.

The lived experience

Shop floor perceptions of TQM at the Carplant

Just prior to the implementation of TQM in 1991, Carplant had made 150 people redundant. In terms of company history the interviewees perceived the period up to 1991 as having been characterized by conflictual relationships between management and trade unions, autocratic management, little shop floor training and strict job demarcation. The analysis revealed that memories and company history were used as a reference point in terms of perceptions of TQM:

> in the past it was the least bit things and the men would down tools. It was very much us and them. The management didn't have much to do with the shop floor. People are pulling together now.

Prior to 1991 the operatives perceived the plant as one in which management and operatives were on either side of battle lines. There was also a perception that this state had contributed to the 1991 redundancies and that engaging in TQM was a way of securing their livelihoods (Guimaraes, 1996). This was seen as preferential to the insecurity and redundancies that they remembered: 'I like the fact that it's a permanent job for the future.'

Many of the operatives viewed a number of aspects of TQM as beneficial. In many ways CCMP had used a 'textbook' approach to TQM, and initial observations and interviews at the factory suggested that TQM was indeed the workplace utopia that the prescriptive authors would maintain. For example, production was arranged on a cell manufacturing basis; individual cells were collecting and displaying information including scrap rates, targets and absence rates; problem-solving groups were brainstorming in specially allocated rooms; team leaders were providing development and encouragement to continually improve quality. The test laboratory manager commented that 'the company is bubbling now, we need to keep the momentum going.'

The operatives' perceptions of TQM were undoubtedly influenced by the TQM training and were continually reinforced via the use of work redesign and new contractual arrangements, which included a complementary system of remuneration. This strategy had been supported by a soft HRM approach and the use of a participative style from the new top management that the operatives had not experienced before. The following comments illustrate common perceptions from the CCMP operatives:

> We're starting to foster a team spirit, more power is dispersed. There's a good relationship between top and bottom, we are empowering people now, people are central.

> There has been an improvement in relationships between management and staff.

> I like the way that we the operators have a say and are not just treated like work objects.

There was a perception that there were better relationships between managers and shop floor workers. The operatives commented that managers were more approachable and this seemed to be in line with their expectations of the management style that was appropriate within a TQM organization. Interviewees identified the increased involvement associated with a change in working practices as a benefit. The involvement centred around problem-solving activities, supported by appropriate training, including operative input into the redesign of work:

> The things that I like best are being in control of how I do my job, being involved in problem-solving and improvements in customer satisfaction. We are involved more than before.

Critics could argue that this merely represents a partial level of meaningful involvement which is primarily of benefit to the company, tying employees more closely to objectives defined by management, without the appropriate level of reward or input into decision-making to reflect the increased responsibilities and changing structures (Wilkinson and Willmott, 1995b; Wilkinson et al., 1991). However, the interviewees at Carplant focused upon the fact that increased involvement had led to intrinsically more interesting work (Hill, 1991). A move from production line to cell manufacturing was perceived to have increased social interactions between peer groups. The new cell working arrangements meant that there was more opportunity for social contact between peers. This was expressed by many as being preferable to the comparative isolation of production line work: 'I like the fact that we're able to work as a team making a lot of our own decisions'; and 'We work as a team and we're being included in what is happening. There's more involvement and we know a lot more of what's going on.'

It was interesting to note that there appeared to be gender differences in the way in which TQM was affecting the working lives of the operatives. The women felt that the TQM initiative had been something of an emancipation in terms of helping them to develop and increase in confidence. In a group interview with women operatives, there was a period of discussion which centred upon how TQM was affecting their personal lives: 'We even take work home now. Sometimes our husbands don't like it.'

The women highlighted the fact that their traditional role within the family had been to look after the domestic chores. In a trend that was linked to the recession, many of them were now the breadwinners. The women discussed how this role reversal, combined with the fact that they were taking work home, was creating pressures within the family unit. The issues of increasing confidence and being challenged to develop their potential were highlighted as a new experience by one of the women interviewed:

> in the past we were encouraged to leave our brains at the back door.

The possibility of gender differences and the impact of these upon the interpretation of TQM initiatives on the shop floor form a rich and interesting area which warrants more research. However, the Carplant study has now finished and unfortunately in the ongoing EngPlant research there are no women shop floor operatives.

Many of the factors highlighted relate to the broader context of the work experience, with certain perceptions being more directly linked to specific TQM techniques of problem-solving and training. It is suggested that TQM was being judged in terms of its impact upon relationships, management style and working practices. The positive comments seemed to be influenced by the fact that TQM had delivered in terms of the expectations that the operatives had of it. The operatives perceived that TQM had succeeded in terms of providing a more interesting and rewarding work experience:

> We've moved on to multi-skilling, but before we had strict job demarcation. We are learning all of the time, it breaks the monotony. We like the flexibility, it makes the job more interesting.

These comments are clearly in contrast to some of the critical perspectives of TQM that have argued that increasing flexibility and responsibility represent the cynical exploitation of shop floor workers (Turnbull, 1988). In contrast, the findings of the Carplant case suggest that a soft approach to HRM within TQM may be seen as beneficial to the employees who have previously experienced, in some cases, many years of boring, mundane and monotonous work.

Perceived pressures

The analysis also picked up a number of tensions, some of which have been highlighted by the critical camp on TQM (see Rees, Chapter 3 in this volume). Garrahan and Stewart (1992) have highlighted that TQM can be used as a vehicle for labour intensification. It would be possible to take the view that the Carplant had achieved this end via work redesign and involvement as part of the TQ-based contract of employment. Whilst there were many comments which were centred around the positive aspects of increased involvement, this particular sword was seen to be double edged:

> We feel more involved now, people are coming up with ideas. More involvement is a good thing in one respect as management have to listen . . . but involvement is a lot of pressure. There's more training now, but we're often stressed out about what we have to do.

One of the most common sources of perceived stress was related to the just-in-time element of the manufacturing process. A common perception was that one of the most stressful aspects of day-to-day work related to late deliveries. If deliveries did not arrive on time, the production process slowed down and targets could not be met. Interestingly enough, the blame for the increase in stress was attributed to unreliable suppliers, rather than the system of work itself or the management of Carplant.

In a parallel example, the cells were collecting data about issues including absence levels. The critical writers have argued that this represents the manipulation of peer pressure as a form of organizational control (Sewell and Wilkinson, 1992). In this case, the interviewees did not comment upon the nature of the information that they were being required to collect, but upon the fact that data collection had led to a vast increase in paperwork and that this was unwelcome.

The findings could be interpreted as a clear example of the peer pressure which is associated with TQM, but the shop floor workers had not perceived it as such and had therefore not resisted it (McArdle et al., 1995). However, the shop floor workers perceived a mix of benefits and tensions that were associated with TQM. They were also very sensitive to any perceived anomalies between their expectations of TQM and their view of reality. It is suggested that the willing acceptance of TQM could have easily changed given a change in circumstances, such as a redundancy programme or a perceived change in management behaviour. This could have led to a situation of 'resigned behavioural compliance' (Ogbonna and Wilkinson, 1990), in which the climate of the plant would have been markedly different.

Whilst the Carplant seemed to have made great strides forward in terms of providing a system that was viewed by many operatives as preferable, the findings suggested that the new relationships of trust and co-operation were fragile in nature (Davies and Wright, 1996). The findings did not support the theory that implementing a system of TQM, however successfully, would remove the pluralistic perceptions of them and us. This aspect was discussed by many of the shop floor workers: 'I still think it's "them and us", we need the trade unions for protection.'

Whilst there were many positive perceptions of TQM at the Carplant most of the interviewees perceived that TQM had not affected the traditional divide between manager and subordinate. There was an overwhelming support for the continuing need for trade unions as a source of back-up for the shop floor. TQM may have been perceived as a welcome intervention in terms of massaging relationships and providing intrinsically more interesting work, but efforts to harmonize conditions, flatten hierarchies and blur divisions between the shop floor and management had not been achieved as far as the respondents were concerned.

In 1994 the head office removed the MD and HR Directors. They had not met their performance indicators quickly enough. Further access to study was denied at this point.

Shop floor perceptions of TQM at EngPlant

Shop floor perceptions of TQM at EngPlant were very different to those described above. This section will highlight some of the major themes at Engplant and the implications of these for TQM at the site.

Past experiences

The issue of company history seemed particularly important in terms of affecting perceptions of TQM at EngPlant. Some of the most emotive comments focused upon the history of working relationships within the plant. During both formal and informal discussions, the operatives would often preface a comment about TQM with the phrase 'You have to understand that', and would then go on to talk about past events in order to explain the context and importance of their comment. At interview, it was common for the respondents to describe what they perceived to be three distinct periods of company history. The first period was described as the mid 1980s when the trades unions on site were very powerful and the shop floor had the upper hand over the management. Secondly, in a management attempt to regain control, there was a period which was characterized by autocratic, 'macho' management, encouraged by the General Manager and reinforced by zealous instigation of the disciplinary procedures. Thus the phrase 'from Butlins to Colditz' was incorporated into the language of the shop floor. In the words of an operative,

> They used a sledgehammer to crack a nut. The men used to be afraid, they were frightened. It's not necessary to treat people like that.

Many of the comments relating to this second period could be summarized as providing a picture of a climate of fear at the plant, with low-trust feelings of 'us and them', and management by coercion, none of which fitted with shop floor perceptions of TQM, as fuelled by the TQM training. Considering this background, the TQM training must have been perceived as presenting a picture of an organization that was many miles from the 'reality' of EngPlant.

The third period is characterized as post-TQM training which was from 1993 onwards. The analysis demonstrated that it was during TQM training that the operatives formed a mental picture of what it was all about, and more crucially, the way in which a TQM organization should operate. When exploring the perceived principles of TQM, the shop floor workers consistently cited the following aspects: striving for quality, teamworking, involvement, communication, everybody pulling together, and 100 per cent trust. The area which was discussed most frequently was the anticipated effect upon relationships between managers and the shop floor. TQM was expected to trigger a change which would help managers and operatives to work more closely together rather than constantly fighting a battle of wits. There was a perception that TQM was potentially a vehicle to draw together management and operatives despite the prior history of adversarial and acrimonious relationships:

> It's got some positive aspects, for example, problem identification and more communication with management. It's common sense; don't manage by fear, try to manage by talking to people. People do come to work to do the best that they can.

A minority felt that TQM was something of an affront in that they had always strived to produce quality goods. The interviewees indicated that there had been a brief period following the training in which hopes had been high at EngPlant that things were going to change for the better. Whilst it was clear that TQM fired expectations, the comments pertaining to this period seemed dominated by the events of January 1994 when the operation was restructured with the ensuing loss of 75 jobs. The redundancies undoubtedly had a direct impact upon the way that shop floor workers at EngPlant subsequently perceived and reacted to TQM:

> People link TQM to reorganization . . . some people were willing, but then it fell flat after reorganization.

> TQM was a good thing . . . a lot of people got behind it but management weren't doing their bit.

Despite the implementation of TQM, the period after this was still characterized by most as being one of low trust, suspicion, a lack of co-operation and barriers between management and operatives. This is perhaps unsurprising considering the proximity of the redundancy exercise to the launch of TQM.

In the period following the redundancies, there were small pockets of operatives within the unit which felt that TQM had led to some beneficial changes, including improved management/shop-floor relationships, increased morale, more awareness of quality issues and improvements in communication: 'Morale has gone through the roof since TQM, we don't have the problems we used to' and 'TQM is there to try and take the business forward, it's helpful in building trust.' The analysis suggested that some perceptions of TQM were influenced by certain line managers who had proactively encouraged TQ activities such as problem-solving, within their own areas, combined with what was perceived as a more participative management style. The element of active participation affecting perceptions of elements of TQM (such as team briefings) has been highlighted by Wood and Peccei (1995); however, the managerial climate in which participation took place seemed to be equally influential.

Current cynicism

Whilst pockets of positive attitudes to TQM existed, the majority of respondents tended to stress negative perceptions. A range of issues were highlighted as being significant in terms of influencing the negative perceptions, and once again these tended to focus upon relationships and management style (Wilkinson and Witcher, 1991). The workers were not opposed to TQM *per se*, but were cynical as to the motives of management in its introduction. The factors which were cited as being inconsistent with their view of TQM included: a blame culture incorporating the excessive use of disciplinary actions against individuals; a lack of honesty between managers and operatives; and a perception that there was a lack of senior management support for TQM. The blame culture was often cited as being inconsistent with the ideals of TQM:

We know more about quality but we're frightened of making mistakes.

TQM doesn't go through the system, punishment is still thrown out.

When something goes wrong it's who not what has gone wrong and how we can stop it in the future.

There was a perception that the management resorted too easily to the formal disciplinary channels if problems occurred. An investigation of the actual number of disciplinary cases indicated that this was not the case, which is a clear example of how a legacy from the past directly impacted on employee perceptions. This emphasizes the issue of perceived reality as highlighted by Hill (1995). Some felt that TQM was now no more than a set of tools that were superficial and had not made any impact upon the organization's status quo:

It's cosmetically trying to do something, but underneath it's us and them, TQM hasn't been taken on board.

In terms of some of the artefacts of TQM, the newsletter was the only factor which was perceived as positive by all. Other initiatives such as the team briefing system and the suggestion scheme were greeted by a more lukewarm response. The problem-solving groups that had initially been set up as part of the TQM launch were perceived to be shrouded in secrecy and many of the operatives were unaware either of how to join a problem-solving group or of what sort of work the groups could be expected to do.

Whilst some of the critical writers such as Delbridge et al. (1992) have pointed to the fact that TQM can be a way of increasing labour intensification, there were only limited signs that the shop floor operatives at the EngPlant were linking TQM to labour intensification. This seemed to be due to the fact that demanning had been an ongoing process over a period of years. There was certainly a perception that individuals were working harder – 'We've cut down so much, everybody does everybody else's job' – but this was not, at the time of study, associated directly with TQM.

A limited number of respondents regarded TQM as a time and motion device, but this perception was not widely held. In general, there was a sense that a honeymoon period had followed TQM training, but this ended in rapid divorce when the 1994 redundancies occurred. Many of the respondents seemed to have expected that trust between management and the shop floor was an integral component of TQM and that a move to TQM would enhance job security. The redundancies of 1994 were viewed as a signifier that any trust that had developed was broken at that point, 'There are deep wounds and a lack of trust, its hard to overcome memories'. Some workers were now increasingly concerned that if TQM meant productivity improvement, then further redundancies may occur (Wilkinson and Willmott, 1995a).

In summary, attitudes to total quality at EngPlant were formed in relationship to past experiences and a constant checking of the expectations of TQM against reality. In contrast to current critical analysis, the disillusionment at the plant in terms of total quality was not attributable to labour intensification, peer pressure or surveillance, but to a frustration that TQM had been perceived as being capable of delivering benefits but had not done so. It is fair to note, however, that the shop floor workers at EngPlant had not experienced a full and determined move to total quality, as found in Carplant. EngPlant retained much of its traditional character and TQM working practices had been supported by partial changes. Perceptions of TQM at EngPlant were more related to images of what might be rather than what was.

Conclusion

This chapter has provided a range of insights into shop floor worker perceptions of total quality management within two brown field site case studies. The impetus for the implementation of TQM in both cases was perceived as being driven by the necessity to compete and survive in increasingly hostile market conditions. Both units were part of large organizations that had been going through a process of reducing headcount over a period of years, and were acknowledged as having a cost-driven focus. The units had a history of adversarial relationships between management and trade unions.

The methodology for the study included the use of qualitative techniques and the interviews were analysed via the use of grounded theory techniques (Strauss and Corbin, 1990). The analysis suggests that individual perceptions of TQM were altered by the constructs which individuals create in order to make sense of their world (Berger and Luckmann, 1971). The model in Figure 4.1 illustrates the main categories that were generated from the shop floor interviews.

The categories are framed within a time context, that is, memories of company history are significant in moulding perceptions. The analysis suggested that the individuals compared their image of what it 'should be' like to work within a TQM company with their memories of company history and current working arrangements. The model suggests that the perceptual process is a continuous, evolving one and that over time perceptions will alter according to different experiences within the workplace.

During the TQM launch, the operatives formed a mental image of what TQM 'should be' and what they expected it to deliver, particularly in terms of working relationships, management style and working practices. These categories were often interlinked in that, for example, a perception of 'meaningful involvement' could be related to the perceived degree of 'fit' between management style and new teamworking practices in the company and an internalized image of TQM.

In both cases, TQM had been 'sold' to the operatives as a developmental-humanist model in terms of its relationship with their working lives. In both cases, the expectation of more satisfying work within a participative management context was well received. If the perceived 'reality', particularly in the three areas identified within the model, did not fit with expectations of TQM, then the operatives would become disillusioned and TQM would be deemed as unable to deliver, a management pipe-dream.

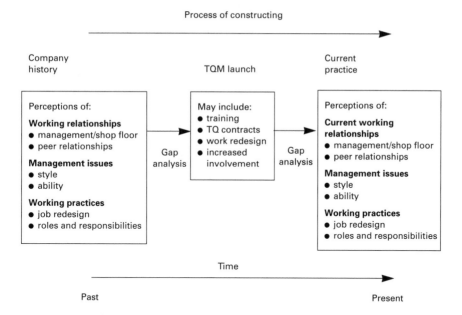

Figure 4.1 *Factors infuencing shop floor perceptions of TQM*

It is not suggested that all interviewees had a consistent mental image of what TQM 'should be'; the terminology associated with TQM is far too complex for that, as highlighted in the initial literature review (Pfeffer and Coote, 1991). However, the 'gap analysis' process of comparing the TQM concept with past history and current working practices did appear to be consistent between the individual interviewees. At this stage the model is offered as provisional (Warr, 1980) and will be refined as the longitudinal study offers more insights into shop floor interpretations of TQM.

The cases provided some contrasting evidence regarding operative perceptions of TQM. Therefore, what are the lessons learnt from the study? Firstly, as detailed above, company history and the interpretation of terminology are important. In terms of research, the questions that need to be addressed include: what model of TQM is being sold during the launch, what substantive changes followed, and is there a perception that the organization delivered what it has promised?

The evidence suggests that the soft approach to HRM combined with a participative management style may be perceived as offering a number of advantages. The Carplant results highlighted that the developmental humanist approach which had been incorporated into the TQM strategy was perceived as having allowed welcome opportunities for learning and involvement. A hard approach to HRM would not have produced the same scenario. The EngPlant case study demonstrated the problems of fuelling expectations and then failing to deliver promises (Wilkinson et al., 1992).

However, the above comments regarding the potentially positive reactions to soft HRM must be couched by other considerations. Our research suggests that both sets of operatives had formed a view that an involvement in TQM would lead to enhanced job security. If TQM incorporates soft HRM as an integral part of its approach then employee commitment may be sought by management as a positive outcome (Guest, 1989). TQM is more likely to generate *real* commitment if it is twinned with job security and trust. The image of TQM enhancing job security was swiftly destroyed at EngPlant by the redundancy programme. In the climate of the 1990s, these two conditions have appeared difficult for companies to deliver.

The research suggested that in contrast to EngPlant, the management at Carplant had not contravened the explicit or implicit promises that they had made to the workforce. They had developed a fragile new relationship between management and shop floor which, at least at the time of the study, was welcomed by the shop floor (Davies and Wright, 1996). The findings suggest that should the trust be broken, then the shop floor could easily revert from commitment to compliance (Ogbonna and Wilkinson, 1990). It is also suggested that if this were the case, the shop floor would be likely to overtly or covertly subvert the progression of the TQM programme.

The findings from both units suggest that the individual style of the manager can be influential in terms of the operatives' perception of TQM. Wilkinson and Marchington (1994) have stated that 'credibility of the [TQM] initiative is partly governed by management's treatment of the workforce.' This can be further complicated by company norms and history: 'In an organisational culture which encourages (or has encouraged) autocratic management . . . it is not an easy task to change entrenched management attitudes' (Wilkinson and Witcher, 1991: 8).

Operatives within both plants were using perceptions of management style and ability as a way of filtering their interpretation of TQM. They expected certain management behaviours as a result of the move to TQM, including a move from autocratic to more participative styles of management. The Carplant case demonstrated, however, that even if managers are successful in terms of nurturing more co-operative relationships through participative management, the short-termist measurement utilized at corporate level by many British businesses may be as potent a barrier for TQM as internal organization politics. This is clearly illustrated by the premature removal of the Managing Director and Human Resources Director of Carplant. The removal of key managers may have a detrimental impact upon any trust that may have built up from the shop floor.

Many individuals at the Carplant were relishing the intrinsically more interesting work that had been brought via job redesign and increased involvement. However, TQM as a model for organizations can be criticized on a number of counts. Some of the prescriptive literature ignores the individuality of people and assumes that the changing of attitudes and behaviour is merely a case of building appropriate systems to deal with the so-called 'soft' side of TQM. Its terminology has the potential to be interpreted in a number of ways. It is a unitarist concept (Fox, 1973) in that it implies there should be no divisions between management and shop floor workers. The end of a management/shop floor divide was certainly not perceived as a possibility at either plant. TQM was not perceived as a vehicle that would lead to increased levels of meaningful industrial democracy, but was seen as having the potential for offering some benefits within the confines of its remit.

The results from the Carplant in particular provided persuasive evidence that TQM, in conjunction with a developmental-humanist approach to HRM, supported by meaningful feelings of job security, can provide a more satisfying work experience for employees who have endured the monotony and boredom of production line work. The study demonstrates, however, that fulfilling operatives' expectations of TQM as a vehicle for improving their working lives is a complex task and requires some reciprocal commitment from the organization to the individuals. In the context of the recession-ridden 1990s it seems appropriate to conclude with a perspective from the shop floor:

TQM is like heaven, a nice place to go but we'll probably never get there.

References

Ackers, P., Smith, C. and Smith, P. (1996) 'Against all odds? British trade unions in the new workplace', in P. Ackers, C. Smith and P. Smith, *The New Workplace and Trade Unionism: Critical Perspectives on Work and Organisation.* London: Routledge.

Berger, P.L. and Luckmann, T. (1971) *The Social Construction of Reality: a Treatise in the Sociology of Knowledge.* London: Penguin.

Collard, R. (1993) *Total Quality: Success through People.* London: Institute of Personnel Management.

Davies, L. and Wright, M. (1996) 'Living downstream of HRM: personnel practitioner and operative views'. Occasional Papers, Leicester Business School, 36, September.

Delbridge, R., Turnbull, P. and Wilkinson, B. (1992) 'Pushing back the frontiers: management control and work intensification under JIT/TQM factory regimes', *New Technology, Work and Employment*, 7 (2): 97–106.

Deming, W. (1986) *Out of the Crisis.* Cambridge: Cambridge University Press.

Fox, A. (1973) 'Industrial relations: a social critique of pluralist ideology', in J. Child (ed.), *Man and Organisation.* London: Allen and Unwin.

Garrahan, P. and Stewart, P. (1992) *The Nissan Enigma: Flexibility at Work in a Local Economy.* London: Mansell.

Gramsci, A. (1971) *Selections From the Prison Notebooks.* London: Lawrence and Wishart.

Guest, D. (1989) 'Personnel and HRM: can you tell the difference?', *Personnel Management*, January: 48–51.

Guimaraes, T. (1996) 'TQMs' impact on employee attitudes', *The TQM Magazine*, 8 (1): 20–25.

Hendry, C. and Pettigrew, A. (1990) 'Human resource management: an agenda for the 1990's', *International Journal of Human Resource Management,* 1 (1): 17–44.

Hill, S. (1991) 'Why quality circles failed but total quality might succeed', *British Journal of Industrial Relations*, 29 (4): 541–68.

Hill, S. (1995) 'From quality circles to total quality management', in A. Wilkinson and H. Willmott (eds), *Making Quality Critical: New Perspectives on Organisational Change.* London: Routledge.

Ishikawa, K. (1985) *What is Total Quality Control? The Japanese Way.* Englewood Cliffs, NJ: Prentice-Hall.

Juran, J. (1988) *Juran on Planning for Quality*. New York: Free Press.

Maiden, R.P. (1993) 'Principles of total quality management and their application to employee assistance programmes: a critical analysis', *Employee Assistance Quarterly*, 8 (4): 11–40.

Marchington, M., Wilkinson, A., Ackers, P. and Goodman, J. (1994) 'Understanding the meaning of participation: views from the workplace', *Human Relations*, 47 (8): 867–94.

McArdle, L., Rowlinson, M., Procter, S., Hassard, J. and Forrester, P. (1995) 'Total quality management and participation: employee empowerment, or the enhancement of exploitation?', in A. Wilkinson and H. Willmott (eds), *Making Quality Critical: New Perspectives on Organisation Change*. London: Routledge.

Mullins, L. (1993) *Management and Organisation Behaviour*. London: Pitman.

Ogbonna, E. and Wilkinson, B. (1990) 'Corporate strategy and corporate culture: the view from the checkout', *Personnel Review*, 19 (6): 10–14.

Peters, T.J. and Waterman, R.H. (1982) *In Search of Excellence: Lessons from America's Best Run Companies*. New York: Harper and Row.

Pfeffer, N. and Coote, A. (1991) *Is Quality Good for You?* London: Harper and Row.

Roberts, K. and Corcoran-Nantes, Y. (1995) 'TQM, the new training and industrial relations', in A. Wilkinson and H. Willmott (eds), *Making Quality Critical: New Perspectives on Organisation Change*. London: Routledge.

Semple, J. (1992) 'Why we need TQM – PDQ', *Management Today*, May: 85–6.

Sewell, G. and Wilkinson, B. (1992) 'Empowerment or emasculation? Shopfloor surveillance in a total quality organisation', in P. Blyton and P. Turnbull (eds), *Reassessing Human Resource Management*. London: Sage.

Storey, J. (1987) 'Developments in the management of human resources: an interim report'. Warwick Papers in Industrial Relations 17, IRRU, School of Industrial and Business Studies, University of Warwick, November.

Strauss, A. and Corbin, J. (1990) *Basics of Qualitative Research: Grounded Theory Procedures and Techniques*. USA: Sage.

Tuckman, A. (1995) 'Out of the crisis? quality, TQM and the labour process'. Paper presented to the 11th Annual Labour Process Conference, Blackpool, April.

Turnbull, P. (1988) 'The limits to Japanization – just-in-time, labour relations and the UK automotive industry', *New Technology, Work and Employment*, 3 (1): 7–20.

Warr, P.B. (1980) 'An introduction to models in psychological research', in A.J. Chapman and D.M. Jones (eds), *Models of Man*. Leicester: British Psychological Society.

Wilkinson, A., Allen, P. and Snape, E. (1991) 'TQM and the management of labour', *Employee Relations*, 13 (1): 24–31.

Wilkinson, A., Marchington, M., Goodman, J. and Ackers, P. (1992) 'Total quality management and employee involvement', *Human Resource Management Journal*, 2 (4): 1–20.

Wilkinson, A. and Marchington, M. (1994) 'TQM: instant pudding for the personnel function?', *Human Resource Management Journal*, 5 (1): 33–49.

Wilkinson, A. and Willmott, H. (1995a) 'Introduction', in A. Wilkinson and H. Willmott (eds), *Making Quality Critical: New Perspectives on Organisation Change*. London: Routledge.

Wilkinson, A. and Willmott, H. (1995b) 'Total quality: asking critical questions', *Academy of Management Review*, 20 (4): 780–91.

Wilkinson, A. and Witcher, B. (1991) 'Fitness for use: barriers to full time TQM in the UK'. Paper presented at the British Academy of Management Conference, Bath.

Wood, S. and Peccei, R. (1995) 'Does total quality management make a difference to employee attitudes?', *Employee Relations*, 17 (3): 52–62.

5

Changing Corporate Culture: Paradoxes and Tensions in a Local Authority

Graeme Martin, Phil Beaumont and Harry Staines

During the course of the 1980s and 1990s it would have been difficult *not* to have come across any medium or large organization in the UK that had failed to experiment with a programme of cultural change. These programmes have their roots in the discourse of excellence associated with the Conservative government philosophy and policies of the 1980s (Du Gay, 1996: 56) and, as such, have been much more than passing fads in managerial theory and practice (Willmott, 1993). A number of features characterize these programmes (Legge, 1995; Mabey and Salaman, 1995; Meyerson and Martin, 1994; Bate, 1996): (1) they were based on the belief that significant organizational change involved 'winning hearts and minds' of employees rather than simply changing formal structures and systems; (2) they were rooted in a view of culture as something organizations *have*, the conscious planning and manipulation of which by senior managers could contribute significantly to performance; (3) they were, in effect, programmes of cultural reconstruction designed to constitute new identities for all levels of employees which were consistent with the overarching 'vision and values' of the organization; (4) they focused on leadership as the engine for creating and changing culture; (5) they employed a remarkably similar vocabulary, with terms such as 'employee empowerment' being particularly prominent; and (6) a set of new or changed human resource management (HRM) policies were assigned a key role in changing employee values and attitudes which would, in turn, produce a new pattern of employee role behaviour, usually involving greater efficiency and job satisfaction.

Invariably in organizations undergoing such programmes of change one encountered individual managers and staff lower in the organizational hierarchy who were less than enthusiastic about the content of such programmes. Initially there was some tendency amongst the architects of these programmes to dismiss the views of such people as representing those who did not understand where their 'true' interests lay (Fox, 1974) or those few who had lost out in the politics of the change process – i.e. their traditional role, status or influence in the organization was being downgraded or constrained. More recently, however, fundamental criticisms of such programmes have begun to appear in the academic literature, though to what practical effect is still open to question. These criticisms concern the conceptual clarity of 'practitioner' views of culture (Meek, 1988), the ideological and ethical nature of culture change programmes (Willmott, 1993; Alvesson and Willmott, 1996) and the empirical justification for their success (Casey, 1996; Legge, 1995: 196–7; Rodrigues, 1996; Van Maanen, 1991). Perhaps the most provocatively titled of the last group of these critical accounts of culture change came from some Harvard researchers who challenged the managerial readership of the *Harvard Business Review* with 'Why change programs don't produce change' (Beer et al., 1990).

This chapter reports some of the key results obtained from an empirical investigation of the impact of a cultural change programme on employee attitudes in a Scottish local authority. The value of this particular study, at least in our judgement, is threefold. Firstly, it is a study of a public sector organization, a sector which has been rather under-represented in the literature concerning the operation and impact of cultural change programmes. And secondly, it seeks to go beyond existing studies which have simply documented the absence of a strong impact of planned change programmes on employee attitudes. Instead it attempts to account for the relative absence of planned changes in employee attitudes (i.e. why little change?) by reporting the results obtained from an explicit investigation of this question. Thirdly, it offers some comments on the theoretical and practical shortcomings of describing and changing organizational culture through survey approaches which, though well documented in the academic literature, appear not to have had much influence on the expanding body of external and internal consultants engaged in change management.

The chapter proceeds as follows. In the next section we examine some of the leading lines of criticism of cultural change programmes. This is followed, in turn, by (i) an outline of the change programme in our local authority; (ii) the presentation of some leading results from an employee attitude survey concerning its impact; and (iii) the findings from a qualitative, follow-up investigation which are concerned with the issue of why change has been limited. Throughout the chapter considerable attention is given to the questions of how to assess the impact of such change programmes, in the sense of what are the relevant criteria involved and how should these be investigated.

The emerging criticism

As noted above, there is a growing body of literature on organizational culture which has important implications for HRM practitioners. Within the more mainstream, 'modernist' tradition, much of this literature is rooted in views of culture which are characterized by either *differentiation* or *fragmentation,* though both concern themselves with the alleged weaknesses of unitary or integratively based cultural change programmes (Frost et al., 1991; Meyerson and Martin, 1994; Martin and Frost, 1996).[1] A brief review suggested at least three major lines of criticism, all of which are outlined below.

Managing cultures

The first line of criticism of cultural change programmes centres on the notion or concept of 'culture' itself, and the potential for 'managing' it effectively. With respect to the concept, the 'integrative' or 'practitioner' school is aligned with a version of culture as something organizations *have*, whilst academic critics argue from a position which sees culture as something an organization *is* (a 'root metaphor'). Those 'purists' who view organizational culture from this latter perspective claim that culture cannot easily be manipulated but only understood and used to interpret the behaviour of participants. Concerning the potential for managing culture, Legge (1995), for example, raises the question of what is actually being managed and how it links to 'positive' organizational outcomes. Thus she notes that the changes which are evident in most cases of cited culture change are of *behavioural* commitment (or compliance) rather than the type of *attitudinal* commitment associated with 'winning hearts and minds'. In any event, as she further notes, the limited research evidence shows only a weak relationship between attitudinal commitment and job performance (1995: 206). Following another line of criticism, Morgan (1986) suggests that managerial attempts to use the concept in a manipulative and ideological manner run the risk of generating resistance, resentment, and mistrust on the part of employees if they 'see through' the unitary sentiments underpinning most culture change programmes. This 'differentiation' perspective has been taken a stage further by some critical theorists (Alvesson and Willmott, 1996) who locate the differences in subcultures in more fundamental divisions in power and conflicts of interests in organizations and highlight the powerful managerial discourses at work in reconstituting new identities for employees (see also Du Gay, 1996). In a similar vein, Anthony has made the following observation:

> One of the realities that must be taken into account in the management of culture is the values and beliefs of those to be submitted to its influence and control. It is a measure of the ideological consensus underlying the discussion of cultural management that, while the significance of management values is taken for granted, the culture of subordinates is seen as an empty space, to be worked upon at will. (1994: 164)

The implication of the above is that the 'integrative' approach to culture, which is based on (i) the functionalist assumption that culture exists to bring about a natural state of organizational equilibrium, and (ii) positivistic research evidence drawn from organizational theory (see Donaldson, 1996), is fundamentally flawed. Instead, as Anthony and others have argued, organization culture and management culture may be treated as two quite separate concepts which are far from being interchangeable terms. This observation raises, among other things, the important question of which groups of employees (broadly defined) are likely to be most (least) responsive to cultural change programmes that essentially seek to align the two notions of organization and management culture. Anthony's perspective seems to suggest that it is groups of employees towards the lower end of the organizational hierarchy who are arguably the least likely to be responsive to the attempt to produce an organizational culture that in essence is management's culture. Indeed, as some researchers (Alvesson, 1993; Rodrigues, 1996) have argued, the focus on changing cultures through value engineering may be self-defeating, or at least misplaced, in so far as such programmes aimed at achieving cultural unity do not fit well with (mainly western) managerial cultures which emphasize hierarchy, control, and instrumental and individualistic values. Finally, Willmott (1993: 517) has given this line of criticism a further twist in questioning the *morality* of such programmes. His argument is that human resource management is engaged in a form of cultural doping, often carried out at a subconscious level, which has the effect (and often the intention) of producing a form of totalitarianism. Thus, when organizations carefully design and promulgate strong cultural values, they are attempting to incorporate employees into a market logic in which they are exhorted to take responsibility for both customers and the organization's competitiveness in order to secure their employment conditions.

> In this way, employees are invited or induced to become 'tied to their identity by conscience or self-knowledge' . . . employees come to *discipline themselves* with feelings of anxiety, shame and guilt that are aroused when they sense or judge themselves to impugn or fall short of the hallowed values of the corporation. (1993: 522–3, emphasis in original)

It should be noted, however, that not all researchers who emphasize the control aspects of culture management accept that employees are 'unwilling dupes'. Casey (1996), for example, adopting a Durkheimian approach, found that new 'designer' cultures are a managerial attempt to recreate the social sphere that has been lost in modern organizations. Although 'designer' cultures are a new form of control, they are often populated by willing or 'smart' believers who 'have been reasonably convinced of the merits of organizational reforms and affectively attracted to the ethos of familial caring and belonging not offered by typical industrial companies' (1996: 334).

The motivation for culture change

The second line of criticism has to do with the *motivation* for the introduction of such programmes. And here it has been suggested that there are simply too many organizations, operating in very diverse circumstances, introducing programmes of cultural change whose aims and content are very similar in nature. Hope and Hendry (1995: 64), for instance, note that organizations with very different products, staff, markets, etc. often have very similar mission or vision statements. These stylized facts point to the possibility, not to say likelihood, of a 'bandwagon' diffusion process being at work. Bandwagon diffusion models essentially highlight 'diffusion processes whereby organizations adopt an innovation, not because of their individual assessments of the innovation's efficiency or returns, but because of a pressure caused by the sheer numbers of organizations that have already adopted this innovation' (Abrahamson and Rosenkopf, 1993: 488). And such bandwagon effects have been attributed in large part to institutional pressures, whereby non-adopters fear appearing different from adopters. An important factor here in spreading the gospel of culture is the role of the growing number of practitioner and academic management 'gurus' (Huczynski, 1993), the uncritical nature of some of the material emanating from business schools (Grey and Mitev, 1995), and the large firms of management consultants who have a vested interest in creating demands for their packaged transformational change programmes (Thompson and Davidson, 1995).

Such institutional pressures (i.e. the 'need to be seen as progressive or innovatory as an organization') for adoption may also be grounded in the personal career ambitions of some of the leading individuals associated with such programmes (Huczynski, 1993). This particular contention parallels Ahlstrand's (1990: 222–4) explanation for the continued use of productivity bargaining initiatives at Esso Fawley, despite the essential absence of evidence concerning their positive impact and effectiveness over time. Moreover, such a motivation would not be inconsistent with the basic nature of management promotion practice in British organizations which attach a great deal of importance to 'individual visibility', arising from the championing of new organizational initiatives. Finally, as Thompson and Davidson note, the language of culture change may provide managers with a rhetoric or 'vocabulary of motive' which legitimizes restructuring and job redesign policies and which 'also helps managers to manage themselves and their relationships with peers and the company' (1995: 31; see also Watson, 1994).

Operating assumptions

From the perspective of change management, culture change programmes have also been criticized for some of their rather questionable operating assumptions. Beer and his colleagues (1990), for instance, argue that the failure of such programmes derives from their all-important assumption that attitude change necessarily leads to behavioural change. In fact they argue that what the organization wants is behavioural change, and that this is better driven (directly) by new roles, responsibilities and relationships (i.e. structural change). This perspective has increasingly led to the proposition that cultural change programmes have frequently left out an important part of the story, namely the role and influence of structure. Eccles (1994), for example, has argued that (i) structure and culture should not be seen as separate, discrete entities; but (ii) in practice changing structure is the more powerful, direct route to behavioural change. As he puts it:

> When radical strategic change is required, one should be sceptical about the efficacy of attitude change programmes. Structure (accountabilities and linkages if you prefer), reward and performance criteria and key appointments are far more potent and immediate weapons to use to galvanize an organization. (1994: 217)

The empirical results reported by Hope and Hendry (1995: 67–70) for a case study organization are certainly not inconsistent with this line of argument.

A related criticism concerns the uses by organizations of a 'snapshot' diagnosis/approach to culture change which fails to take into account the 'spatial and temporal dimensions of culture'. As Bate argues, 'any theory of change needs a theory of changing' (1996: 29). Culture patterns are a *recurrence* of historical circumstances and culture change requires a focus on the past as well as the present and the future; in other words, a longitudinal approach to understanding why organizational change emerges, develops, grows and terminates over time (Huber and Van de Ven, 1995: vii).

Finally, three other more *ad hoc* observations have been made about making cultural change programmes work which have relevance for this case study:

1　Seeking to produce behavioural change indirectly via attitude change is likely to be a relatively long process, involving a timescale of change (i.e. results coming through) which may not comfortably fit with the traditional 'short-termism' of British organizations (Legge, 1995: 135–7).
2　The broad-brush values which are central to cultural change programmes may be difficult to operationalize, in the sense of being adequately represented in behavioural terms by management: in short, in current US parlance, it may be difficult 'to walk the talk'.
3　There is a need to secure some 'early wins' in order to assist the internal process of diffusing the new culture (Pettigrew, 1990; Kotter and Heskett, 1992).

With this background in mind we now turn to outline the nature of the cultural change programme in our local authority.

Cultural change in the local authority

In the early 1990s the administration of our medium sized Scottish local authority (which we refer to as 'the council'), prominently led by a newly appointed chief executive officer (CEO), embarked on a large-scale cultural change programme. This particular initiative was reportedly motivated by the following factors:

● It was an integral part of a larger programme of change designed to deal with the economic problems of the area, which included a declining population, increasing levels of unemployment and significant pockets of urban poverty.
● It was closely tied up with the reorganization of local government and the moves towards unitary authorities in Scotland in 1995–6 (i.e. four authorities in the area were to be reduced to three by 1995–6 with a consequent loss of jobs). The CEO publicly stated his desire to place his own organization in good standing with the Scottish Office by acting as a pacesetter and role model of a well-managed authority. In doing so it was hoped the programme would enhance the organizational career of the authority and also the individual career prospects of staff whose jobs were threatened by the reorganization.

- The Local Government Act 1988, which required local authorities to put many of their services out to public tender through compulsory competitive tendering (CCT), exposed the authority to increased private sector competition and resulted in the creation of separate divisions within local authorities between those acting in a client and those in a contractor role.

To meet these challenges and with the help of a management consultant, the CEO and his leadership team developed a broad vision or mission statement 'to put the heart back into the city'. At this juncture, it is worth noting the importance of the management consultant whose guru-style role in selling the culture 'dream', often through anxiety-provoking performances during training sessions, resembled the image of a 'witchdoctor' described by Salaman and Clark (1996). However, the effects of this approach were contradictory: according to some interviewees, the consultant's message seemed, on the surface at least, to seduce the CEO and some senior managers, but had the reverse effect on certain councillors and the more sceptical managers.

In addition to these 'softer' aspects of the programme, more tangible changes included advance factory building, and housing and environmental improvements. Within the larger context of this strategic response (the 'Leadership Plan') the council specifically committed itself to (i) maintaining the council's record in winning CCT contracts, (ii) improving the council's accessibility and responsiveness via effective communication with citizens and service users, and (iii) ensuring that the council lived up to its mission and values established in the Leadership Plan.

The Leadership Plan, which was formally launched in March 1992, set out the mission and values framework identified by the council as a core element of their larger objective of creating 'a strong and vibrant regional centre which attracts and retains people'. Table 5.1 provides a summary statement in this regard.

Using the services of the management consultant, a benchmark survey was undertaken in the period December 1992 to March 1993. This involved a questionnaire being issued to all employees, which was designed to evaluate the extent to which employees identified with the council's mission, and how they felt about existing organizational problems, internal communications, individual development opportunities, and how people were treated, managed and recognized. Moreover, a 'leadership working party', consisting of the nine chief officers and chaired by the Head of Corporate Planning, was established to steer and progress the programme of change. The basic aims here were to maximize external publicity and internal involvement in the programmes. To these ends a series of public, corporate and departmental launches were held over time involving presentations, the distribution of documentation and question/answer sessions.

Furthermore, a variety of policy and practice initiatives were concentrated in the two-year period March 1993 to March 1995. These were broadly reflective of the style of 'new people management' which began to characterize the public sector in the 1990s (Farnham and Horton, 1995) and were essentially as follows:

Table 5.1   *The council's mission and values statement*

Mission
We shall lead the way to new horizons for the city of . . ., where the quality of life makes people proud to stay.

Values

1   *Communications*
   ● We value openness, honesty and understanding in all our communications.
   ● We recognize communication as a positive two-way process which is sensitive and responsive to the views of others.

2   *Change*
   ● We value innovation and recognize the need for continuous improvement.
   ● We recognize that our actions affect others and we value their right to consultation.

3   *Organization*
   ● The council values the culture of a caring, listening, developing organization which adapts to change.
   ● We value the acceptance of authority and responsibility at every level.

4   *Recognition*
   ● We value the recognition of achievement.

5   *People*
   ● We will show respect and consideration for everyone and the environment in which we live.
   ● We value the attainment of fairness, dignity and equality.

6   *Individual*
   ● We value the development of individuals and will support them in reaching their full potential.
   ● We value individuals' knowledge of what is expected of them and their freedom to discuss ideas and views.

7   *Team*
   ● We believe we can only achieve our goals for the city through teamwork.
   ● We value team building and the fostering of loyalty.

8   *Mission and values*
   ● We value our mission which puts the people of the city at the heart of our actions on which we will be judged.

Delayering   A policy decision was taken to ensure that there were to be no more than five levels of management between the CEO and employees. This was to involve 'stripping out' between one and three layers of management in all divisions dependent on their size. The delayering was to have been achieved through non-replacement of managers as they left or retired rather than through compulsory redundancies.[2]

Business planning   This was introduced into all divisions of the council with each department within the divisions required to produce an annual action plan. These were to be linked to the five-year corporate planning framework. All chief officers attended full-day workshops on each of the following: leadership, mission and values, business (or leadership) planning, and performance indicators.

Training and development   Over 700 managers and team leaders attended a series of seminars on 'action-centred leadership' (three days), 'communication and delegation' (two days), 'problem-solving' and 'time management' (one day each).

Team briefing and teamworking   Team briefing was introduced into all major divisions, and each department was encouraged, with the help of facilitators, to develop high-performance work teams which would involve empowering staff at all levels.

Leadership improvement proposals   A major programme of employee empowerment was introduced through an elaborate structure for encouraging improvement proposals. These arrangements involved employees being able to make job-specific, divisional or organization-wide suggestions which would be either implemented immediately or passed on to higher levels of management for consideration. This approach was to be assisted by departmental facilitators and a leadership improvement proposal steering group. Targets were set for the programme with the aim being to have each employee on average submitting two proposals per year by 1995–6.

The initial leadership strategy document had given a commitment to audit the changes every two years, and in November 1994 the first such assessment was undertaken. It is the results of this particular exercise which will be reported and discussed later in the chapter. For the moment, however, we need to raise some issues concerning the evaluation of cultural change programmes.

Some issues associated with evaluation

The two issues raised here are, firstly, the criteria for judging whether a change programme has been successful (or not) and, secondly, the methods used to gather the information which constitutes the basis for that judgement.

In relation to the first issue, some academics have questioned whether a simple success/failure dichotomy adequately reflects the rather mixed reality of many organizational change programmes (Bate, 1994; Stacey, 1996). For instance, Goodman and Deane have argued as follows:

> The problem in some of the literature on change is the use of the words success or failure. This language clouds the crucial issue of representing and explaining degrees or levels of institutionalization. Most of the organizational cases we have reviewed cannot be described by simple labels of success or failure. Rather we find various degrees of institutionalization. (1982: 229)

Goodman and Deane further argued that variation in the degree of institutionalization can be represented by the presence (absence) of the following facets: (i) knowledge of the behaviour; (ii) performance of the behaviour, (iii) preferences for the behaviour; (iv) normative consensus; and (v) values.

This being said, most studies of cultural change programmes utilize essentially a success/failure dichotomy, based on (i) whether the programme survives the test of time (i.e. is institutionalized for at least a certain period) and/or (ii) whether employee attitudes have reportedly changed as a result of the programme. In utilizing the latter approach (as here) the following points should be noted:

- It is desirable, indeed arguably essential, at least to engage in a form of comparative statics and compare the results of at least two surveys of employee attitudes (i.e. a self-control or before/after comparison approach) over the course of time.
- The relative absence of reported attitude change between the two surveys may result from management's exaggerated expectations concerning the (realistic) pace of change which, in turn, are often fuelled by management consultants' timescales.
- Even if attitude change is observed there is still the all-important question as to whether this will translate into (desired) behavioural changes (Beer et al., 1990) or the more pervasive and deep-rooted changes in values (Ogbonna, 1992).

In addition to these points we need to recognize some of the well-known limitations of periodic employee surveys for assessing the extent of attitude and culture change. From an 'objectivist' perspective, these limitations include the following:

1   Such a research design, though providing an element of longitudinal self-control, can, by definition, produce only a 'snapshot' involving a single point-of-time set of results. Generalizing from such 'snapshots' can (i) often ignore the influence of timing or the context in which the survey was undertaken, in this case during a period of reorganization and employee worries about job security; (ii) ignore the potentially biasing effects of experimentation or maturation of the respondents; and (iii) lack the necessary controls to test whether the effects are also present in other groups (Fink, 1995).

2   The results obtained can be extremely sensitive to the precise wording of particular questions, covering letters and the overall appearance of questionnaires.

3   There is an overall problem of generating high and consistent response rates from the survey. Any observed variation in response rates between differing parts of the workforce may derive in substantial measure from differing (initial) levels of expectation.

From a 'subjectivist' perspective, it is often argued that complex, multidimensional constructs cannot be probed in any in-depth, qualitative fashion. For example, Despres (1995) criticizes attitude surveys on the grounds that they present respondents with sets of items that reflect the knowledge structure and values of the researcher rather than those of the respondent. More fundamentally, Chia (1995) argues that surveys are rooted in a view of organizations as 'being' rather than in the process of 'becoming'. The associated emphasis on structure at the expense of process presents a static and linear view of organizational culture change.

As well as the above, we would also suggest that any employee attitude survey is a relatively 'blunt' instrument in the sense that it can offer relatively few insights as to why attitude change has been observed or not. As a consequence, we felt it was essential to go beyond the results of the surveys to examine in a more qualitative fashion some of the reasons for the pattern of results obtained.

The extent of attitude change

The key findings presented in this section arise from an employee audit undertaken in 1994. In considering the findings to be presented, the following points should be noted:

- This assessment was undertaken by a group of academics, rather than the management consultant originally involved in the change programme. The feeling amongst the leadership working party was that any audit of the programme would be better undertaken by an independent group rather than by the original consultant or an internal department. The general aims of the assessment or audit were to provide the leadership working party, managers and all employees with some feedback on how deeply the change initiatives had embedded themselves into the new culture and to provide the basis for further improvements.
- The questionnaire developed by the academics included many of the same questions used in the original (1992) benchmarking survey so that comparisons over time could be made. However, some additional questions (mainly biographical ones) were included, in order to facilitate examination of any revealed differences across the workforce as a whole. And it was this new information that allowed us to examine the question of which types of employees had been most (least) responsive to an attempt to align management culture and organizational culture.
- The response rate to the questionnaire in 1994, which covered all 3000 employees, was 64 per cent (compared with 42 per cent for the original benchmark survey), although this varied considerably between divisions: in general, a low response rate came from the manual dominated divisions (e.g. Public Works 30 per cent, Parks 55 per cent), with much higher return rates coming from the white collar divisions (e.g. Housing 78 per cent, Planning 80 per cent).

For reasons of space, the full set of tabulated responses to all the questions cannot be presented here. However, some of the key findings obtained for the *workforce as a whole* are set out in Table 5.2.

The basic message of Table 5.2 is remarkably clear, namely that although some positive messages could be taken from the survey, the extent of attitude

Table 5.2   *Assessment of the change programme: some key findings for the workforce as a whole*

---

1   *Overall job satisfaction*
    The overall level of satisfaction ranged between 75% and 63% (depending on the particular question answered).

2   *Organizational commitment*
    The levels of identification, involvement and loyalty appeared relatively high. For example, 60% articulated an active pride in the council, only 14% would not recommend a friend to work for the council, and 77% agreed with the statement that 'In my work, I like to feel I am making some effort not just for myself but for the council as well.'

3   *Leadership improvement programme*
    Here 88% of staff were aware of the programme, and 41% claimed to have made suggestions for improvement, although only 30% felt that the scheme had been a major factor in encouraging them to make suggestions.

4   *Recognition of achievement*
    In general, staff/employees felt that their views were listened to and their achievements recognized by supervisors and managers, but not by senior management.

5   *Change and innovation*
    In general, employee satisfaction with the level of consultation, communication, encouragement of new ideas and ability to question decisions has, if anything, declined over time.

6   *Teamworking*
    Perceptions concerning effective teamworking reveal a decline over time, with little sense of team spirit between managers and workers in departments being reported.

7   *Individual development*
    The growth in the content and quality of training is noted and approved of, although dissatisfaction exists concerning longer-term career development and the performance of managers as coaches.

8   *Communication*
    Compared to the benchmark surveys, no significant improvements in information flows within departments are reported, and managers are not seen as being more approachable than before.

9   *Mission*
    There was no apparent improvement in perceptions concerning the extent to which colleagues and managers understand and act out the mission of the council.

---

change in the direction desired by senior management has been very limited. Indeed there are a number of indications of change in exactly the opposite direction. Moreover, it has to be said that although senior management were disappointed with the findings, many, especially in the leadership working party, were not unduly surprised. During feedback sessions by the researchers, the impression gained was of a resigned acceptance on the part of managers that such programmes, whilst strong on rhetoric, were weak in practice (Watson, 1996). Explanations were given which highlighted unrealistic expectations concerning the pace of change; the failure of some of the most senior managers in the council to act out the message of culture change, with the consequent effects that this had on some departmental managers

Table 5.3   *Variation in responses within the workforce*

1   Older staff, senior managers and employees in professional grades were more likely to be imbued with a sense of mission, feel that the public have a positive image of the council and believe that their department actively listens to feedback from customers.
2   Manual employees in unpromoted posts had significantly more negative perceptions concerning the effectiveness of departmental and interdepartmental communications.
3   Senior managers and professional employees had significantly more positive views of the extent to which new ideas were encouraged.
4   Male workers were more likely to adopt 'extreme' views concerning the recognition of achievement than female workers; this was a general tendency throughout the questionnaire.
5   Improvement suggestions were less likely to have been made by male workers, manual workers and employees in unpromoted posts.
6   The large DLOs, employing mainly manual workers whose jobs were dependent on securing contracts in competition with the private sector, usually exhibited lower levels of satisfaction than divisions which were mainly staffed by professionals such as Art Galleries and Museums and the Architects Department.

who were negatively influenced by the gap between the *espoused theory* and the *theory in use*; and, finally, the antagonistic/'old-fashioned' nature of some divisions and/or departments.

With respect to the last of these, and as anticipated, there was considerable variation in the extent of reported attitude change between the different parts of the workforce. Some of the key findings in this regard are set out in Table 5.3.

Thus, the sort of attitude change sought by senior management has been relatively limited, an outcome that is particularly apparent towards the lower end of the organizational hierarchy.[3] However, this survey-based information was able to provide little insight as to why this had been the case. Accordingly, in the next section we pursue the theme of why change was limited, drawing on the qualitative findings of a series of focus group exercises conducted in one particular division of the council.[4]

Why limited change?

Following the attitude survey results presented (admittedly in summary fashion) in the previous section, all departments were instructed to respond to the problems identified, and were advised to conduct further, more qualitative research with employees. The latter was seen to have three major purposes:

1   It would assess the accuracy of the survey results by seeking the views of employees through the use of an alternative method.
2   It would provide an opportunity to establish the feelings and perceptions which led to employees answering in the way they did.
3   It would provide the first step towards the future by inviting employees to suggest ways by which practice could be improved by senior management.

The qualitative findings reported here are primarily concerned with point 2, and derive from three focus groups involving a total of some 33 employees in the Housing Department. In considering the nature of the material to be presented here the following points should be noted about the Housing Department: (i) in size terms it is a very important department, employing more than 500 people out of a total workforce of some 3000; (ii) it is very much a white collar employee dominated department, which meant that both the response rate to the questionnaire and the extent of reported 'positive' change were above that for the council as a whole.

As to the focus group methodology itself, a great deal of attention was given to various issues associated with the design of the exercise. The basic aim was to obtain the views of an essentially randomly chosen group of employees, but with adequate representation of the various sections and salary grades within the department. Moreover the nature of the discussion/feedback process was designed to illuminate the reasons for the pattern of findings set out in Table 5.4.

The results of the focus group exercise (three groups involving a total of 33 individuals in a three-day interview period) clearly and strongly further highlighted the closely intersecting influence of *workload, uncertainty, and inconsistencies between espoused theory and theory in use* in shaping the pattern of responses outlined in Table 5.4.

For instance, workload pressures were viewed as a major factor which had limited the ability of people to pursue individual development initiatives. The following quotes are illustrative in this regard.

- I've been in this office for five years and I haven't been on a single day's training. I'm always needed for cover.
- Most of us don't bother asking to go on day release at college because my manager always says we're too short-staffed to let anybody away for an afternoon every week for a year at a time.

Table 5.4   A comparison of the Housing Department survey results

Leadership element	First survey Dec. 1992 to March 1993 (positive %)	Second survey Oct. to Nov. 1994 (positive %)
Mission	71	52
Communication	29	43
Individual	31	42
Team	69	66
Change	41	40
Recognition	52	46
Organization	39	42
People	76	50

This workload pressure was held in large measure to derive from the freeze on recruitment in the run-up to local government reorganization. This being said, variation was perceived to exist within the department: 'There are some sections where everybody seems to be on some course or another.' This inter-sectional variation was clearly a strong centre of employee grievance in many quarters. To some individuals it was a *counter-productive* effect of the change programme. That is, they held that intra-team co-operation had increased, but to the detriment of inter-team co-operation. As one individual put it:

> Phones ring and ring and no one answers them. We just do our own work and let everybody else worry about theirs. We've no time to help anybody else out. Nobody helps us.

In addition, the inter-section variation was very much laid at the door of supervisors. There were frequent references to supervisors not practising what they preach: 'They come away with all the jargon but it doesn't make any difference to what they do.' To some individuals, supervisors' attitudes had changed little:

> There are good ones and bad ones. The good ones were good before all this and are still good. The bad ones are still bad.

> Our boss sits in his office less than ten feet away but can't actually talk to us. All we get is memos . . . When we do well on our monthly targets . . . he even says 'well done' in a memo.

Another typical complaint about supervision concerned the lack of consultation over business planning and target setting:

> We see it [the plan] once a year when our principal officer tells us what he is putting in it. I think he wants it done as quick as he can to get it out of the way.

However, to some the uncertainty surrounding local government reorganization had made things worse, by deflecting the attention of supervisors. There were frequent references to supervisors planning their future careers rather than concentrating on the job of managing their teams. As one individual put it:

> They're all queuing up to see where they can get a slot for themselves. They're not worried about whether there's anywhere for us to go.

Employees were consistently critical of the fact that senior management were unaware of the extent of supervisory/sectional variation, or at least did little to try and correct it. Indeed many went further in pointing to the recent announcement that the Director of Housing post was to be increased in salary by a third. This was viewed as symptomatic of the inequality and mistaken priorities of the organization: 'The Director gets another £15,000 and we can't get a part-time GS1/2 for lunch cover.'

An overall assessment

The principal aim of this chapter has been to make a contribution to the more critical literature on the management of organizational culture through the analysis of a culture change programme in a Scottish local authority. Despite the heavy investment by the organization in an essentially 'top-down' programme, in accounting for the relative lack of change we hope to have got beyond the managerial rhetoric which often accompanies such programmes and to have provided what we believe to be a more typical example of the short-lived, 'faddish' nature of many HRM-based initiatives and the ambiguous, often paradoxical, nature of culture change programmes .

We began by noting some of the *emerging criticisms* of organizational culture change, briefly outlining the lack of understanding by managers of what they are trying to change, the (frequently political) motivation for such programmes, and the problems of 'managing' fundamental or second-order changes in culture (Bate, 1994). We also touched on the issues concerning the *evaluation* of culture change. On the assumption that the architects of these programmes wish to reach beyond the level of HRM rhetoric and the unreflective, self-referential standards of proof that often pass for evidence in HRM-based programmes, it was also proposed that the principal method of assessing culture change – the use of attitude surveys – embodies some questionable assumptions and is subject to severe implementation problems.

The first and most notable point to emerge from the case study evidence concerns the problematic notion of a homogeneous or integrative organizational cultural paradigm. The evidence on attitudinal change, as one might have expected, reflected a more differentiated and diverse notion of culture with considerable variation evident between the different departments/divisions within the authority. These variations reflected the extent to which the different units and subunits were dominated by white collar, professional staff or by blue collar, manual workers. It was also transparent from the survey statistics that employees in the large manual direct labour organizations (DLOs), whose jobs were most subject to the vicissitudes of competitive tendering, were the least enchanted with the message (and reality, up to that point) of the culture change programme. However, such scepticism of the culture change initiatives was not restricted to manual workers, as demonstrated by the focus group comments of the professionally dominated, white collar employees in the Housing Department. Inconsistency and inequality of treatment between different levels in the hierarchy were frequently commented upon. Moreover, and consistent with the differentiated view of culture, the focus group evidence hinted at a looser coupling of subunits, paradoxically brought about by the change programme itself. On the other hand, the survey results do provide evidence that many managers and particularly older professional staff were more in sympathy with the vision and values framework. Such data are consistent with the view that culture change programmes work best with 'easy converters' (Hopfl, 1993) since they provide managers with a rhetoric for change (Watson, 1994) in the uncertain context of competitive tendering and reorganization.

Furthermore, the case study reveals the tensions between programmes aimed at securing an organizational unity based on a strong corporate culture and the low-trust assumptions embedded in the fundamentally unchanged hierarchical nature of bureaucratic organizations (see Coopey and Hartley, 1991), especially those which emphasize individualistic and competitive market values as distinct from the more high-trust, professional/public service values of the old-style public sector (Farnham and Horton, 1995).

The second theme of the case study concerns the evidence on the effective management of culture change programmes, especially that which highlights the problems of achieving major, top-down changes in short-term timescales. In this regard, Bate (1994: 204–5) has outlined several criteria for assessing the effectiveness of culture change. These are:

Expressiveness   The extent to which the approach has compelling vision.

Commonality   The extent to which the approach generates a communion of purpose.

Penetration   The extent to which the approach permeates through different levels.

Adaptability   The ability of the approach to adjust to changing circumstances.

Durability   The ability of the approach to create a durable change in culture.

Whilst the case study provides evidence that the local authority programme may have engendered some initial enthusiasm amongst many managers, professional staff and a substantial minority of staff in lower grades, it is clear that its ability to achieve *commonality* between the various departments and to *penetrate* the various levels in the hierarchy was limited and even self-defeating. The general feeling amongst the steering group (the leadership working party) and the academics who undertook the research was that expectations had been raised by the top-down, highly publicized nature of the programme but had remained largely unfulfilled amongst staff in the lower levels of the hierarchy and in departments whose managers were sceptical of its ability to convince workers that a new caring and listening culture was possible, or even desirable, in the changed competitive circumstances of CCT. As Bate has put it, culture change strategies must take into account the aspirations and ambitions of all parties involved and

> it is all too easy to get carried away with the 'big' idea . . . [they] must ask themselves whether they are being too ambitious, whether there will be too much resistance or indifference, whether the timing is right and whether there is sufficient political support and momentum to achieve the desired objective. (1996: 39)

Such evidence, firstly, points to a need for structural changes to accompany culture changes (Anthony, 1994). Secondly, it highlights the potential pitfalls of top-down, 'big-bang' programmes which are based on buzz-words like leadership and empowerment and also the belief that planned programmes will behave in a linear and predictable fashion. These programmes, it is argued, do not address the fundamental complexity of organizational problems, do not provide training at all levels in the hierarchy, and do not achieve the changes through organization-wide consensus because they are spread from the top (Beer et al., 1990). Finally they fail to address the turbulent nature of organizational environments which make long-term planning difficult, if not impossible. The implication of this line of reasoning, which is consistent with the work of Pettigrew (1990) and others, is that fundamental change in large and diverse organizations takes many years to achieve rather than, in this case, over a period of the three years for which the authority was to remain in existence. At the same time, however, these authors point out the need for short-term successes in some departments to act as models for others and to sustain the momentum of the programme as a whole.

The third, and final, theme of the chapter concerns the motivation for introducing culture change programmes and the assumptions about culture change held by the designers of such programmes. The case study shows that such programmes are frequently motivated by non-rational reasons such as internal and external politics rather than addressing organizational problems in a reflective and particularistic manner. As noted previously, Hope and Hendry (1995) and Huczynski (1993) have argued that organizational competition, 'bandwagon diffusion' and individual career interests are often at the heart of why such programmes are adopted. Managers as consumers and consultants as producers of such programmes are frequently observed to consciously or unconsciously collude in applying packaged solutions to complex problems. In this case, the publicly stated motives of the CEO and the management consultants who devised the package (and the resigned acceptance by members of the leadership working party of the negative results) provide justification for such scepticism. Indeed, given that both the leadership and the consultants knew, because of the *fact* of local government reorganization in 1996, that the life of the authority was to be short, one is inevitably led to speculating on the motives underlying the programme.

The most obvious point of departure for such speculation is that the CEO-led initiative was a rationally 'wise' and politically aware (Cooper and White, 1995) attempt at image building through an ambitious second-order change programme designed for two different 'publics'. The first of these comprised ministers and officials at the Scottish Office, who were perceived to value such a change because it embraced 'modern', private sector thinking (indeed, there is circumstantial evidence that that was the case). The second 'public' were the majority of employees who, faced with the prospect of reorganization and possible losses of jobs, needed to be 'redesigned' to fulfil the authority's organizational and individual careerist aims. As Willmott points out, culture management is much more powerful than 'theory Y' management, its neo-human relations predecessor, in so far as no underlying organizational consensus is assumed:

> corporate culture is more responsive to the value conflicts within modern ... organizations, conflicts which it interprets as a sign of cultural weakness that can be corrected ... Instead of assuming a consensus of values, corporate culturism aspires

to build or manufacture consensus by managing the content and valency of employee values. (1993: 525)

The question remains: why did so many employees respond in an 'irrational' fashion by becoming more disenchanted as the programme was implemented and as reorganization loomed large? This can be explained in different ways. Firstly, in implementing a large-scale, top-down programme of change, little, if any, thought may have been given to the art of the possible and the 'politics of acceptance' (Bate, 1994: 164) with respect to employees in the lower levels in the hierarchy, particularly those in the DLO departments. Such an explanation further highlights the shortcomings of the 'integrative' paradigm of culture change which stresses planned change and the importance of leadership-led initiatives. Alternatively, the possibility remains that such employees may never have been intended to benefit from the programme because of the predictable, but tacitly acknowledged, view held by senior managers that a complete organizational culture change, involving the various interest groups, was unlikely to work in the timescale left open to the authority. The 'planned' goal may well have been limited to the more short-term, image building exercise with the Scottish Office rather than any longer-term, widespread organizational culture change. This, more political, explanation is consistent with managers (and researchers) holding a 'differentiated' view of culture. A final explanation is derived from a third cultural paradigm, that of 'ambiguity' or 'fragmentation'. For, as Meyerson and Martin have argued, 'ambiguity [is] accepted . . . irreconcilable interpretations [of culture] are simultaneously entertained; paradoxes are embraced' (1994: 122). Thus 'confusion, paradox and even hypocrisy' characterize this view of culture. Change is seen as a constant rather than temporary state of affairs and is thought to be relatively uncontrollable since it is 'largely triggered by the environment or other forces beyond an individual's control' (Martin and Frost, 1996: 609). This processual view of management (Whittington, 1993) is characterized by inconsistent decisions and accidental discoveries as managers incrementally adjust to the emerging situations. In doing so they are changed by and also change the organizational cultures in which they live.

Conclusions

In this chapter we have addressed the relative failure of a planned approach to culture change in a Scottish local authority. In doing so we hope to have made a contribution to the literature on culture change and HRM. The chapter set out the context, content and process of a programme of change – new people management – which is becoming almost paradigmatic in the public sector (Audit Commission, 1995; Farnham and Horton, 1995). However, as Stacey (1996) argues, when managers share the same paradigm, they are driven to practise a form of 'ordinary management' which is both rational and designed to secure harmony in closed or contained situations. Such ordinary (human resource) management is also likely to evaluate success in either/or terms and engage in single-loop learning. Paradoxes and tensions are dealt with by being either removed or defined out of existence. In doing so, managers are in danger of becoming 'skilled incompetents'.

However, under the arguably more typical conditions described in this case study, which were far from certain, planned change programmes are much less likely to work and management is only likely to be effective in its 'intuitive, judgmental and political forms' (Stacey, 1996: 46–7). Organizations under conditions of uncertainty are likely to be characterized by paradoxes which cannot be resolved but only embraced and 'endlessly rearranged'. Thus the practice of 'extraordinary management' requires that managers (and researchers) are able to work with multiple models and to see problems through different lenses (Morgan, 1986; 1993). In developing a more complete view of organizational culture change 'we must consider the complex dynamics of culture as well as those inter-related change processes from such a multi-paradigm approach' (Meyerson and Martin, 1994: 128).

A final point concerns the nature of change programmes. Increasingly, as planned change strategies are being questioned as to their likelihood of producing intended outcomes, the point is made that such planning can lead to vicious circles of dysfunctional behaviour. As Bate puts it: 'the axiom should be: don't plan but be prepared. People who make rigid plans are all too often the ones who are least adequately prepared' (1996: 33).

Postscript

Just prior to the final draft of this chapter, local government reorganization became a reality in Scotland. The CEO secured the top job in the new unitary authority, as did most of the key players in the culture change programme. One might reasonably speculate from this result that the culture change programme had indeed fulfilled the personal agenda of the CEO. It is also interesting to note that in the new unitary authority, the notion of a leadership programme became 'taboo'. Though a corporate culture programme is being instituted, it is evident that some organizational learning has taken place as the new programme is to be much more incrementalist and less top-down in nature.

Notes

1 We recognize the importance of postmodern critiques of organizational culture but, as most writers in this tradition might acknowledge, their goal is not to offer better theories of culture change or assistance to organizations and their employees but 'rather to challenge the foundations of modern cultural scholarship' (Martin and Frost, 1996: 612). Our aims are more prosaic and practical.

2 At the time of the second survey, little actual progress had been made in implementing this policy.

3 This result was out of line with the conclusions of recent attitude surveys of 13 public sector organizations (including a number of local authorities) which showed that manual workers were more likely to feel satisfied with their jobs than white collar and principal officer grades,

despite the increase in CCT (LGMB/MORI, 1994), and a similar longitudinal survey of 1000 health board staff which found the middle, supervisory grades least satisfied with the change programme (Mabey and Mallory, 1995).

4 The authors greatly acknowledge the assistance of a part-time masters student who, under the supervision of one of the authors, conducted the focus group research. For understandable reasons, he does not wish to be named.

References

Abrahamson, E. and Rosenkopf, L. (1993) 'Institutional and competitive bandwagons: using mathematical modelling as a tool to explore innovation diffusion', *Academy of Management Review*, 18 (3): 487–517.

Ahlstrand, B.W. (1990) *The Quest for Productivity: a Case Study of Fawley after Flanders*. Cambridge: Cambridge University Press.

Alvesson, M. (1993) *Cultural Perspectives on Organizations*. Cambridge: Cambridge University Press.

Alvesson, M. and Willmott, H. (1996) *Making Sense of Management: a Critical Introduction*. London: Sage.

Anthony, P.D. (1994) *Managing Culture*. Milton Keynes: Open University.

Audit Commission (1995) *Calling the Tune: People, Pay and Performance in Local Government*. London: Audit Commission.

Bate, P. (1994) *Strategies for Cultural Change*. Basingstoke: Butterworth Heinemann.

Bate, P. (1996) 'Towards a strategic framework for changing corporate culture', *Journal of Strategic Change*, 5 (1): 27–42.

Beer, M., Eisenstat, A. and Spector, B. (1990) 'Why change programs don't produce change', *Harvard Business Review*, 67 (November–December): 158–66.

Casey, C. (1996) 'Corporate transformations: designer culture, designer employees and "post-occupational solidarity"', *Organization*, 3 (3): 317–40.

Chia, R. (1995) 'Managing complexity or complex managing?' Paper presented to the British Academy of Management, Sheffield, 11–13 September.

Cooper, C. and White, B. (1995) 'Organizational behaviour', in S. Tyson (ed.), *Strategic Prospects for HRM*. London: IPD.

Coopey, J. and Hartley, J. (1991) 'Reconsidering the case for organizational commitment', *Human Resource Management Journal*, 1 (3): 18–32.

Despres, C.J.-N. (1995) 'Culture, surveys, culture surveys and other obfuscations: questionnaire approaches and the culture-fallacy approach', *Journal of Strategic Change*, 2 (4): 65–76.

Donaldson, L. (1996) *For Positivist Organizational Theory*. London: Sage.

Du Gay, P. (1996) *Consumption and Identity at Work*. London: Sage.

Eccles, T. (1994) *Succeeding with Change*. London: McGraw-Hill.

Farnham, D. and Horton, S. (1995) 'The new people management in the UK public services: a silent revolution'. Paper presented to the International Colloquium on Contemporary Developments in Human Management, ESC Montpellier, 9–13 October.

Fink, A. (1995) *Survey Design*. Thousand Oaks, CA: Sage.

Fox, A. (1974) *Man Mismanagement*. London: Hutchinson.

Frost, P., Moore, L., Louis, M.R., Lundberg, C. and Martin, J. (eds) (1991) *Reframing Organizational Culture*. Newbury Park, CA: Sage.

Goodman, P.S. and Deane, J.W. (1982) 'Creating long-term organizational change', in P.S. Goodman, *Change in Organizations*. San Francisco: Jossey-Bass.

Grey, C. and Mitev, N. (1995) 'Management education: a polemic', *Management Learning*, 26 (1): 73–90.

Hope, V. and Hendry, J. (1995) 'Corporate culture change: is it relevant for the organizations of the 1990s?', *Human Resource Management Journal*, 5 (4): 61–73.

Hopfl, H. (1993) 'Culture and commitment: British Airways', in D. Gowler, K. Legge, and C.

Clegg (eds), *Case Studies in Organizational Behaviour and Human Resource Management* (2nd edn). London: Paul Chapman.

Huber, G. and Van de Ven, A. (eds) (1995) *Longitudinal Field Research Methods*. Thousand Oaks, CA: Sage.

Huczynski, A. (1993) *Management Gurus*. London: Routledge.

Kotter, J. and Heskett, K. (1992) *Corporate Culture and Performance*. New York: Free Press.

Legge, K. (1995) *Human Resource Management: Rhetoric and Realities*. Basingstoke: Macmillan.

LGMB/MORI (1994) *Employee Attitudes in Local Government*. Local Government Management Board.

Mabey, C. and Mallory, G. (1995) 'Structure and culture change in two UK organisations: a comparison of assumptions, approaches and outcomes', *Human Resource Management Journal*, 5 (3): 28–45.

Mabey, C. and Salaman, G. (1995) *Strategic Human Resource Management*. Oxford: Blackwell.

Martin, J. and Frost, P. (1996) 'The organizational culture war games: a struggle for intellectual dominance', in S. Clegg, C. Hardy and W. Nord (eds), *Handbook of Organizational Studies*. London: Sage. pp. 599–621.

Meek, V. L. (1988) 'Organizational culture: origins and weaknesses', in G. Salaman (ed.), *Human Resource Strategies*. London: Sage. pp. 192–212.

Meyerson, D. and Martin, J. (1994) 'Culture change: an integration of three different views', in T. Tsoukas (ed.), *New Thinking in Organizational Behaviour*. Oxford: Butterworth Heinemann. pp. 108–32.

Morgan, G. (1986) *Images of Organization*. Beverly Hills, CA: Sage.

Ogbonna, E. (1992) 'Organizational culture and human resource management: dilemmas and contradictions', in P. Blyton and P. Turnbull (eds), *Reassessing Human Resource Management*. London: Sage. pp. 74–96.

Pettigrew, A. (1990) 'Is corporate culture manageable?', in D. Wilson and R. Rosenfeld (eds), *Managing Organizations*. London: Heinemann. pp. 267–72.

Rodrigues, S.B. (1996) 'Corporate culture and deinstitutionalization: implications for identity in a Brazilian telecommunications company', in G. Palmer and S. Clegg (eds), *Constituting Management*. Berlin: de Gruyter. pp. 113–38.

Salaman, G. and Clark, T. (1996) 'The management guru as organizational witchdoctor', *Organization*, 3 (1): pp. 85–108.

Stacey, R. (1996) *Strategic Management and Organizational Dynamics* (2nd edn). London: Pitman.

Thompson, P. and O' Connell Davidson, J. (1995) 'The continuity of discontinuity: managerial rhetoric in turbulent times', *Personnel Review*, 24 (4): 17–33.

Van Maanen, J. (1991) 'The smile factory: work at Disneyland', in P. Frost, L. Moore, M. Louis, C. Lundberg and J. Martin (eds), *Reframing Organizational Culture,* Newbury Park, CA: Sage. pp. 58–76.

Watson, T.J. (1994) *In Search of Management*. London: Routledge.

Watson, T.J. (1996) 'How do managers think? Identity, morality and pragmatism in managerial theory and practice', *Management Learning*, 27 (3): 323–42.

Whittington, R. (1993) *What is Strategy and Does it Matter?* London: Routledge.

Willmott, H. (1993) 'Strength is ignorance; slavery is freedom: managing culture in modern organizations', *Journal of Management Studies*, 30 (4): 515–52.

Part III

THE PERCEIVED IMPACT OF HRM ON PERFORMANCE AND PRODUCTIVITY

As we have outlined, the main purpose of this book is to give voice to the other players in HRM strategies, i.e. those on the receiving end. An important aspect of this is the differences in perception which exist between each of the groups involved, for example those who implement initiatives and those who are affected by them and the impact that this has on the success or otherwise of HRM. Although each of the following three chapters considers a different type of HRM intervention they all include an exploration of the views held by the various participants in the scheme which often prove to be contradictory.

The chapter by Heyes focuses on training, frequently cited within the literature as a cornerstone of HRM. The author identifies the benefits which are widely expected to accrue from investment in training and concludes that the implication is that training can be seen as a 'positive-sum game' providing benefits to both employees and the companies within which they work. Heyes challenges this depiction of training and development, arguing that it has resulted in a neglect of the social significance of skill at the workplace, specifically the processes underlying the acquisition and deployment of skills and the centrality of skill to job controls. Using a detailed ethnographic study of a chemicals plant, the chapter demonstrates that training is fundamentally bound up with struggles and accommodations around the frontier of control. The findings are used to explore the linkages between training and development, reward systems and performance outcomes while addressing the broader issue of how shop floor order is constructed under new management initiatives.

In their chapter Kelly and Monks consider a performance-related pay (PRP) scheme introduced in an Irish food manufacturing organization which had recently moved from the public to the private sector and sought to be more performance oriented. Despite the steady growth of PRP schemes since the beginning of the 1980s the authors note that there has been limited empirical exploration of the issues involved in their implementation. Through this study they consider the implementation of such a scheme from two key perspectives: that of the architect of the scheme, the HR Director, and that of the group of managers affected by it. The results of the study, a combination of quantitative and qualitative approaches, highlight important differences of perception about the scheme's objectives, the appropriateness of performance measures and rewards, even the extent to which it had been successful.

Significantly these differences existed not only between the HR Director and the managers but within the management group itself.

Strategic alliances or networks are a means by which small and medium enterprises can pool resources and skills for mutual benefit in an increasingly competitive world. The study by Connell and Ryan considers one such network in Australia which, as a group, adopted a government sponsored cultural change programme known as 'best practice' in an attempt to increase flexibility and productivity. As in the case of the Irish PRP scheme the network found that there were inherent dangers in assuming shared perspectives and needs, with the uniformity of the programme eventually becoming a source of friction. Nor did the pursuit of a common change programme have the same results across the group: although the firms adopted a similar approach, the impact of elements of the programme differed not only between firms but also in the way that managers and non-managers perceived the changes within each of them.

6

Training and Development at an Agrochemical Plant

Jason Heyes

A remarkable consensus currently exists amongst employers, trade unions, academics and policy-makers concerning the benefits of investing in training and development.[1] To a large extent, interest in skill formation is being driven by concerns relating to the position of the British economy in the international division of labour and the enduring competitive malaise affecting much of manufacturing industry. Differential levels of training activity are frequently cited as central in explaining the superior performance of overseas companies when compared with their British counterparts (Daly et al., 1985; Mason et al., 1994; Steedman et al., 1991; Lynch, 1994). The alleged emergence of new production systems has further served to intensify interest in workforce skills (Piore and Sabel, 1984; Best, 1990; Cappelli and Rogovsky, 1994). In contrast to the deskilled jobs and Taylorist working practices characteristic of the Fordist past, competitive success in the future is argued to be dependent on a reintegration of conception and execution within a continuous learning environment. The emerging requirement is argued to be for a workforce with the types of 'broad and high' skills which allow for flexible adaptations in the face of volatile product markets and uncertain production requirements (Streeck, 1989). Training and development is also seen as central to the concerns of human resource management (HRM); indeed at least one commentator has identified training as the 'vital component', the strategic function without which no organization can meaningfully be said to be practising HRM (Keep, 1989). Training not only facilitates flexible working practices and rapid adaptation but, it is argued, can also be an important means of motivating employees and securing commitment to company goals.

Organizational outcomes of this kind are, however, thought likely to be foreclosed to British employers because of systematic under-investment in skill formation. In explaining such apparent indifference to the benefits of a highly trained workforce commentators frequently point to institutional failure, citing, for example, poor management training, 'arm's length' relations between the City and industry, and a failure by the state to take an appropriate interventionist stance in training provision (Finegold and Soskice, 1988; Keep, 1989). Together, these forces have entrapped the British economy within a 'low-skills equilibrium' (Finegold and Sockice, 1988) which militates against the adoption of HRM and competitive strategies based around the production of high-quality, high-value-added goods and services.

While this type of structural account appears to be subject to a more or less general consensus (see, for example, Hyman, 1992; Storey and Sisson, 1993), a focus on the determining influence of state and societal institutions on training provision has coincided with an almost complete neglect of the workplace. Yet, as this chapter argues, it is only by looking at the workplace that the linkages between training provision and performance outcomes can be understood (see in addition, Heyes, 1993; Heyes and Stuart, 1994). The chapter represents an investigation into the social processes surrounding the acquisition and deployment of skills at the workplace. The issue of training is also used as a vehicle for exploring broader concerns regarding the way in which shop floor order is constructed and reconstructed under management initiatives associated with HRM. The chapter begins by outlining the causal connections which are commonly assumed to exist between training and development and organizational outcomes such as employee commitment. Conceptual problems relating to the implied neutrality of training provision, the neglect of skill as an important basis for job controls, and the under-developed theorization of the linkages between training and development and other aspects of HRM are then discussed. The second section of the chapter explores these issues more fully through a presentation of ethno-graphic data collected during a six-week period spent as a non-participant observer in a chemical plant. The case study explores worker responses to attempts by management to achieve greater 'flexibility' in the way jobs were performed and rewarded and the strategic role of skill in this context. The findings demonstrate how struggles and informal accommodations at the point of production served to shape the performance outcomes arising from managerial initiatives with respect to training and development.

Training, HRM and performance outcomes

The apparent lack of priority placed on skill formation within much of British industry stands in marked contrast to the primacy afforded training and development issues in the HRM literature. The importance of training and development is said to reside in its function in transforming the 'perfor-mance potential of employees and managers' (Hyman, 1992: 258), and in the way in which it serves to constitute employees as strategic resources as opposed to disposable commodities (Keep, 1989). This occurs in at least two ways. Firstly, training is the means by which employers create technical com-petencies within the workforce, facilitating the adoption of new technologies and the development of flexible working practices. To this end, it is argued that firms should seek to emphasize 'broad and high' skills (Streeck, 1989), or multiple competencies which allow for an expansion of job boundaries and the ability to switch between tasks, rather than narrow, low-level skills. This in turn should allow for a closer matching between firms' labour utilization policies and production requirements. The second way in which training is thought to impact positively on performance is through its potential to play a key role in harnessing employee commitment (Sisson, 1989: 34). Commitment, taken to include worker attachment, loyalty, involvement and identification with company goals (Keenoy, 1990: 372; Du Gay and Salaman, 1992; Guest, 1992: 118), is usually seen as central to that which HRM seeks to achieve (Walton, 1985: 79). The HRM ideal of worker commitment is also typically taken to include a behavioural dimension involving workers 'going beyond contract' or 'going the extra mile' in pursuit of customer service or organizational goals (Storey, 1995: 8). According to Keep:

> These motivational aspects of HRM are bound up with investment in training and development in so far as such investment is a powerful signalling device, which enables employers to confirm to their employees that they are being regarded as important to the company's future success. (1989: 112)

Essentially, the treatment of training and development within the HRM literature implies a 'positive-sum game' in which employers benefit from a more committed, motivated and flexible workforce while employees experience psychological rewards from more interesting, varied and challenging work. There is a risk, however, of over-simplifying the causal connections between training provision and performance outcomes. In effect, the treatment of training provision within HRM corresponds to a human capital model (Becker, 1975) in which inputs in the form of training investment produce outputs in the form of skills, superior productivity, affirmative attitudes and so forth. Yet, by treating training provision in basically value neutral terms, the social dimension of skill and skill formation is neglected (Green, 1992). The essential significance of training under HRM is not that workers should be provided with cognitive and non-cognitive capabilities, but that the knowledge they acquire should be at *management's disposal*, that it should be used in the pursuit of management defined goals (Thompson and O'Connell Davidson, 1995). Indeed, the training process may itself represent an opportunity for management to directly attempt to strengthen employees' identification with corporate values in the hope of encouraging co-operative forms of behaviour (Willmott, 1993: 524). Most HRM commentators recognize of course that employee co-operation cannot be simply assumed and that complementary strategies of reward and appraisal are needed to ensure that training is put to 'productive' use. However, important implications of this argument, such as the possibility that workers might use their skills as a tactical resource to pursue non-managerial goals and that training and development may therefore present management with certain risks, have been insufficiently addressed.

The implied political neutrality of skill and processes of skill formation found in the HRM literature stands in marked contrast to the treatment of these issues within the labour process debate. Struggles around the definition, control and remuneration of skill have here been seen as crucial in understanding the organization of work and production (Braverman, 1974; Elger,

1979). Studies such as those by Coyle (1982) of the clothing industry and Cockburn (1991) of the printing industry demonstrate that the definition of skill at the workplace has an important relational component whereby the recognition of one group of workers as 'skilled' may result, and indeed depend on, another group of workers being defined as 'unskilled'. The value of studies of this kind also lies in their recognition that job knowledge encompasses not only those skills which are formally imparted and recognized by management, but also 'tacit' skills (Manwaring and Wood, 1985) and 'trade secrets' (Marglin, 1984: 159) which may form the basis for job controls and sanctions against management. The issue here is less one of a notional concern with investment in human capital and more the fundamental question of how employees are encouraged to comply and co-operate in the search by employers for surplus value.

Within the HRM literature, securing commitment and co-operation is frequently treated as simply a matter of pursuing the 'right' strategies, often associated with a shift away from 'collectivism' and towards greater 'individualism' in employee relations (Purcell, 1993a: 519). Emphasis is placed on the development of employees as individuals through initiatives such as goal setting, performance appraisal and performance-related pay. As a number of commentators have noted, however, there is a risk of overlooking the 'collective' dimension of HRM, as embodied in initiatives such as teamworking and quality circles, and the tensions which may potentially arise between the individual and collective aspects (Legge, 1989; Keenoy, 1990). For purposes of analysis, Storey and Bacon (1993) have proposed that individualism and collectivism at the workplace be explored along the dimensions of industrial relations, work organization and human resources. One problem with this approach, however, is that these labels are used mainly to describe various management strategies and objective characteristics of work organization: what is less clear is how the character of shop floor relations is shaped by these. Does a more individualistic approach to human resources herald the emergence of more individualized forms of conflict? What does 'individualization' within work organization mean for workers' propensity to challenge managerial control either individually or collectively? How do the categories of individualism and collectivism help in understanding the linkages between specific HRM strategies and their associated performance outcomes?

Training within the internal labour market

An initial starting point for exploring some of these issues is to focus on the role of workplace institutions and governance structures in regulating social relations at the point of production. In the context of training and development, the role of the internal labour market in particular is frequently seen as crucial to ensuring that skills are effectively developed, rewarded and utilized (Sisson, 1989; Purcell, 1993b: 21). The internal labour market is usually taken to refer to an internal administrative structure governing the pricing and allocation of jobs. By encouraging job tenure, the internal labour market reduces the risk to firms of losing costly investments in human capital through employee quits or the 'poaching' activities of rival firms. International comparisons point to the importance of internal labour markets and low levels of inter-firm mobility in explaining the adoption of high-skills strategies in Germany and Japan (Caillods, 1994; Soskice, 1994). Other accounts have also emphasized the importance of internal labour markets in structuring shop floor relations and ameliorating conflict. Burawoy (1979), for example, has argued that internal labour markets are an important component of what he terms the 'internal state',[2] providing workers with identifiable rights and helping in the co-ordination of employers' and workers' interests. Thus 'The rewards of seniority – better jobs, improved fringe benefits, job security, social status and so forth – engender a commitment to the enterprise and its survival' (1979: 106). Burawoy argues that the internal labour market promotes worker co-operation by imposing constraints on the free exercise of management prerogative while encouraging 'possessive individualism' amongst the workforce. Workers in the engineering workshop studied by Burawoy were able to 'bid off' unattractive jobs or 'bump' less senior workers off jobs in the event of a layoff. Mobility within the internal labour market had the effect of mitigating conflict between workers and managers while promoting tensions between individual workers.

Seniority rules of this kind, while characteristic of internal labour markets in parts of the US manufacturing sector, cannot, however, be seen as generic characteristics of internal labour markets *per se*. Other accounts have stressed the importance of the collective properties of internal labour markets in explaining co-operation on the shop floor. Pertinent in this respect is Williamson's (1975) work on transactions costs. His analysis of alternative forms of labour contracting emphasizes the potential for internal forms of organization to deliver more efficient technical and social outcomes than available under purely market-mediated exchange relations. Internal organization is not, however, necessarily sufficient to *eliminate* transaction costs, particularly where production is characterized by a significant degree of 'task idiosyncrasy', a term Williamson uses to refer to job knowledge which can only be acquired through experience or through the disclosure of job knowledge by incumbent workers in the context of on-the-job training. Williamson claims that where pay is individualized, incumbent workers may choose to strategically (or 'opportunistically') withhold information, thus exploiting the bargaining leverage their job knowledge gives them in the production process. Such problems can, it is argued, be ameliorated by the creation of an internal labour market within which wages are attached to jobs rather than to workers, thus precluding individual wage bargaining and reducing the incentive for workers to behave 'opportunistically'.

The past decade has, however, witnessed an erosion of internal labour markets in some industries. In place of the 'broad' and 'long' promotion ladders characteristic of companies in the public sector and manufacturing in the post-war period, shorter, 'truncated' internal labour markets comprising fewer job slots and opportunities for promotion have emerged (Lovering,

1990). In the public sector, the policies pursued by the state have been instrumental in promoting the compression of internal labour market structures (Nolan and Walsh, 1995), while in the private sector attempts by management to achieve greater flexibility in production have resulted in changes to established job descriptions, fewer and broader job grades and greater variation in pay within bands (Kessler, 1995). Increasingly, companies have sought to relate pay to individuals rather than to the jobs they do through the introduction of systems of reward closely associated with HRM such as performance-related pay (Purcell, 1993b; Kessler and Purcell, 1995). For some commentators, remuneration strategies of this kind represent an *extension* and *consolidation* of internal labour markets (Purcell, 1991). Yet as others have argued, individualizing rewards in this way may undermine the collective organizational foundations on which internal labour markets are established (Walsh, 1993). Case study research suggests that discriminatory pay practices may conflict with established notions of fairness and equity and undermine the basis for co-operation in production (Geary, 1992). Williamson's work also suggests the possibility that a haemorrhaging of internal labour structures may be detrimental to on-the-job training and co-operative skill deployment as workers hoard job information and use their skills as a tactical resource in the pursuit of 'opportunistic' gains. The following case study directly engages with these issues by examining the relationship between structures of reward, worker behaviour and the outcomes arising from management initiatives with respect to training and development.

Training at the workplace

Research context

The fieldwork was conducted over a six-week period spent as a non-participant observer on one site of a chemical company which we shall call 'Reaction'. A transnational corporation formed as a product of a demerger in 1993, Reaction's core activities centred around the production of pharmaceuticals, agrochemical products such as fungicides and insecticides, and specialities such as colour dyes, biocides and fine chemicals. The factory in which the research was conducted, which we shall call 'Agro', specialized in the production of agrochemicals and dyestuffs. Agro had been operating since the early 1970s and, compared with other, more modern plants on the site, required considerable manual intervention in the production process.

Of the 1400 people working at Reaction, 695 were employed in processing and maintenance roles and 57 of these worked within Agro. Production was organized around a system of continuous shifts. Each shift crew comprised a Shift Manager, one Process Controller (PC), one Group Leader, an Ice Plant Technician (IPT) based in the adjoining ice production plant, and three Chemical Process Technicians (CPTs). In addition, the day shift team was augmented by one Engineering Support Technician (EST), although these worked to a separate shift pattern. The study group within Agro consisted of one particular team of male shift workers (F-shift), although the changing composition of the group through absence and sickness cover afforded opportunities to conduct research with workers from other shifts. Although I did not participate in the production process, I was given complete freedom to observe and interact with the shift crew in every part of the factory from the control room to the shop floor. While my presence was initially treated with extreme suspicion, particularly by the shop steward, I was eventually included in general conversation, banter, smoke breaks and 'rituals', such as the takeaway meals which were consumed on the weekend night shift. Additional information was acquired through a series of semi-structured interviews with senior and middle management representatives and senior shop stewards.

The search for flexibility: from WSA to LWA

The research took place in 1994, shortly after the introduction of a new agreement on working practices and training and development. The Local Working Agreement (LWA), jointly agreed at company level between management and the signatory unions, represented the latest in a series of attempts dating back 20 years by management to achieve greater flexibility between and within craft and process work. In the early 1970s, the company had introduced the Weekly Staff Agreement (WSA) which led to the development through job evaluation of an internal labour market structure attaching rewards to specific jobs. Within Agro, the grading structure for process workers encompassed three grades: grade 4 'ground floor' who discharged the finished product; grade 5 'top floor' workers, dedicated to charging raw materials to the reactors; and grade 8 Process Controllers and Group Leaders. On the craft side, tradesmen acquired grade 7 status on completing their apprenticeship.

Despite sporadic attempts by management to increase the degree of freedom in matters of labour deployment, the job definitions established under WSA remained relatively intact until the late 1980s when, under increasing competitive pressures in the markets for dyes and agrochemicals, Reaction undertook an extensive review of working practices. The resulting 1993 LWA, brought in with the assistance of a 14 per cent bonus payment, introduced greater flexibility in the deployment of labour, task enlargement, annualized hours and a commitment to ongoing training and development. The grading structure established under WSA was disrupted, the notion of progression through the internal labour market being subsumed beneath an expansion of existing job definitions. Management sought to expand task boundaries by promoting grade 4 process workers to grade 5 in the expectation that all process workers would both load and discharge chemicals from then on. In addition, a new production role of Chemical Process Technician (CPT) was created. The CPT crews incorporated the existing process workers, along with the majority (100) of the maintenance workers who were redeployed into process activities under the LWA agreement. This development, however, had the effect of disrupting established pay differentials.

Table 6.1   *Pay relativities at Reaction's Agro plant: annual salary (£000)*[1]

Grade	1992	1993	1994
4	14.3	15.0	15.4
5	15.1	15.8	16.2
6	15.9	16.7	17.2
7	13.4	14.3 (17.8)[2]	14.,8 (18.3)[2]
8	17.9	18.9	19.4

[1] The figures do not incorporate overtime earnings but do include a shift disturbance allowance (paid only to process workers at a flat rate) and working conditions payments (paid to all workers as a percentage of grade value).

[2] Figures in parentheses refer to the basic salary for those grade 7 craft workers redeployed into CPT shift crews in 1993. The difference between the bracketed and unbracketed figures represents a shift disturbance allowance of approximately £3500.

Despite the higher grade and basic salary of craft workers under WSA, their actual earnings had been significantly less than those of the process workers. This was primarily because the process workers worked on shifts and received a supplementary shift disturbance allowance, amounting to approximately £3500 per annum, paid on top of their basic salary. During negotiations for LWA, the craft unions had argued that any tradesman redeployed into process work should be allowed to keep his grade 7 status instead of having his pay gradually scaled down to the grade 5 CPT rate (before shift disturbance allowance) as would otherwise have been the case under the existing redeployment rules. The company, anxious to elicit the engineering union's support for LWA, agreed that any craftsman redeployed into a shift CPT crew should retain his grade 7 status and associated basic salary. However, as the former craftsmen now received shift disturbance allowance, their redeployment also meant an effective reversal of the earnings differential which had previously existed between the grade 5 and grade 7 workers (see Table 6.1). In addition, the 14 per cent bonus payment for flexibility was paid as a percentage of grade value, thus causing a further differential to open up as payments were phased through. In short, inequalities in reward were introduced for workers performing the same job.

Training for empowerment

Management believed that by accepting the LWA, workers had committed themselves to 'continual and ongoing change' in which further changes to working methods could be introduced without negotiation. To facilitate 'continual and ongoing change', considerable emphasis was placed on the development of a new two-phase training programme. The first phase was directed predominantly at facilitating horizontal task enlargement within the CPT crew, providing workers with the technical competencies required to cope with redeployment and flexible working. Process workers received training in craft skills, essentially consisting of the simple fitting, electrical and instrument skills required to keep the plant running, while the redeployed craft workers were taught the process skills required in their new role as CPTs. The second phase of the training programme was directed at vertical task enlargement, which management referred to as 'empowerment'. Empowerment involved the CPTs in being trained to perform tasks traditionally performed by PCs and Shift Managers. Senior management presented the training programme in terms of 'personal development' with each worker 'going as far as he wants to'. Ultimately, however, management exercised complete discretion over who to train and in what areas. According to Agro's Operations Manager: 'Anyone can do anything is the rule, as long as it's safe to do so, it's good business sense, and it's not best done another way.' In practice, this amounted to developing the skills needed for simple plant maintenance and materials ordering rather than offering workers opportunities for continuous development.

According to Reaction's Personnel Manager, each CPT had been trained in five new areas of competency since the introduction of LWA. Yet, notwithstanding the considerable amount of training activity which had taken place, there was little evidence to suggest that workers felt empowered. The most common attitude expressed on the shop floor was one of demoralization at the changes wrought by management. Many of the former craft workers felt that their work and skills had been devalued – that they had been forcibly dispossessed of their trade. As one former fitter put it: 'I feel as I've been robbed. LWA . . . it's not right nice, not for tradesmen. They say you should get pride out of this job, but anyone can do this.'

The truncation of the internal labour market through the merging of 'top' and 'ground' floor work into a single graded job also generated a considerable amount of discontent among incumbent grade 5 workers. Part of the attraction of progressing to grade 5 in the past had been the opportunity to escape the more effort-intensive 'ground floor' jobs of the grade 4 worker. At the same time, top floor men considered the pay differential they enjoyed over the ground floor men fair recognition of the greater responsibility they carried (a failure to charge the chemicals correctly could result in a spoiled batch, or a potentially hazardous situation). The merging of the two roles, however, resulted in incumbent grade 5 workers becoming once more involved in activities they felt they had legitimately 'escaped' through internal promotion. The introduction of broader job bands coupled with the enlargement of job definitions conflicted with traditional notions of equity and fairness.

Training and the frontier of control

The first phase of the training programme introduced under LWA was heavily dependent on process workers' willingness to train former craft workers in an on-the-job context. Following Williamson (1975), it might be predicted that the fragmentation of reward structures that accompanied the redeployment of the craft workers into CPT roles would have resulted in incumbent process workers becoming less prepared to disclose job knowledge. Yet this was not the case. Despite pay fragmentation, process workers were happy to pass on their skills. In explaining this it is necessary to understand the organization of work and the terms on which process workers sought to exert a measure of control over the effort bargain.

Although the computer dictated the times at which materials should be charged and discharged, thus taking an important structuring element in the effort bargain beyond the control of the CPTs, a measure of control over the average level of effort intensity could nevertheless be achieved by preparing jobs in advance. In this way, work-related activity could be interspersed with rest periods on a basis more suitable to the men. The ability to structure the pace of work in this way depended, however, on team members' willingness to co-operate fully in the preparation and execution of tasks. The establishment of a steady pace of work also occasionally called for workers to engage in rule breaking. Examples of this included washing minor chemical spillages down the drains and washing 'excess' chemicals away rather than waiting for a reactor to become available. Such practices required a significant amount of complicity between team members.

> Gary (a grade 5 process worker) and Sam (a former fitter) were waiting to discharge a product but needed four extra poly-tubs (containers). They located four 'tubs' containing non-conforming acid which they should have taken up to the top floor and emptied into a pan. Instead they emptied the contents onto the floor and washed them down the drain with the hose. 'We just tell them [the PCs] we've charged it to the pan,' said Sam. 'The pH level at the effluent plant'll go up, that's all,' added Gary, 'they'll treat it with alkaline.'

The willingness of the process workers to train the former craft workers can therefore be understood as an expression of self-interest. If all team members were able to perform to an equal level, the CPTs could successfully achieve a measure of control over their collective efforts and thus achieve a degree of respite from the shop floor. Job knowledge (including that relating to the safety of various 'fiddles') was used as a strategic resource, enabling workers to gain a measure of control over the production process and the pace of their efforts. Such behaviour suggests that it is not only the transmission of job knowledge which needs to be considered in the analysis of training provision, but also the *nature* of that knowledge and how it is used.

Although pay fragmentation did not discourage skill transmission and acquisition, rigidities did appear in the way in which skills were used. Incumbent process workers demonstrated a clear reluctance to use their new maintenance skills to further company objectives. Senior management were reluctant to admit this, arguing instead that the grading system established under WSA had led to rigid job demarcations which LWA had since broken down. Yet there was evidence that management had over-stated the extent to which labour arrangements under WSA had resulted in rigidities in the organization of production, for both process and craft workers alike would regularly perform tasks outside the terms of their job definitions.[3] Process workers would, for example, remove valves (officially fitters' work) from the pipework if this was necessary to clear a blockage. Conversely, fitters would clear a blockage (officially process work) once they had broken into the line. According to one PC:

> People have *always* been flexible. There were never any real demarcations between process and trade. They [process workers] did do [maintenance] jobs if they needed to be done . . . [and] if a process operator broke into a line, the fitter would make it legitimate by doing the necessary paperwork for you.

Working across demarcations was always a matter for day-to-day negotiation and tacit agreement between the workers themselves. In reducing the time spent waiting for minor maintenance tasks to be done, it had allowed for jobs to be completed more swiftly and hence enabled workers to structure their rest time more effectively. Any positive effects on down time, productivity and performance were essentially by-products and dependent on continued worker co-operation. It is important to note at this point that flexible working under WSA should not be seen as having had the status of a custom and practice rule. The customary rule in operation related to the maintenance of the right to *choose* whether or not to engage in flexible working. Workers could, and would, resist managerial efforts to force them into performing work outside the remit of their job descriptions even though they might regularly perform such work voluntarily. As one Shift Manager commented:

> Shift Managers would see operators doing certain small jobs outside the job description. But if you told him [the process worker], for example, to change a valve, 90 per cent of the time he'd say 'that's not my job' and you wouldn't have an argument.

The flexibility achieved through the voluntary efforts of workers under WSA was formalized within the LWA implying, *prima facie,* a shift in the frontier of control in management's favour. However, incumbent process workers fought to retain control over the terms on which they used their skills, demonstrating a marked reluctance to perform jobs outside the remit of their old WSA job definitions. Skill deployment, particularly with respect to fitting work, was subjected to a process of struggle and accommodation which eventually resulted in the construction of a new shop floor order. The basis for this can be illustrated by explaining instances in which process workers performed fitting work, and those in which they chose not to do so. These are referred to as 'the act of acceptance' and the 'act of refusal', respectively.

The 'act of refusal' reflected concerns over pay fragmentation and resulting inequalities in reward between process workers and former craftsmen as outlined above. The feelings of the grade 5 process workers towards the former tradesmen was articulated by one CPT who, when asked if he expected the grade 7 workers to work harder than himself, replied:

> I don't expect them to work harder, but I *do* expect them to do any fitting or control work if there is any. I don't see why I should do it if there's a bloke being paid a hundred pound more than me.

This attitude also needs to be understood in the context of a further grievance of process workers which centred on the implications arising from the 'formalization' of the rules governing flexibility. The transference of these rules from the arena of informal negotiation to that of formal agreement under LWA constituted a threat to workers' ability to regulate their own work effort. Yet, while management succeeded to some extent in expanding process workers' job boundaries, there was a clear disjuncture between the terms of the LWA agreement and shop floor behaviour. Fitting work, for example, continued to be subject to 'unofficial' demarcation with grade 5 process workers acting to maintain their *right to refuse* such work as existed under WSA.

The degree of autonomy afforded CPTs in the production process was important in explaining the basis upon which the 'act of refusal' was affected. The division of tasks was decided on by the men at the start of a shift and peer pressure could be exerted to induce former fitters into performing any maintenance work. Although the Shift Manager was obligated under LWA to ensure that the burden of fitting work was shared between incumbent process and former craft workers, the Shift Manager on F-shift did not seek to pressure grade 5 workers into fitting. Shift Managers at Agro accepted grade 5 workers' 'act of refusal' since continuing demarcations around fitting work did not conflict with their own interest in continuous output.

The autonomy afforded process workers, and their success in continuing to regulate the terms on which fitting work was performed, were also central in explaining their occasional willingness to work flexibly: it remained, to a large extent, their choice. Once again, the behaviour of the Shift Manager was crucial. Occasional efforts to cajole incumbent process workers into fitting work by reference to the terms of the LWA were met by workers articulating their grievances concerning the wage disparity between themselves and the former tradesmen and by the withdrawal of co-operation. The deployment of fitting skills by grade 5 process workers was dependent, therefore, on the Shift Manager's willingness to respect their 'act of refusal'. So long as this remained the case, the performance of fitting tasks was not seen by the process workers as threatening a precedent which the Shift Manager would then attempt to enforce. Moreover, process workers enjoyed benefits from the 'act of acceptance' as fitting provided respite from the boredom caused by the periods of inactivity which inevitably punctuated a shift. Although, as noted above, the achievement of a steady pace of work was an important goal to workers, in a computer controlled production process this was not always possible. The decision to be inactive was sometimes beyond the workers' control and fitting, particularly on the night shift, could provide an illusion of time passing more swiftly.[4] Furthermore, waiting for a job to be done could interfere with workers' ability to structure their shift if, for example, it caused process jobs to be moved back too close to the end of the shift, or if it brought jobs too close together. The occasional performance of fitting work by grade 5 workers can therefore be understood in terms of an adaptation to the deprivations associated with the process of production (Baldamus, 1961: 52–77).

Summary and conclusions

This chapter has highlighted the utility of distinguishing between skill acquisition and skill deployment in understanding the connections between training and development and performance outcomes. The failure in the HRM literature to distinguish between these two separate but related processes has encouraged a depiction of skill as essentially a value neutral, productivity enhancing factor input stripped of any broader social significance. Once the workplace is included within the scope of analysis, however, the limitations of such a narrow interpretation of training become clear. The experience of Reaction suggests that for both workers and management, training is enmeshed in a broader set of concerns relating to effort, reward and control. The training process, and the resulting implications for productive efficiency, must therefore be understood by reference to social processes on the shop floor wherein skill acquisition and deployment represent enactments of interest furtherance through which broader sets of power relationships are reflected. Training investment does not, in other words, automatically translate into improved performance; rather this result is dependent upon how, and in whose interests, skills are utilized.

A key concern of HRM is to ensure that skills are deployed in such a way as to secure managerially defined objectives such as flexibility, quality and high productivity. Ensuring workers co-operate to this end is argued to require appropriate complementary strategies of reward, appraisal and so forth which aim to develop workers as individuals and encourage motivation (Purcell, 1993a: 518). In the case of Reaction, however, the severing of the association between tasks and rewards caused by the redeployment of the craft workers into the CPT teams created tensions on the shop floor which acted to discourage flexibility, teamwork and co-operation in pursuit of management goals. Rather than working 'beyond contract' in the manner implied by the HRM ideal of commitment, pay fragmentation encouraged the emergence of rigidities where they had previously not existed. This finding also needs to be understood in terms of the way in which LWA had changed the meaning attached to working 'beyond contract'. Under WSA, working flexibly across job boundaries had enabled workers to have a measure of control over the pace of work; the benefits provided to management were coincidental. Under LWA, however, working across job boundaries became a formal expectation, with 'multi-skilling' threatening an intensification of work and a shift of the frontier of control in management's favour.

The response of the workers to these challenges was complex and multifaceted. Although inequalities in reward fostered divisions within the workforce which militated against the deployment of skills in the pursuit of management defined objectives, skills were at the same time used collectively by workers to achieve their own goals. The creation of a 'multi-skilled' CPT grade provided an imperative for the incumbent process workers to pass on their skills to the former craft workers so as to maintain some degree of control over the pace of work. 'Multi-skilling' in this sense produced a recognition of shared interests and formed a basis for collective job controls. However, the lateral tensions which were simultaneously produced on the shop floor through the disruption of the internal labour market also encouraged the process workers to pursue other job controls (those surrounding the deployment of maintenance skills) at the expense of the former craft workers. As we have seen, the construction of order on the shop floor in the wake of LWA was dependent on a willingness by Shift Managers to tolerate the continuation of process workers' controls over the manner in which their skills were deployed. This in turn was important in explaining why process workers would occasionally consent to work flexibly.

This complex picture of solidaristic and sectional struggles and accommodations points to a difficulty in understanding the linkages between training provision and performance outcomes in isolation from social processes at the point of production. It also indicates the problems involved in operationalizing categories such as 'collectivism' and 'individualism'. The central problem relates to a tendency for the contradictory nature of the employment relationship to disappear in the search for ways in which to map changes in management approach. As a consequence, regulatory processes and institutions at the level of the workplace tend to be insufficiently addressed. In contrast, approaches such as those of Burawoy and Williamson, notwithstanding their very different interests, orientations and methodological approaches, place the employment relationship at the centre of the analysis. In doing so, they provide suggestive insights into how the connections between management strategy, changes in the organization of work and production, and resulting technical and social outcomes might be explored. As the present discussion of training and development has sought to establish, such an analysis also needs to give full recognition to the continued importance of job controls and other forms of purposive behaviour by workers at the point of production. Empirical inquiry at the level of the shop floor can, potentially, serve a valuable purpose in this regard by helping to reconnect the study of HRM strategies and outcomes to social and regulatory processes within the workplace.

Notes

1 The limits of a consensual approach by trade unions towards training and development have been critically assessed by Claydon (1993), Kelly (1996) and Stuart (1996).

2 This term is equivalent in many respects to the concept of the 'factory regime' employed in Burawoy's (1983; 1985) later work. Both terms refer to a conceptual distinction between the labour process and the regulatory institutions which shape the character of struggles at work.

3 WSA had in fact allowed process workers to perform up to 15 minutes' worth of fitting work per hour on a shift. However, few workers within Agro were able to provide me with a definitive version of the rules surrounding fitting work. This evidence is suggestive of the liberality with which the rules had been interpreted in the past.

4 The sensation described by Baldamus (1961: 59) as 'traction'.

References

Baldamus, W. (1961) *Efficiency and Effort: an Analysis of Industrial Administration*. London: Tavistock.

Becker, G. (1975) *Human Capital* (2nd edn). New York: Columbia University Press.

Best, M. (1990) *The New Competition*. Cambridge: Polity.

Braverman, H. (1974) *Labor and Monopoly Capital: the Degradation of Work in the Twentieth Century*. New York: Monthly Review Press.

Burawoy, M. (1979) *Manufacturing Consent: Changes in the Labor Process under Monopoly Capitalism*. Chicago: University of Chicago Press.

Burawoy, M. (1983) 'Between the labor process and the state: the changing face of factory regimes under advanced capitalism', *American Sociological Review*, 48 (October): 587–605.

Burawoy, M. (1985) *The Politics of Production*. London: Verso.

Caillods, F. (1994) 'Converging trends amidst diversity in vocational training systems', *International Labour Review*, 133 (2): 241–58.

Cappelli, P. and Rogovsky, N. (1994) 'New work systems and skill requirements', *International Labour Review*, 133 (2): 205–20.

Claydon, T. (1993) 'Training and the new bargaining agenda: the limits to co-operative joint regulation within the firm'. Paper presented at the British Universities Industrial Relations Association Conference, York University.

Cockburn, C. (1991) *Brothers: Male Dominance and Technological Change* (2nd edn). London: Pluto.

Coyle, A. (1982) 'Sex and skill in the organisation of the clothing industry', in J. West (ed.), *Work, Women and the Labour Market*. London, Boston: Routledge and Kegan Paul.

Daly, A., Hitchens, D. and Wagner, K. (1985) 'Productivity, machinery and skills in a sample of British and German manufacturing plants', *National Institute Economic Review*, 111: 48–61.

Du Gay, P. and Salaman, G. (1992) 'The cult(ure) of the customer', *Journal of Management Studies*, 29 (5): 615–33.

Elger, T. (1979) 'Valorisation and "deskilling": a critique of Braverman', *Capital and Class*, 7: 58–99.

Finegold, D. and Soskice, D. (1988) 'The failure of training in Britain: analysis and prescription', *Oxford Review of Economic Policy*, 4 (3): 21–52.

Geary, J.F. (1992) 'Pay, control and commitment: linking appraisal and reward', *Human Resource Management Journal*, 2 (4): 36–54.

Green, F. (1992) 'On the political economy of skill in the advanced industrial nations', *Review of Political Economy*, 4 (4): 413–35.

Guest, D.E. (1992) 'Employee commitment and control', in J.F. Hartley and G.M. Stephenson (eds), *Employment Relations*. Oxford: Blackwell.

Heyes, J. (1993) 'Training provision and workplace institutions: an investigation', *Industrial Relations Journal*, 24 (4): 296–307.

Heyes, J. and Stuart, M. (1994) 'Placing symbols before reality? Re-evaluating the low skills equilibrium', *Personnel Review*, 23 (5): 34–49.

Hyman, J. (1992) 'Training and development', in B. Towers (ed.), *The Handbook of Human Resource Management*. Oxford: Blackwell.

Keenoy, T. (1990) 'HRM: rhetoric, reality and contradiction', *International Journal of Human Resource Management*, 1 (3): 363–84.

Keep, E. (1989) 'Corporate training strategies: the vital component?', in J. Storey (ed.), *New Perspectives on Human Resource Management*. London: Routledge.

Kelly, J. (1996) 'Union militancy and social partnership', in P. Ackers, C. Smith and P. Smith (eds), *The New Workplace and Trade Unionism*. London: Routledge.

Kessler, I. (1995) 'Reward systems', in J. Storey (ed.), *Human Resource Management: a Critical Text*. London: Routledge.

Kessler, I. and Purcell, J. (1995) 'Individualism and collectivism as theory and practice', in P. Edwards (ed.), *Industrial Relations: Theory and Practice in Britain*. Oxford: Blackwell.

Legge, K. (1989) 'Human resource management: a critical analysis', in J. Storey (ed.), *New Perspectives on Human Resource Management*. London: Routledge.

Lovering, J. (1990) 'A perfunctory sort of post-Fordism: economic restructuring and labour market segmentation in Britain', *Work, Employment and Society*, 4 (2): 9–28.

Lynch, L.M. (1994) 'Introduction', in L.M. Lynch (ed.), *Training and the Private Sector: International Comparisons*. Chicago: University of Chicago Press.

Manwaring, T. and Wood, S. (1985) 'The ghost in the labour process', in D. Knights, H. Willmott and D. Collinson (eds), *Job Redesign: Critical Perspectives on the Labour Process*. Aldershot: Gower.

Marglin, S. (1984) 'Knowledge and power', in F. Stephen (ed.), *Firms, Organization and Labour: Approaches to the Economics of Work Organizatio*n. London: Macmillan.

Mason, G., Van Ark, B. and Wagner, K. (1994) 'Productivity, product quality and workforce skills: food processing in four European countries', *National Institute Economic Review*, 147: 62–83.

Nolan, P. and Walsh, J. (1995) 'The structure of the economy and the labour market', in P. Edwards (ed.), *Industrial Relations: Theory and Practice in Britain*. Oxford: Blackwell.

Piore, M. and Sabel, C. (1984) *The Second Industrial Divide: Possibilities for Prosperity*. New York: Basic Books.

Purcell, J. (1991) 'The rediscovery of the management prerogative: the management of labour relations in the 1980s', *Oxford Review of Economic Policy*, 7 (1): 33–43.

Purcell, J. (1993a) 'The challenge of human resource management for industrial relations research and practice', *The International Journal of Human Resource Management*, 4 (3): 511–27.

Purcell, J. (1993b) 'The end of institutional industrial relations', *Political Quarterly*, 64 (1): 6–23.

Sisson, K. (1989) 'Personnel management in transition?', in K. Sisson (ed.), *Personnel Management in Britain*. Oxford: Blackwell.

Soskice, D. (1994) 'Reconciling markets and institutions: the German apprenticeship system', in L.M. Lynch (ed.), *Training and the Private Sector: International Comparisons*. Chicago: University of Chicago Press.

Steedman, H., Mason, G. and Wagner, K. (1991) 'Intermediate skills and the workplace: deployment, standards and supply in Britain', *National Institute Economic Review*, 136: 60–76.

Storey, J. (1995) 'HRM: still marching on, or marching out?', in J. Storey (ed.), *Human Resource Management: a Critical Text*. London: Routledge.

Storey, J. and Bacon, N. (1993) 'Individualism and collectivism: into the 1990s', *The International Journal of Human Resource Management*, 4 (3): 665–84.

Storey, J. and Sisson, K. (1993) *Managing Human Resources and Industrial Relations*. Buckingham: Open University Press.

Streeck, W. (1989) 'Skills and the limits of neo-liberalism: the enterprise of the future as a place of learning', *Work, Employment and Society*, 3 (1): 89–104.

Stuart, M. (1996), 'The industrial relations of training: a reconsideration of bargaining arrangements', *Industrial Relations Journal,* 27 (3): 253–65.

Thompson, P. and O'Connell Davidson, J. (1995) 'The continuity of discontinuity: management rhetoric in turbulent times', *Personnel Review*, 24 (4): 17–33.

Walsh, J. (1993) 'Internalisation v. decentralisation: an analysis of recent developments in pay bargaining', *British Journal of Industrial Relations*, 31 (3): 409–32.

Walton, R.E. (1985) 'From control to commitment in the workplace', *Harvard Business Review*, March/April: 76–84.

Williamson, O.E. (1975) *Markets and Hierarchies: Analysis and Antitrust Implications*, New York: Free Press.

Willmott, H. (1993) 'Strength is ignorance; slavery is freedom: managing culture in modern organizations', *Journal of Management Studies*, 30 (4): 515–52.

7

View from the Bridge and Life on Deck: Contrasts and Contradictions in Performance-Related Pay

Aisling Kelly and Kathy Monks

The complexities surrounding the issue of reward management can be seen as indicative of the contradictions that exist within the discipline labelled human resource management (HRM). For example, Storey's (1992: 27) distinction between 'hard' and 'soft' HRM identifies the need for 'strategic interventions designed to elicit commitment and to develop resourceful humans' (soft HRM) and 'strategic interventions designed to achieve full utilization of labour resources' (hard HRM). The current state of knowledge on reward systems suggests that these are often designed to attempt both strategic interventions together; how successful they are on either count is perhaps less well documented. This tension within HRM has been noted by several writers and the processes currently used to reward individuals have been well scrutinized (Smith, 1992; Legge, 1995; Kessler, 1995). In the final analysis, it appears that many of the reward initiatives pursued represent no more than a 'shuffling of the pack' (Kessler, 1995: 274) rather than any innovative, integrated strategy which could be considered part of a distinctive HRM approach.

This chapter considers one aspect of the current debate on reward systems by examining the operation of a performance-related pay (PRP) scheme in a food manufacturing company in Ireland. The research is presented from two contrasting viewpoints. The first, the view from 'the bridge', is that of the Human Resource (HR) Director involved in designing and administering the scheme. The second, from those 'on deck', is that of the managers who are experiencing the scheme. The differences between these two views give an insight into the contradictions which may arise in the operation of PRP. Before considering these views in detail, the chapter first of all considers some of the evidence available on the operation of PRP systems and describes the background to the study and the methodology used in the research.

PRP: the literature evidence

The traditional personnel textbooks are noted for their prescriptive approach to most matters with issues neatly labelled and packaged for consumption by students and practitioners. PRP is no exception to this rule, with the advantages and disadvantages of such schemes neatly displayed, guidelines for their introduction and operation clearly laid out and solutions to envisaged problems helpfully provided (Armstrong, 1991; Armstrong and Murlis, 1994). More recent textbooks and the evidence provided by empirical research (Mabey and Salaman, 1995; Geary 1992) tend to present a less optimistic picture of the viability of the off-the-shelf schemes which are promoted by the textbooks and suggest that successful performance management schemes, of which PRP may be one dimension, may need to be organization specific. However, both the textbook writers and the empirical researchers are agreed that the issues surrounding the operation of PRP schemes are complex.

PRP as a motivator

Armstrong suggests that 'it is fair to provide financial rewards to people as a means of paying them according to their contribution' (1993: 86). The primary argument in favour of PRP is that it acts as a motivator, through both recognition of achievements and monetary reward. Further benefits cited include the fact that individuals can identify closely with their employers' goals and that this can increase productivity and encourage quality, flexibility and teamwork (Armstrong and Murlis, 1994; Wright, 1991). In addition, PRP can contribute to the successful recruitment and retention of staff. However, many researchers (Dwyer, 1994; Kessler and Purcell, 1992; Marsden and Richardson, 1994) have questioned the extent to which PRP actually acts as a motivator, or, indeed, the extent to which money itself can motivate: 'Most managers are aware of Herzberg's view that the job itself is the source of true motivation, not the pay or even the conditions of work' (Dwyer, 1994: 17). A study by Kovach (1987) reported a mismatch between managerial and employee views concerning what motivates; while managers attributed high financial needs to employees, staff cited pay as fifth on a list of ten factors, while the first four were concerned with intrinsic motivators.

Expectancy theory (Vroom, 1964) has been used to explain the motivational force in performance: 'Expectancy theory hypothesizes that it is the anticipated satisfaction of valued goals which causes individuals to address their behaviour in a way which is most likely to lead to their attaining them' (Mabey and Salaman, 1995: 190). More specifically, expectancy theory claims that motivation is a multiplicative function of three components: expectancy, the belief that one's effort will result in performance; instrumentality, the belief that one's performance will be rewarded; and valence, the perceived value of the rewards to the recipient.

Reasons for the introduction of PRP

There are a variety of reasons for the introduction of PRP schemes. Several writers note that a pay system can be used as a vehicle for organizational change. For example, Armstrong suggests that PRP can 'act as a lever for cultural change in the direction of accountability for results and orientation toward high performance' (1993: 86). However, PRP may simply be one of a number of initiatives designed to achieve cultural change. Procter et al. suggest that 'the necessary culture may already have to be in place for a system of PRP to work effectively' (1993: 73), as PRP alone may be incapable of becoming the primary driving force of cultural change. PRP may also serve the purpose of providing a statement to employees regarding what Kessler and Purcell (1992: 21) describe as the 'kind of company we are' and may reinforce existing organizational values and expectations. The strategy of culture change may also encompass broader objectives which aim to change the relationship between management and employees. Thus, it has been suggested (Ribbens, 1988; Kessler and Purcell, 1992; Procter et al., 1993) that the individualistic nature of PRP can be used to side-step the collective bargaining process, thereby reducing the influence of the trade union in an effort to re-establish managerial control.

The success of PRP schemes

The objectives in introducing PRP can have a significant impact on the success, or otherwise, of the scheme. Crowe suggests that 'each scheme will need to be assessed in the light of each organization's objectives' (1992:124). Furthermore, the manner in which a scheme is formulated and implemented, and the extent of employee participation in this process, will also have an impact on the scheme's success. Case study research (Lawler and Hackman, 1969; Schefflen et al., 1971) demonstrates that plans will be more conducive to both acceptance and success if employees are involved in their formulation.

The success of a PRP scheme does not lie solely with employee involvement in the initial stages, or indeed even with a particular set of procedures designed to administer such schemes. According to Beer et al., 'the motivational and satisfactional value of a reward system is a function of the perceived equity of the reward system' (1984: 124). Without the presence of this perceived fairness, trust in the system is likely to be low and there is the distinct risk that the contingent link between performance and pay will not be accepted. For example, it has been noted that managers are often unhappy with their wage system because they do not perceive the relationship between how hard they work (productivity) and how much they earn (Hamner, 1975: 17). The issue of fairness is even more critical in flatter organizations where opportunities for promotion may be limited.

Several antidotes for this problem of 'perceived unfairness' have been suggested. These include the extent to which employees have the opportunity to participate in pay design decisions, the quality and timeliness of information provided, the degree to which the rules governing pay allocations are consistently followed, the availability of channels for appeals, and the organization's safeguards against bias and inconsistency (Greenberg, 1986). Hamner points out that the 'more frequent the formal and informal reviews of performance and the more the individual is told about the reasons for an increase, the greater his preference for a merit increase system and the lower his preference for a seniority system' (1975: 20). Frequent reviews, coupled with the opportunity to air grievances through a formal appeals process, may therefore eliminate many of the difficulties associated with employees' perceptions of unfairness.

In addition to the issue of fairness, problems associated with PRP include a tendency toward a short-term focus on quantifiable goals to the neglect of more long-term issues. There may also be measurement difficulties, both in measuring the work of professionals and in attaining a fair and consistent means of assessing employees which will avoid the risks of subjectivity (Murphy and Cleveland, 1995; Kessler, 1994; Beer et al., 1984). Philpott and Sheppard (1992) identify a lack of communication as the principal failing and further difficulties may be created by a lack of agreement on objectives and standards of performance and insufficient feedback (Armstrong, 1993; Mabey and Salaman, 1995). Storey and Sisson (1993) argue that PRP would appear to undermine utterly the whole concept of teamwork. From research in multinationals operating in Ireland, Geary (1992) found evidence of the contradictory nature of management's strategy which attempted to develop simultaneously a collective identity focused around teamwork, while discriminating between individual contributions.

In summary, the available research does not suggest that PRP has been particularly successful as a reward strategy and there seem to be many pitfalls associated with its operation. There has been little research carried out in Ireland on this topic and it is therefore difficult to estimate the success or otherwise of PRP schemes in the Irish context. However, from the limited evidence available, it does appear that PRP is an issue for Irish organizations (Gunnigle et al., 1993; Geary, 1992) and that it is used in a considerable number of firms. The findings of the Price Waterhouse Cranfield study (Filella and Hegewisch, 1994) indicate a take-up of merit-related or performance-related pay for managerial staff in 51 per cent of the European organizations studied, with private sector companies more likely than their public sector counterparts to employ this type of pay system. PRP was less likely to be used for other types of staff with 44 per cent of organizations using it for professional/technical staff, 27 per cent for clerical and 12 per cent for manual employees.

The research

The company

The research was undertaken in an Irish multi-divisional organization involved in the production and distribution of food products. The 15 subsidiary companies which comprise the organization are decentralized, though the executives remain accountable to head office. The establishment and acquisition of these subsidiaries took place at various times and, as a consequence, the firms have different histories and organizational cultures. The company's status recently changed from that of a public sector organization to one of a private limited company (PLC).

The company provided funding to research the success factors in PRP. Company sponsorship can encounter several difficulties (Bailey, 1996; Hedrick et al., 1982). While most research clients want to support sound, well-executed research and are generally sympathetic to its integrity, some will inevitably have political, organizational or personal agendas which push the researcher to produce results supporting a particular position. This did not prove to be the case in the organization in question. The Human Resource Director who had initiated the research project was generally very helpful in providing information and access to both documentation and respondents, while not trespassing on the confidentiality of respondents' views and opinions. The only obstacle encountered was when an interview was requested with the trade union representatives in the company. This request was refused and the researcher was forced to rely on an interview with an official from the union involved in order to gain an understanding of the union's position in relation to PRP.

The PRP scheme

The PRP scheme in operation within the company was first introduced in 1992 and then reviewed in December 1993. According to a company memo on the management performance bonus scheme (1993), it aimed:

> to increase the level of individual and team performance which will, in turn, increase the operating profit of each company and the overall group. The increased level of profit will provide the capacity to pay a bonus to designated managers.

The scheme further aimed:

> to reward initiative, leadership, commitment, the development of good management practices and to foster a spirit of continuous improvement throughout the organization.

The scheme was based on two elements: a base salary and a variable incentive payment. Base salary was no longer to be determined by the national pay awards, the centralized bargaining system in Ireland, but was to be influenced by the ability of the business to fund increases, by market trends, by national norms in pay increases and by individual performance. The incentive payment provided the opportunity to earn an additional 15 per cent of base salary through the achievement of both individual and company targets. Managers were allocated between four and six personal targets. These were intended to be related to the overall goals of the company, to be measurable, to encourage teamwork and to be prioritized. Targets were revised at the end of six months and managers were reviewed on an annual basis. These reviews were carried out by both their supervisor and their supervisor's line manager. The PRP scheme was considered to be part of a wider performance management system and managers were invited to assess their own performance. However, this was considered an optional feature of the scheme.

Research design

The research utilized a combination of both quantitative and qualitative techniques in the collection of data. The HR Director responsible for introducing and administering the scheme was interviewed and documentation relating to the operation of the scheme was collected. A postal questionnaire was then sent to the 107 managers involved in the scheme and 70 replied, a 65 per cent response rate.[1] The questionnaire was developed from ones which had been used in other surveys of PRP (Fletcher and Williams, 1992; Marsden and Richardson, 1994). Following analysis of the data using the SPSS package, interviews were conducted with a cross-section of managers, with the administrators of schemes in two other firms and with a trade union official in order to explore in more detail issues which had emerged from the questionnaire findings.

The remainder of the chapter deals with the issues faced by the company in implementing the PRP scheme and are explored from the perspectives of both the HR Director as designer and administrator of the scheme and the managers as participants. The discussion focuses on two areas which have been highlighted in the literature as critical to the success of PRP schemes: the way in which the scheme is introduced and the fairness of the scheme as perceived by those at the receiving end. These issues are discussed in terms of the contrasts and contradictions between the HR Director and the managers in their understanding of the factors surrounding the introduction of PRP, and between the managers themselves in their acceptance of and enthusiasm for changes in their pay system

The introduction of PRP

From the HR Director's perspective, the scheme had a number of objectives: the design of a fair and cost effective reward system, a means of motivating staff, a means to improve performance and a recognition of the managers' contribution to the transformation of the company from a public sector organization to a PLC:

> It was also introduced partly to recognize that the company was now a PLC, and enable people to share in that sense, and to recognize that the managers were the biggest influence. (HR Director, 1994)

Additional aims in designing the scheme were to reduce trade union influence, to eliminate collective bargaining and to provide an individualized pay system. Managers, by accepting PRP, were expected to give up all rights to national pay agreements negotiated by the social partners:

> At management level, unions wanted more rewards, not necessarily for higher performance, they just felt that they were underpaid. The lack of a reward system held back pay levels. The company was profitable and had the potential to be more profitable but there was a view that the unions were going to hold out for more money. (HR Director, 1994)

Table 7.1   *First-ranked objectives of the scheme*

Objectives	%
Improve performance of the organization	57
Reward good performance	15
Motivate employees	9
Increase commitment to the organization	9
Improve recruitment and retention of staff	5
Reinforce existing culture, values, and performance expectations	2
Promote organizational change	2
Remove the bargaining process away from trade unions	1

$N = 70$

The multiplicity of objectives proposed for the PRP scheme stemmed from the fact that there was a perceived need within the company to focus attention on performance and continuous improvement. As a semi-state company it had not been performance driven; PRP was seen as a vehicle for focusing attention on performance once the company became a PLC.

The managers did not totally share the HR Director's perceptions of the objectives of the scheme. As Table 7.1 shows, the HR Director's objectives of improving organizational performance, rewarding individual performance, and motivation were mentioned. However, there was little importance given to the promotion of organizational change, which could describe the process of transforming the organization into a PLC. Only 2 per cent of all respondents ranked the promotion of organizational change as the top objective, while 59 per cent ranked it among the bottom three objectives. The reduction of trade union influence, identified by the HR Director as an objective of the PRP scheme, was ranked as a priority by only 1 per cent of managers.

Employee involvement in introduction of PRP

It has been suggested that there should be consultation before the implementation of PRP, together with the inclusion of an appeals mechanism (Beer et al., 1984). The HR Director had not involved employees in the design process. During the interviews he indicated that the Board of Directors had instructed that a scheme had to be implemented within a two-month period and that this meant that there was little time for consultation with staff. The HR Director explained that he later realized the existence of mounting suspicion and a basic lack of trust for the scheme and then appointed consultants to allay any fears regarding the scheme's introduction:

> We brought in an outside consultant, who went back and talked to everyone about how the system is working, did some of the consultation that should have been done beforehand, allowing them the input that should have been there initially. (HR Director, 1994)

The HR Director felt that as a direct consequence of the consultancy, all difficulties with the scheme had been overcome. However, the managers appeared less convinced of the supposed lack of difficulties, with a total of 80 per cent agreeing with the statement 'The PRP scheme has yet to overcome some difficulties.'

An appeals system is one mechanism which may counteract suspicions of unfairness within PRP, but no such system existed within the company. The HR Director indicated that he felt little need for an appeals forum of any kind as assessments were examined by head office. Here assessments were scanned to ensure a fair distribution of ratings and any unusual patterns or the excessive use of one particular rating were identified and resolved. The ratings were expected to be evenly distributed across a wide spectrum from poor to excellent. If this were not the case, the particular assessor was asked to explain the reasons underlying the ratings. This head office scrutiny was considered to act as a 'second court'.

The managers did not share the HR Director's view that scrutiny by Head Office was an effective substitute for an appeals mechanism and 65 per cent of respondents indicated that a formal system was required. Managers with longer service were more likely to view an appeals system as important. Given that 45 per cent of managers had disputed the fairness of their previous assessment, there did appear to be a need for some formal appeals mechanism.

The fairness of the PRP scheme

From the HR Director's perspective the scheme had proved itself a success, in improving both productivity and overall profitability, and he considered that the initial difficulties arising from the lack of consultation and suspicion surrounding the scheme's introduction had since been overcome. However, managers proved less convinced that this was the case. Table 7.2 identifies the drawbacks they perceived with the scheme, ranked in order of importance.

Table 7.2 *Drawbacks with the scheme ranked in order of importance*

Drawbacks with the scheme	%
Measuring individual performance objectively	42
Encouraging a narrow focus on short-term quantifiable goals while neglecting longer-term issues	21
Lack of pay in order to substantiate change in performance	12
Assumes that money is the best reward	9
Unsuccessful in improving employee motivation	8
Negatively affects teamwork, and co-operation can suffer	6
Principally unfair in discriminating between individual employee contributions	2

$N = 70$

Measurement of performance

The first difficulty identified with the scheme was the objective measurement of performance. When interviewed, the HR Director argued that the measurement of performance was vital to the scheme's overall success and that this required clear, specific and quantifiable objectives. He felt that the identification of these objectives would eliminate any element of subjectivity as employees would be judged on whether or not these were achieved. When responding to the statement 'My work objectives are clear and specific, I know exactly what my job is', 87 per cent of managers considered that their objectives were clear and specific. However, 78 per cent still ranked 'measurement of performance' as one of the top three disadvantages with the system, indicating they believed that clear objectives do not necessarily result in an adequate measure of performance. In both the comments on the questionnaires and in the follow-up interviews, measurement of performance emerged as the primary cause of concern and dissatisfaction with the PRP scheme:

> I think that personalities will always play a big role in any individual's assessment and until somebody devises a method to overcome this then I think we will have to live with under-performance and over-performance but I think that is where a potentially very good system will become unstuck. (Manager, 1995)

Many managers expressed concern with regard to the extent to which the maximum reward was achievable:

> There is a tendency [for the company] to find ways of not awarding the maximum reward even if all the goals are achieved. (Manager, 1995)

Additional difficulties with the measurement of performance were also evident in the comments which reflected the problems involved in defining and measuring goals for managerial positions:

> True goals are hard to clarify and harder still to judge. (Manager, 1995)

Short-term goals

In discussing the issue of short- versus long-term goals, the HR Director indicated that the targets set tended to focus on the short-term, but this was not perceived to be a disadvantage as short-term goals were designed to fit with the long-term plan.

However, 51 per cent of managers agreed with the statement that 'There is an over-emphasis on short-term work objectives', while only 33 per cent disagreed. This over-emphasis on short-term objectives, however, did not appear to be quite as harmless as the HR Director perceived and many managers commented on the stifling effect it was having in relation to innovation:

> One of my objectives was a five-year budget, I was told to be cautious, make it easy to achieve. It creates a negative effect, planning for what is achievable rather than an entrepreneurial attitude. (Manager, 1996)

Some managers also indicated that targets may become irrelevant as a result of circumstances beyond the manager's direct control. As one respondent commented:

> It does not take into consideration the unexpected which necessitates an extremely high level of work on targets outside those set which might leave you in a position of not having achieved the set targets while having worked extremely hard. (Manager, 1995)

This comment summed up the feelings of many respondents on this issue and appeared to be the cause of much frustration among employees. Part of this sense of frustration may have stemmed from the lack of feedback available to managers. Thus, when asked for their opinions on the statement 'I am provided with a great deal of feedback and guidance on the quality of my work', only 30 per cent agreed. Many voiced their grievances with respect to the lack of regular reviews or feedback available, and there appeared to be a higher level of frustration directed toward the inability to obtain an adequate explanation with regard to the achievement of a particular reward:

> Each year to date I have outperformed all the objectives set and have not achieved higher than 70 per cent reward. I don't know what I have to do and nobody can tell me – I have asked. (Manager, 1995)

Lack of rewards

The HR Director perceived no difficulty with the reward system. In his opinion the rewards available were substantial and 'worth striving for'. In addition, he considered that pay was a prime motivator of people and this belief underpinned the operation of the PRP scheme. Not all managers shared his views on these issues. Thus, when asked if the extra effort involved in attaining the maximum reward was worth striving for, 43 per cent replied 'no':

> Amount of money that can be earned in a good year is small (after tax) and does not incentivize me. (Manager, 1995)

In addition, the level of reward available was ranked third in importance in the list of drawbacks with the scheme. As Table 7.3 shows, there were mixed opinions as to whether the production of high-quality work would actually

Table 7.3   *Links between performance and pay*

Statement	Strongly agree (%)	Agree (%)	No view (%)	Disagree (%)	Strongly disagree (%)
Producing high-quality work is rewarded with more pay	1	46	20	24	9
PRP has no effect on my work performance	11	32	17	39	1
The most important thing about a job is pay	3	21	15	49	12

$N = 70$

result in more pay and whether the PRP scheme affected work performance. In addition, only 24 per cent of managers shared the HR Director's view that pay is the most important element of a job, thus confirming Kovach's (1987) view that a mismatch may occur between management and employee views on what motivates.

Difficulties with teamwork

The issue of teamwork was another source of contrasting viewpoints. The HR Director considered the achievement of teamwork as one of the most successful aspects of the scheme and further added:

> It's helping teamwork, because of the way it is structured, relating to a company's overall performance. Each function within the company has to make a contribution. What objectives are there for people, that requires the co-operation to set objectives. (HR Director, 1995)

Comments expressed by the managers, however, did not suggest a shared perception of this issue:

> Individuals will sacrifice team goals for their own glory. (Manager, 1995)

When asked to rank their opinions on the statement 'PRP has contributed to more effective teamwork', 48 per cent agreed and 32 per cent disagreed, while 20 per cent held no view on the matter. Furthermore, many commented on the lack of co-operation as a result of the PRP system, and its failure in achieving a sense of team spirit. The issue of teamwork may be affected by the type of motivation provided by PRP:

> It helps to motivate certain individuals with competitive instincts. It doesn't motivate people who will do a good job come what may. It can therefore be divisive on a team with two types of personalities. (Manager, 1995)

Improvement in performance

Though PRP had disadvantages for some managers, there were others who supported both its underlying principles and its operation. Individuals indicating a positive response to the statement 'With PRP my individual efforts and achievement are recognized' seemed to be far clearer about their work objectives and how their work contributed to the organization. They also appeared to be well informed about the company's plans and performance and had few difficulties with PRP. Table 7.4 shows a matrix correlation which indicates the relationship between these matters.

In the follow-up interviews it became clear that there were differences between managers working in different subsidiaries in their perceptions and experience of PRP. Managers in the more recently established subsidiaries appeared to accept the changes in the reward system wrought by PRP, but in the older and more traditional organizations PRP was largely resented. Comments made by managers in these companies suggest a negative change in culture since the scheme's introduction:

Table 7.4   *Matrix correlation of individual effort and achievement*

With PRP my individual efforts and achievements are recognized	Correlation
My work objectives are clear and specific: I know exactly what my job is	0.38
	p = 0.001
I can see how my work contributes to the organization as a whole	0.54
	p = 0.000
I have a clear idea about how the organization is performing overall	0.49
	p = 0.000
I am generally told what is going on in the company	0.60
	p = 0.000
I've got a clear idea of what this organization's goals and plans are for the future	0.42
	p = 0.000
PRP has yet to overcome some difficulties in this organization	−0.35
	p =0.004

$N = 70$

> The culture today is not as good as it was before. It used to be a vibrant place to work. Now minimum standards are set and [there's an attitude of] I'm not going to go beyond those . . . We see ourselves as a separate identity . . . it has broken a sense of group pride. Pride can contribute to performance when you feel like you're in a successful group . . . We're denied a cross-fertilization of ideas, morale. (Manager, 1996)

The comments of another manager suggest that PRP may be inappropriate in the older, more traditionally established organizations:

> The mechanics and principles of PRP I fully subscribe to. The architecture and structure of the organization are not part of the PRP culture. (Manager, 1996)

These views contrast to those expressed by a manager working in one of the younger organizations within the group:

> We have seen a change in the culture of the organization, slowly from a static hierarchical structure to an active team-based structure. (Manager, 1996)

A manager in one of the younger subsidiaries summed up the contrasting attitudes to PRP in stating:

> It's different in different parts of the group. Others in the group it might have been alien to, in a more commercial organization it was a normal sort of a thing. (Manager, 1996)

Discussion

This chapter provides some interesting contrasts between the views of the HR Director involved in implementing and administering a PRP scheme and the managers at the receiving end. In addition, contradictions emerged amongst the managers themselves. The managers did not share the same set of perceptions of the scheme, nor did they share the same value system: for some the most important element in their jobs was pay and PRP did have a strong effect on performance, for others the reverse was the case. These differences could not be explained by factors such as age, length of service, trade union membership or gender, but had to be sought in the companies within which these managers worked.

Contrasting cultures

As already described, this company comprised 15 subsidiaries, each with its own history and culture. Some were fairly new organizations, others were long established, yet the same PRP scheme had been implemented in each. From the HR Director's perspective, one of the objectives of the scheme was to reinforce and reward the changes involved in moving the company from a bureaucratic, public sector organization to one which would embrace a performance driven, enterprise way of thinking. However, given the diversity of companies operating within the group, it is not surprising to find that a uniform reward scheme was unable to achieve this purpose.

Contrasting objectives

The HR Director had a large number of objectives in introducing the PRP scheme, only some of which were recognized and shared by the managers at the receiving end. This raises the issue of whether it is possible to pursue such wide ranging and diverse objectives in the implementation of a PRP scheme; energies may be dissipated in the pursuit of multiple aims rather than focused firmly on one particular issue. In the case of this company, the dilution of trade union influence was seen by the HR Director as an objective of the PRP scheme. Yet less than half of the managers were in fact union members and trade union membership failed to account for any of the differences found in the views and attitudes of managers. It was difficult to gauge the extent to which the HR Director was successful in his efforts to reduce union influence through the PRP scheme, as access to the company's trade union representatives was denied to the researcher. However, it would appear, from follow-up interviews with the managers and an interview with the trade union official of the union representing these managers, that PRP had failed to have any effect on the union's position within the organization.

Contrasting views on performance

It has long been recognized that it is difficult to find an objective measurement for managerial tasks. This study found a distinct contradiction between what the HR Director termed as an adequate measure of performance and what management considered would suffice. Contrary to the HR Director's perceptions, the managers considered that there was a need for regular feedback and reviews and the use of such mechanisms could provide safeguards against bias and inconsistency and contribute to a fairer means of measuring performance. Their use would also provide the means by which to adapt targets to suit changing demands and would reduce the risks of focusing on irrelevant targets. In addition, this study indicated that the source of multiple grievances with the scheme may have been avoided had the managers had opportunity to voice their queries and complaints and to receive feedback in relation to these. The absence of consultation and an appeals mechanism led to suspicion among managers and a lack of trust in the system.

Contrasting views on pay

The study indicated contrasting views on the value of money as a motivator, thus confirming the research evidence on the difficulties of identifying decisively the motivational impact of PRP schemes (Kessler and Purcell, 1992; Marsden and Richardson, 1992). Only some managers shared the HR Director's view of money as a prime motivator. In addition, there were contrasts between what the HR Director regarded as a sufficient reward and what managers considered sufficiently desirable in terms of increased effort. Within an expectancy theory framework (Vroom, 1964), the concept of 'valence' describes the need for the reward to be attractive to an individual; if the concept of valence is absent there is an unlikely prospect of increased effort. The reward must also be sufficiently seductive to motivate employees to strive for it. In the case of some of the managers, neither of these requirements were met. In addition, the setting of targets that are difficult to achieve or which focus on short-term objectives may not result in sustained productivity and performance. Thus, the overall success of the scheme must be bound up with a shared understanding of good performance.

Conflicting viewpoints: inevitable outcomes of PRP?

The contrasting views on PRP encountered in this study reinforce the accepted wisdom that the design of reward systems, particularly where a performance-related element is involved, is a complex matter. But this also helps to determine more clearly which factors of a pay system will have repercussions for the overall success of the scheme. First, it appears that the way in which PRP is introduced will have a significant bearing on the degree of suspicion with which it is viewed and the subsequent acceptance of the scheme: there appears to be a need to inform all participants in the scheme of the reasons for its introduction and its objectives. Second, the evidence suggests that it may not be feasible to pursue wide ranging and multiple objectives through a PRP scheme: a few narrowly focused objectives may be much more successful. In addition, the study confirms Procter et al.'s (1993) view that the necessary culture may have to be in place for a system of PRP to work effectively. The Irish study seems to suggest that PRP may not work effectively as a prime agent of culture change. Third, much of a scheme's success appears to be dependent on employees' perceptions of the equity of the scheme. Some mechanisms may increase the likelihood of perceived equity: joint consultation in the formulation of targets and regular feedback on these targets, coupled with sufficient flexibility to amend targets to meet changing circumstances. Managers need to be competent to set targets with their staff and training and development requirements for both appraisers and appraisees should be identified. A further protective mechanism includes the installation of an appeals process to allow employees the opportunity to voice any grievances with the scheme, either directly or through representation. Fourth, PRP is unlikely to achieve full success in isolation; instead it requires the supporting infrastructure of a performance management system which incorporates objective setting, feedback, measurement of rewards, training and development and appeals procedures. Finally, PRP is more likely to be successful in certain types of environments and with certain types of employees. In this study the ethos of paying for performance appeared to be widely accepted in younger organizations, whereas in other, particularly older, organizations, it was resented. PRP schemes may also need to be tailored not only to the needs of specific companies, but also to the specific needs of individuals.

Conclusions

This chapter has presented contrasting perspectives on PRP by examining the views from both 'the bridge' and 'the deck'. The difficulties faced by the HR Director in implementing the PRP scheme may have stemmed from the fact that from his viewpoint on 'the bridge', he perceived only one 'deck'. From an administrative perspective, the 107 managers covered by the scheme represented a reasonably small, distinct grouping and there seemed to be no reason to suggest that one PRP scheme would not suit them all. The research revealed that the managers were not the homogeneous grouping that the HR Director perceived: they were working in very different environments and did not necessarily share either the HR Director's view of what constituted good performance, or a general managerial view of such performance. This suggests that while PRP is one response to the age-old problem of motivation, it is not necessarily the most effective. PRP relies for its success on rewarding good performance; determining the exact nature of good performance is more difficult.

Notes

1 Copies of the questionnaires and interview schedules used in the research can be obtained from the authors.

References

Armstrong, Michael (1991) *A Handbook of Personnel Management*. (4th edn). London: Kogan Page (1st edn 1977).

Armstrong, Michael (1993) *Managing Reward Systems*. Buckingham: Open University Press.

Armstrong, Michael and Murlis, Helen (1994) *Reward Management: a Handbook of Remuneration Strategy and Practice* (3rd edn). London: Kogan Page (1st edn 1988).

Bailey, Carol (1996) *A Guide to Field Research*. USA: Pine Forge Press.

Beer, M., Spector, B., Lawrence, P., Mills, D. Quinn and Walton, R. (1984) *Managing Human Assets*. New York: Free Press.

Crowe, David (1992) 'A new approach to reward management', in M. Armstrong (ed.), *Strategies for Human Resource Management*. London: Kogan Page.

Dwyer, John (1994) 'Performance pay: pain or gain?', *Works Management*, 47 (6): 16–18.

Filella, J. and Hegewisch, A. (1994) 'European experiments with pay and benefits policies', in C. Brewster and A. Hegewisch (eds), *Policy and Practice in European Human Resource Management*. London: Routledge. pp. 89–106.

Fletcher, C. and Williams, R. (1992) Performance Management in the UK: *An Analysis of the Issues*. London: IPM.

Geary, John (1992) 'Pay, control and commitment: linking appraisal and reward', *Human Resource Management Journal*, 2 (4): 36–54.

Greenberg, J. (1986) 'Determinants of perceived fairness of performance evaluations', *Journal of Applied Psychology*, 71: 340–2.

Gunnigle, P., Flood, P., Morley, M. and Turner, T. (1993) *Continuity and Change in Irish Employee Relations*. Dublin: Oak Tree Press.

Hamner, W. (1975) 'How to ruin motivation with pay', *Compensation Review*, 7 (3): 17–27.

Hedrick, T., Bickman, L. and Rog, D. (1982) *Applied Research Design: a Practical Guide*. Newbury Park: Sage.

Kessler, Ian and Purcell, John (1992) 'Performance related pay: theory and practice', *Human Resource Management Journal*, 2 (3): 16–33.

Kessler, Ian (1995) 'Reward systems', in J. Storey (ed.), *Human Resource Management: a Critical Text*. London: Routledge.

Kovach, K.A. (1987) 'What motivates employees? Workers and supervisors give different answers', *Business Horizons*, September–October: 58–65.

Lawler, E.E. III and Hackman, J.R. (1969) 'Impact of employee participation in the development of incentive plans: a field experiment', *Journal of Applied Psychology*, 53: 467–71.

Legge, K. (1995) *Human Resource Management: Rhetoric and Realities*. London: Macmillan.

Mabey, Christopher and Salaman, Graeme (1995) S*trategic Human Resource Management*. London: Blackwell.

Kessler, Ian (1994) 'Performance Pay', in Sisson, K. (ed.), *Personnel Management in the UK: A Comprehensive Guide to Theory and Practice in Britain*. Oxford: Blackwell.

Marsden, David and Richardson, Ray (1992) *Does Pay for Performance Motivate? A Study of Inland Revenue Staff*. London: IPM.

Marsden, David and Richardson, Ray (1994) 'Performing for pay? The effects of "merit pay" on motivation in a public service', *British Journal of Industrial Relations*, 32 (2): 243–61.

Murphy, Kevin and Cleveland, Jeanette (1995) *Understanding Performance Appraisal*. Beverly Hills, CA: Sage.

Philpott, Lawrie and Sheppard, Louise (1992) 'Managing for improved performance', in M. Armstrong (ed.), *Strategies for Human Resource Management*. London: Kogan Page.

Procter, S., McArdle, L., Rowlinson, M., Forrester, P. and Hassard, J. (1993) 'Performance related pay in operation: a case study from the electronics industry', *Human Resource Management Journal*, 3 (4): 60–74.

Ribbens, G.F. (1988) 'Personnel managers as social engineers: harmonisation and new technology', *Personnel Review*, 30 (5): 27–33.

Schefflen, K.C., Lawler, E.E. III and Hackman, J.R. (1971) 'Long term impact of employee participation in the development of pay incentive plans: a field experiment revisited', *Journal of Applied Psychology*, 55: 182–6.

Smith, I. (1992) 'Reward management and HRM', in P. Blyton and P. Turnbull (eds), *Reassessing Human Resource Management*. London: Sage. pp. 169–84.

Storey, John (1992) *Developments in the Management of Human Resources*. Oxford: Blackwell.

Storey, John and Sisson, Keith (1993) *Managing Human Resources and Industrial Relations*. Buckingham: Open University Press.

Vroom, Victor H. (1964) *Work and Motivation*. New York: Wiley.

Wright, V. (1991) 'Performance related pay', in F. Neale (ed.), *The Handbook of Performance Management*. London: IPM.

8

Culture Change within a Regional Business Network

Julia Connell and Suzanne Ryan

A strategic alliance, or network, is the 'coming together of a group of enterprises to use their combined talents and resources to achieve results which would not be possible for the enterprises operating individually' (NIES, 1993). Much of the literature on strategic alliances has concentrated on organization design and marketing aspects (Buttery and Buttery, 1992; Dean et al., 1996) with little attention being given to the labour management aspects. However, as Iles maintains, 'alliances and partnerships involve more than sharing money, technology and products; they also involve sharing people and HRD practice' (1996: 81).

The focus of the study described in this chapter is the 'sharing of practices' among a network of five small to medium firms in Australia (herein referred to as SubNet) that embarked on a common cultural change programme known as 'best practice'. The study sought to measure the impact of the culture change in each of the member organizations and to make some comparisons across the network.

The chapter begins with a summary of views on strategic alliances and the controversies surrounding organization culture and culture change programmes such as 'best practice'. These provide the context for the detailed description of the study, its findings and the subsequent discussion.

Strategic alliances: flexible specialization or modern marketing tool?

Strategic alliances or networks involve a range of stakeholders operating at both 'macro' and 'micro' levels. At the 'macro' level stakeholders may include suppliers, contractors, customers and competitors, and at the 'micro' level stakeholders are the individuals co-ordinating and co-operating between firms (Limerick and Cunnington, 1993). Handy (1990) referred to networks as the 'federal' form of organization, which he predicted would become increasingly popular in the future as small firms join together to form a 'strategic mass' in order to compete with larger firms. The strategic mass allows firms to use their relationships with other firms, be they suppliers, customers or competitors, to enhance individual business capabilities and provide greater access to market opportunities.

In Australia, networks have been promoted as a positive organizational response to globalization and the international market. Advocates cite benefits such as information sharing, improving performance and efficiency, cost sharing in market investigation, research and development, training and market entry, broadening the product range, strengthening of negotiating and purchasing power, and fostering of specialization (NIES, 1993).

Networks vary in both size and composition, the two most common forms consisting of regional industry-based networks, or networks based on one major firm with supplier and customer links. In the regional industry networks, small and medium firms form collaborative links which allow them to compete with large firms, while remaining small enough to be flexible and innovative and maintain individual independence. Piore and Sabel (1984) were among the first to refer to regional networks as a means to achieving 'flexible specialization', or strategic responsiveness to subtle changes in market demand. They pointed out that 'flexible specialization' required flexible production, which in turn required flexible labour and labour management, including flexible work practices, skill use and management competency.

However, as Limerick and Cunnington (1993) recognize, the formation of an alliance or network cannot, in itself, transform a member firm into a dynamic organization. They emphasize the importance of organization development as a necessary ingredient for the change to a more entrepreneurial/flexible culture. Herman also stressed the need for attention to intra-firm relationships: 'An issue which is often overlooked by networking advocates is that regarding relations inside the firm. This intra-firm dimension is as important as inter-firm relationships and a successful, long-term competitive strategy cannot ignore the labour-management arena' (1991: 3).

Defining organizational culture

Since its 'discovery' as an ingredient for high productivity and organization effectiveness (Deal and Kennedy, 1982; Peters and Waterman, 1982), organization culture has become a much debated topic within the management and employment relations literature. The literature tends to polarize between two extremes. At the one extreme is the pragmatic, managerial approach and at the other the anthropological/sociological approach. Mabey and Salaman described the literature of the former group as 'consultancy-based, popular, bland and prescriptive, aimed at managers' and the literature of the latter group as 'more theoretical and descriptive, aimed at scholars' (1995: 276). Definitions of organization culture are similarly diverse, ranging from the pragmatists' view of culture as a shared system of values (Schein, 1985) to the purists' view of culture as the behaviours, values and attitudes that distinguish one society from another (Vecchio et al., 1996).

The pragmatists consider culture to be an attribute of an organization which can be manipulated by management strategy (Darmer, cited in Bate,

1994; Meek, cited in Whiteley, 1995). Culture change initiatives, often labelled 'revitalization, renewal, large scale systems change, transformation or re-engineering' (Porter and Parker, 1992) represent attempts to alter not only how work is performed, but also employee commitment to work and to the organization. Such initiatives imply that culture can be changed to achieve improved organization performance; culture is perceived as the product of management strategy able to affect productivity depending on the strength of the culture (Wierner, 1988). Payne (1990) maintains that the strength of an organization's culture reflects the degree of consensus among its members. Deal and Kennedy (1982), espousing the virtues of a strong organization culture, suggest that strong cultures communicate to the workforce the appropriate way in which to behave. Implicit within these views is the concept that the workforce exists within a unitary framework, bound together by common tasks and accepting of management's views and values. This pragmatic view of culture centres on the proposition that effective organizations consist of 'a unitary system bound together by a common task and values' (Green, cited in Bate, 1994: 56).

Critics of the pragmatic approach to culture have variously described such manipulation as a sophisticated control mechanism (Legge, 1989) and incipiently totalitarian (Willmott, cited in Waring, 1995). They challenge the view that organizations have a unified culture, maintaining that organizations contain, in fact, a number of subcultures. Smircich (1983) suggests that organization culture is the perspective of the individuals who constitute the organization, and it cannot by definition be manipulated by one sector of the organization. Concepts of 'sharedness' and 'commonality' are not relevant within this environment. Cultural change is organization change; thus any focus on cultural change must examine the social relationships, attitudes and perceptions of the individual members of the organization (Bate, 1994).

Anthony's (1994) view of organization culture as the perceptions or 'negotiated realities' of an organization's members represents a more balanced perspective between the pragmatic and purist culture literature. Anthony separates organization culture into 'workplace culture' and 'corporate culture'. The former refers to the realities of life in the organization, perceived by all members, while the latter refers to the way management would like the organization to be. This perspective is supported by Robbins: 'individuals behave in a manner based not on what their external environment actually is, but, rather, on what they see or believe it to be . . . It is the employee's perception of a situation which becomes the basis on which he or she behaves' (cited in Whiteley, 1995: 22). While management cannot manipulate perception, it can change its own behaviour in such a way that employees may want to negotiate a new reality.

Schein's (1985) work adds yet another dimension to the organization culture debate, suggesting that there are three levels of cultural phenomena in organizations: overt behaviours, values and basic assumptions. Schein argues that a change in behaviour leads to a change in values, and eventually to deep cultural change. Subsequently there has been considerable debate as to whether observable behavioural change represents cultural change, or whether deeper value change must precede cultural change. Gagliardi (cited in Ogbonna, 1992) argued that core values are not so easily changed and that, while behaviour at work and attitudes toward work may change, values need not be affected. Ogbonna (1992) questions whether it matters if cultural change is only behavioural if management's interest is in behavioural change to achieve labour flexibility and product quality improvements.

For the purpose of this study, organization culture is viewed as the perception of employees towards various aspects of their work content and context. Cultural change is considered as a change in attitude towards the same aspects over time. This approach to organization culture avoids the superficiality of simply describing behavioural change, while also avoiding 'the excursion into the unknown' which can be encountered when measuring value change (Ogbonna, 1992: 90).

Best practice: the change programme

Between 1991 and 1995, the Australian federal Labor government actively promoted 'best practice' as a preferred method of achieving world class performance (Department of Industrial Relations, 1994). The term referred to a programme of workplace change which aimed to increase competitiveness through improving productivity, efficiency and quality in each business function. The key elements of a 'best practice' programme (Department of Industrial Relations, 1994) included:

- use of benchmarking as a central management tool to determine performance gaps and differences in production processes, and establishment of data bases around which commitment for change can be gathered
- improvement in quality, cost and delivery and customer focus
- development of closer relations with suppliers to reduce inventories and ensure quality
- adoption of appropriate technology strategies
- implementation of flatter organization structures to promote greater speed and directness in decision-making
- adoption of a team-based approach to work and problem-solving
- involvement of the workforce in problem-solving and planning decisions
- development of innovative human resource policies aimed at removing demarcations, establishing career paths, and providing significant training to develop a skilled and committed workforce.

Wood uses the term 'high-commitment management' (HCM) to describe culture change programmes and practices such as the 'best practice' programme where 'behaviour is primarily self-regulated rather than controlled by sanctions and pressures external to the individual' (1996: 55). Culture change programmes are commonly promoted as a means of enhancing the power of the worker, through an emphasis on participative work practices and 'empowerment' (Piore and Sabel, 1984). Critics have argued, however, that they are a means of increasing work intensity and gaining greater managerial control over labour (Bramble, 1995; Legge, 1989). Many of the arguments against 'lean production' and the associated work intensity, might apply equally to both HCM and 'best practice' (Hampson et al., 1994).

Guest (1987) maintained that HCM was antithetical to workers' interests, as it excluded the possibility of collective bargaining in favour of a unitary system. He argued that under HCM workers would be committed to management's vision, and that management would favour individual contracts over collective agreements as a means of furthering worker commitment and dependence, thus making unions redundant. When subsequent studies (Storey, 1992) established that HCM and unionism could and in fact did coexist, Guest (1992) defended his earlier position by maintaining that the unions involved with HCM organizations could not be strong unions because, *inter alia*, they allow management to communicate directly with the workforce, thus undermining the union's role. Guest (1989) argued that the tensions between unionism and HCM must eventually erupt, as unions ultimately would not allow the desired levels of flexibility and job redesign required for the programme to be successful. In a study of 135 manufacturing organizations in the UK, Wood (1996) tested the proposition that HCM is associated with either non-unionized workplaces or those with weak unions. He found no relationship between HCM and union presence and/or strength.

The observations of Storey (1992) and Wood (1996) in the UK, that an increase in HCM is not necessarily accompanied by union redundancy, are supported by the Australian experience. In the metals manufacturing sector particularly, the national employer association and the metal workers' union were the joint leaders in advocating the need for workplace change in the face of global competition. In the 1990s, these efforts turned to 'best practice' programmes and various forms of strategic alliances varying from loose coalitions to formalized networks.

The background to the study

This study was based in the Hunter region of New South Wales, Australia. The Hunter is one of the oldest industrial regions in Australia, its history being firmly rooted in coal mining, steel manufacturing and engineering. The region has had a strong tradition of trade unionism with union leaders playing prominent roles in regional affairs. The subjects of the study were five small to medium engineering and manufacturing firms (herein referred to as SubNet), which were part of a larger alliance of 29 engineering and engineering-related firms (herein referred to as the Network). The Network was established as a registered co-operative in 1991 to assist local firms in developing their capacity to export and tender for defence and other large contracts. The Network's strategic plan emphasized the development of member capability, increased market opportunity and reducing the cost of supplying services. Network members were in multiple relationships with each other, the most common being competitor and customer relationships.

Following a major downturn in steel and heavy engineering in the early 1980s, the trade unions and employer associations made a determined effort to maintain the industries and assist in finding new markets both nationally and internationally. In 1994 the federal government, as part of a broad industry restructuring policy, offered development funds for small to medium businesses to adopt 'best practice' programmes. Under this scheme a grant of $250,000 was awarded to the five Network members who had formed SubNet. The adoption of 'best practice' was assisted by information and organization support from trade unions and by grants and publicity from the federal government. When the federal government established a Best Practice Consultancy (BPC) to assist with workplace reform, the Australian Council of Trade Unions, as well as the metal trades unions and the metal trades employer association, were represented on its National Board.

The contention that small, owner-managed firms are the 'bleak houses' of worker exploitation (Sisson, cited in Wood, 1996: 55), as a result of non-unionization, did not describe the situation of the five SubNet firms. A union–employer partnership formed part of the agreement whereby SubNet received government assistance for the 'best practice' programme. Unionization of small and medium engineering firms is common in the Hunter region, which has higher union coverage than the state or national averages. It was not unusual, therefore, that three of the SubNet firms were fully unionized, with the majority of workers at the other two firms being union members. Contrary to Guest's (1987) hypothesis, union representatives on the SubNet committee perceived their involvement with 'best practice' as a proactive response to the globalization of markets, and as a means of maintaining union power and survival.

A 1994 survey of Network general managers revealed the reasons they gave for joining the Network were related to maintaining and improving competitiveness through sharing management know-how, training costs and programmes, engaging in joint tendering and increasing market share (Fulop and Kelly, 1995). The survey concluded that the major benefits from belonging to the Network were information sharing, increased business opportunities and contact with competitors and suppliers. Most improvements arising from Network membership had been made in the areas of marketing and quality assurance. Survey respondents acknowledged that although human resource management was a key factor in productivity improvement, little had been achieved in this area. The SubNet firms' implementation of the 'best practice' culture change programme reflected a conscious effort to address the human resource area. SubNet commenced the 'best practice' culture change programme in late 1994, and the researchers were invited to carry out this study one year later.

The Best Practice Consultancy model

The aim of the SubNet firms in implementing the 'best practice' programme was to 'create a program of cultural change, integrating management with the shop floor in day to day business' (Hissey, 1994: 4), with the intention that cultural change would eventually lead to greater labour flexibility and productivity. The SubNet 'best practice' culture change programme was facilitated by the national 'Best Practice Consultancy. BPC's (1993) organization change model consisted of the following steps, many of which were designed to occur simultaneously:

1 climate setting through two-way communication about the programme with all employees
2 the establishment of a management–union partnership to manage the programme
3 the appointment and training of internal facilitators
4 leadership training for owners and senior managers
5 the creation of cellular work teams
6 the introduction of quality assurance measures
7 five-day training for teams
8 project management by teams.

Key aspects of the BPC model were: the appointment of internal facilitators in each firm; the shift to semi-autonomous work teams; and the introduction of benchmarking. Two full-time and three part-time facilitators were appointed to the five firms from internal applicants. Although the facilitators' backgrounds ranged from the trades to clerical and professional positions, they were selected according to their interpersonal skills and their ability to communicate and problem solve effectively. BPC consultants initially trained the internal facilitators, who then trained other employees and engaged in 'on-the-job' mentoring and liaison between work teams.

Mabey and Salaman argue that a successful strategic training and development model should include senior management support, the involvement of line managers and the motivation of trainees linked to the 'shared diagnosis of training need and relevance to training and development activities chosen' (1995: 131). The initial training programme, designed by BPC, was presented as a 'recipe' for success with consultants stressing that if one vital ingredient was left out or changed, the 'recipe' would fail to work. This approach did not allow for individual differences within each firm such as size, technology, development and preparedness for change, and eventually the uniformity of the programme became a source of friction between the consultancy and the SubNet firms.

Additional problems were caused by the focus on quality improvement processes inherent in the BPC model. One of the SubNet firms, with a mostly overseas market, was already well advanced in quality improvement and, believing the BPC programme had little to offer it in terms of business improvement, made an early withdrawal from the 'best practice' training programme. Over time, however, the facilitators became more confident in their roles and began to customize aspects of BPC's training model to suit the individual firm, moving away from the original 'recipe'. While the BPC consultants provided the direction for the 'best practice' programme, it was the internal facilitators who directed the process in the workplace, and liaised between the firms, the consultants and the SubNet management committee.

A longitudinal assessment of culture change

In order to evaluate the extent of the culture change which has taken place the study sought to measure the perceptions of the employees, managers and owners of the SubNet firms. An attitude survey was used to measure the change in attitude of employees within the five SubNet firms. Given the difficulty in conceptualizing 'organization culture' and the subsequent complexities associated in the measurement of values, an attitude survey in the form of a questionnaire was chosen as it allowed for the greatest consistency across and among firms. This approach also had the benefit of offering a level of confidentiality not possible with other methods, e.g. focus groups, particularly important for employees working in very small firms.

A questionnaire developed by Broadfoot and Ashkanasy (1994), based on an evaluation of 18 commonly used organization culture survey instruments, was modified for use in the study. The original Broadfoot and Ashkanasy survey consisted of 65 items covering 11 dimensions (the 11 dimensions are herein referred to as the B&A dimensions). Modifications to the Broadfoot and Ashkanasy instrument for this survey included the addition of 8 further items covering 5 new dimensions (herein referred to as the additional dimensions). The Appendix provides a full definition of all the dimensions.

A five-point Likert scale was used for responses. The closer a score was to five, the more positive the employee's perception towards a given dimension; conversely, the closer a score to one, the more negative the perception towards a given dimension. Two exceptions to this were the unionism dimension, where a score of one would indicate a lack of union presence and five would indicate a strong union presence; and the work intensity dimension, where five would indicate a very heavy workload. Additionally, the questionnaire sought demographic data on gender, length of employment within the firm, and employment position (management or non-management). Respondents were given space to add general comments if they so desired.

In order to assess change over a 12-month period, each question required respondents to rate their current (1995) attitude to a given statement and their attitude 12 months previously (1994). While the researchers acknowledge the limitations in asking respondents to remember their opinion of one year ago, given the absence of survey data before the programme began, it was considered the most expedient and objective means of obtaining information in a uniform manner across all the firms.

Owing to the need to maintain confidentiality, a background profile of each firm is not provided apart from the information requested on the survey questionnaire. Survey forms were hand delivered to respondents by the researchers which meant that employees who were absent from work, and/or on night shift, were excluded from the survey. The five firms varied in size ranging from 16 to 100 employees. The number of surveys distributed was 210 to which the response rate was 163 or 78 per cent. Of the 163 responses, 12 per cent were female and 79 per cent (129) were male, reflecting the gender bias in the engineering industry. The remaining 8.5 per cent did not state their gender. Non-management respondents accounted for 72 per cent (117) of the total, management 18 per cent (29) and 10 per cent did not state their position. The median number of years respondents had been employed in a firm was 4, with a range from 0 to 22 years. All firms had experienced low turnover and three of the four firms had experienced growth over the previous two years. Four of the five firms were privately owned, and the subject of close owner involvement in the business.

The results were analysed for each firm in terms of overall significant differences in attitude toward the 16 dimensions over the 12-month period and differences in perception between managers and non-managers. Responses were initially analysed using descriptive statistics to find means, distributions and frequencies. Paired T tests were used to ascertain changes in 1994 and 1995 responses, and the Wilcoxon scores (rank sums) test for independent samples to find any differences between the responses of managers and non-managers. Written responses in the 'general comments' section varied from 50 per cent of respondents in one firm to just one response in another. Most comments were negative or cynical about management. When the survey was complete and the data were analysed for each firm, the results were discussed with each general manager, and a summary was provided as information for employees.

Analysis of cultural dimensions

Firstly, the data from all five SubNet firms were analysed by score and by significant differences in attitude between 1994 and 1995 (see Table 8.1). Secondly, the data were separated into management and non-management groups in order to test significant differences between the perceptions of both groups in 1994 and 1995 (see Table 8.2).

The total average scores indicated both change and improvement at the aggregate level of the five firms. Over the 12-month period, 27 out of a possible 55 statistically significant changes occurred across the five firms with one only change being in a negative direction. The most positively perceived B&A dimensions, that is those with the highest average 1995 scores, were in descending order: environment (3.55), leadership (3.34) and planning (3.29). The most negatively perceived dimensions, those with the lowest average scores, were in ascending order: communication (2.85), workplace relationships (2.87) and induction (2.88). Of the additional dimensions, those with the

Table 8.1   *Perceived change in workplace culture and non-culture dimensions in the previous 12-month period*

	Firm 1	Firm 2	Firm 3	Firm 4	Firm 5	Average score: now then
B&A dimensions						
Leadership	*	*	*		*	3.34 3.20
Structure		*				3.09 3.09
Innovation		(***)			**	3.26 3.05
Job performance	***	**	*		*	3.19 2.98
Planning	***	***	*		**	3.29 2.92
Communication	***	***	**	*	***	2.85 2.37
Environment	**	***	**		***	3.55 3.32
Workplace relationships			*			2.87 2.71
Training		***			***	3.08 2.87
Induction						2.88 2.80
Commitment						3.19 3.11
Average score: now	3.18	3.15	3.23	3.41	2.98	3.15
then	2.89	2.93	2.98	3.39	2.72	2.95
Additional dimensions						
Quality	**	***			***	3.77 3.26
Job satisfaction			*	(*)		3.21 3.19
Job autonomy	**					3.07 2.89
Unionism					***	2.65 2.49
Work intensity	**					3.86 3.73

*   Indicates significance at the 0.05 level.
**   Indicates significance at the 0.01 level.
***   Indicates significance at the 0.001 level.
( )   Indicates change in a negative direction.

Table 8.2 *Significant differences between management and non-management towards culture and non-culture workplace dimensions*

		Firm 1	Firm 2	Firm 3	Firm 4	Firm 5
B&A dimensions						
Leadership	now		**		*	
	then		**		*	
Structure	now		**			
	then					
Innovation	now	*	*		*	
	then	**				
Job performance	now		***		**	
	then		*			
Planning	now	**	**		***	
	then	*			*	
Communication	now	**	**		**	
	then	**	*		*	
Environment	now				***	
	then					
Workplace relationships	now	***	**		**	
	then	**	**		*	
Training	now	*	***		**	
	then	*	**		*	
Induction	now				***	
	then	*			***	
Commitment	now	***	***		***	
	then	***	***		***	
Additional dimensions						
Quality	now	*			*	
	then					
Job satisfaction	now	**	**		**	
	then	*			***	
Job autonomy	now	**			*	
	then	*	*		*	*
Unionism	now	**	**	**	*	
	then	**	***	*		
Work intensity	now				*	
	then					

*   Indicates significance at the 0.05 level.
**   Indicates significance at the 0.01 level.
***   Indicates significance at the 0.001 level.

highest scores were work intensity (3.86) and quality (3.77). The lowest average was unionism (2.65) which indicated that unions were not perceived to have a strong presence within the SubNet firms.

The five dimensions in which significant change occurred in at least four of the five firms were communication (the dimension with the lowest average score, and the only dimension in which all five firms experienced significant change), environment, planning, leadership and job performance. No significant changes occurred in induction and commitment. Despite the importance of training in the 'best practice' programme, only two firms recorded a significant change in that dimension. Of the additional five dimensions, three firms experienced a strong change in quality. Work intensity and job autonomy, although having the highest average scores, increased in only one firm.

A summary of the results for each firm is as follows. Firm 1 had the greatest total average score differences on the B&A dimensions, suggesting it had experienced the most change of all the SubNet firms between 1994 and 1995. Although firm 1 had fewer dimensions on which significant change occurred, four of the changes indicated that although the impact of change had been narrow, it had been deep. Firm 1 had three changes on the additional dimensions of quality, job autonomy and work intensity. This was more than for the other firms, where the latter two dimensions had not changed at all. Differences between management and non-management occurred on 11 of the 16 dimensions, a relatively high number considering firm 1 was not engaged in enterprise bargaining at the time of the survey.

Firm 2 had the total average scores closest to the aggregate average, but the highest number of significant differences on the B&A dimensions, where 8 out of 11 dimensions changed. A strong negative change occurred in the innovation dimension. Quality was the only significant change among the additional dimensions. Differences between management and non-management groups appeared on 12 of the 16 dimensions but, of these 12 differences, 5 were in 1995 only, possibly reflecting the enterprise bargaining which was taking place at the time of the survey.

Firm 3 was above the average total scores between 1994 and 1995 and had 6 out of 11 significant differences on the B&A dimensions, although the changes were not as strong as some of the other firms. Firm 3 was the only firm to experience a significant increase in job satisfaction. With one exception, unionism, firm 3 had no differences between the management and non-management groups.

Firm 4 had the highest total average scores for both 1994 and 1995, but the least number of significant differences over the period. Communication was the only B&A dimension to change. The only other change was in job satisfaction, which decreased. This suggested that people at firm 4 held the most positive view of their work and workplace, but that the 'best practice' programme had made little impact. Differences between management and non-management occurred on 15 of the 16 dimensions, structure being the only dimension in which there was no difference; 7 of the 15 differences occurred in 1995 only, again reflecting the possible influence of enterprise bargaining.

Firm 5 had the lowest total average scores for 1994 and 1995. Significant differences occurred on 7 of the 11 B&A dimensions and in quality and unionism among the additional 5 dimensions. As in firm 3, there were no differences between management and non-management on the B&A dimensions. On the additional dimensions there was one difference in job autonomy in 1994 between management and non-management.

Discussion

The findings indicate some interesting deviations from the organization culture literature. The pragmatists' view of organization culture, as a tool of management used to promote employee commitment to management's goals, was not confirmed by the results. Neither employee commitment nor the degree of unitarism as measured by the differences between management and non-management was affected by the culture change programme. In fact, two of the firms experienced greater diversity in the views of management and non-management after the 12 months of the programme. The large number of differences between management and non-management on almost every dimension, in three of the five firms, seems to support the view that a unified 'corporate culture' is not 'workplace culture' (Anthony, 1994).

There was also little evidence to support the 'strong/weak' culture notion suggested by Wierner (1988), Deal and Kennedy (1982) and Payne (1990). Wierner (1988) maintained that the non-unitary cultures were weaker than those with greater consensus where culture is learned and can be consciously changed by managers to improve organization performance. An interesting paradox emerged as firm 5, the firm with the most negative culture in terms of the lowest average score, had the 'strongest' culture in terms of the consensus between management and non-management on all dimensions. On the other hand, firm 4, the firm with the most positive culture in terms of average scores, had the greatest number of differences between management and non-management. The pragmatist's assumption that 'strong' (unitary) cultures are 'good' cultures was not, therefore, confirmed.

The results demonstrate that management has the ability to affect change through changing its own behaviour and the formal practices of the firm. Significant changes in leadership, communication and participatory management practices indicated a change in management style which, combined with training, led to significant changes in job performance, quality and sensitivity to the external environment. While these aspects of organization culture changed, other aspects, such as workplace relations and commitment, did not, which lends support to Gagliardi's proposition that core values need not be affected by workplace culture change (cited in Ogbonna, 1992).

The 'best practice' programme had been in operation for only one year when this study was carried out. For at least four of the five firms, the programme had been successful in producing change in the areas of quality improvement, benchmarking, customer focus, training, and worker participation in planning and problem-solving. In the areas of employee commitment, workplace relations, structure, greater job autonomy, and job satisfaction, the programme had little or no effect. Further, the results do not support the suggestion that 'best practice' had been a means of increasing management control and work intensity through self-regulation (Bramble, 1995; Hampson et al., 1994).

Only one firm recorded a significant increase in both job autonomy and work intensity, and the increase in work intensity was reported by both management and non-management. No other firm experienced an increase in either job autonomy or work intensity. Nor did the results support a relationship between employee participation and greater job satisfaction. Despite four firms experiencing significant increases in participatory practices, as measured by the planning dimension, there was no increase in job satisfaction. Guest's proposition that cultural change programmes exclude the possibility of workplace bargaining was not supported by the results, as two firms were in the middle of enterprise bargaining when the survey was carried out. In addition, all the firms were unionized and the 'best practice' programme was managed by joint union–management committees at both the SubNet and individual firm levels.

The major elements of the 'best practice' programme implementation included internal facilitation and training. Internal facilitation was the primary means of introducing best practice training. In addition, the internal facilitators provided on-the-job mentoring and coaching. The two firms with the greatest number of changes, and the firm with the highest overall change, employed full-time facilitators who worked closely together. The firm which experienced almost no change throughout the programme did not have a full-time, active facilitator and the training programme was cut short on the basis that the firm was sufficiently advanced in improving quality assurance.

Conclusion

The SubNet alliance was a vehicle for the 'best practice' programme. Being part of an alliance allowed Network members access to the resources necessary to implement a culture change programme. Eventually the alliance proved valuable not only in 'sharing the practices' involved in the programme, but also in 'sharing the people' (Iles, 1996) through inter-firm meetings and training programmes. After one year of a 'best practice' culture change programme, the fact that four of the five firms experienced positive change in several common aspects of workplace culture suggests the programme was effective, at least in terms of communication, environment, planning, job performance and leadership. Commitment, workplace relations and job satisfaction were not affected, which suggests that while changes occurred in the behavioural aspects of culture, they did not affect the deeper value aspects. Despite the common programme and the positive changes in workplace culture, the degree of change varied between firms, and between management and non-management within firms, suggesting that organization culture need not be consensual, nor need the outcomes of culture change programmes be similar in intensity. The evidence seems to support the joint union–management partnership approach to managing workplace change, an approach in which both parties agree to practical change for pragmatic reasons while each maintains its own interests and identity.

Appendix: Explanation of the organization culture profile dimensions

Broadfoot and Ashkanasy dimensions

Leadership   Related to leadership and how management acts as a role model for the workforce through its actions and commitment to customer service and organization values and goals.

Structure   Related to policies and procedures and whether they are widely known, helpful and up to date and allow individuals a degree of autonomy, or whether organizations are bureaucratic in nature.

Innovation   Related to the degree of risk taking and individual initiative.

Job performance   Related to the degree of emphasis on achievement and performance measurement.

Planning   Related to the degree of clarity of and participation in strategic planning.

Communication   Related to the quality and frequency of formal and informal communication in the organization.

Environment   Related to the degree of customer focus and sensitivity to the external environment.

Workplace relationships   Related to the degree of individual respect and camaraderie in the organization.

Training   Related to the degree of training and development in the organization.

Induction   Related to the degree of formal socialization of new employees into the organization.

Commitment   Related to the degree of individual commitment to the organization.

Additional dimensions

Quality   Related to the organization's commitment to quality.

Job satisfaction   Related to the degree of job satisfaction individuals perceived they experienced.

Job autonomy   Related to the degree of individual autonomy over job-related decisions.

Unionism   Related to union presence in the organization.

Work intensity   Related to the degree of work intensity in the organization.

References

Anthony, P. (1994) *Managing Culture*. Buckingham: Open University Press.

Bate, P. (1994) *Strategies for Cultural Change*. Oxford: Butterworth Heinemann.

BPC (1993) *Best Practice Culture Change Document*. Newcastle, Australia: Best Practice Consultancy.

Bramble, T. (1995) 'Labour-use strategies in the context of recession: provisional evidence from

1990–93'. Paper presented to Staff–Graduate Seminar Series, Department of Economics, Newcastle, Australia.

Broadfoot, L. and Ashkanasy, N. (1994) 'A survey of organizational culture measurement instruments'. Paper presented at the Annual Meeting of Australian Social Psychologists, Queensland.

Buttery, E. and Buttery, A. (1992) *Business Networks: Reaching New Markets with Cost Effective Strategies*. Melbourne: Longman.

Deal, T. and Kennedy, A. (1982) *Corporate Cultures: the Rites and Rituals of Corporate Life*. Reading, MA: Addison-Wesley.

Dean, J., Holmes, S. and Smith, S. (1996) 'Business networks: growth options and manufacturing and service sector comparisons'. Paper prepared for the Joint SEEANZ and Institute of Industrial Economics, Newcastle, Australia.

Department of Industrial Relations (1994) *Best Practice Forum Document*. Canberra: Australian Government Publishing Service.

Fulop, L. and Kelly, J. (1995) 'A survey of industry network initiatives in NSW'. Paper prepared for the Strengthening Local Economic Capacity (SLEC) Project, Newcastle, Australia.

Guest, D. (1987) 'Human resource management and industrial relations', *Journal of Management Studies*, 24: 503–21.

Guest, D. (1989) 'Human resource management for industrial relations and trade unions', in J. Storey (ed.), *New Perspectives on Human Resource Management*. London: Routledge. pp. 41–55.

Guest, D. (1992) 'Human resource management, trade unions and industrial relations', in J. Storey (ed.), *Human Resource Management*. London: Routledge. pp. 109–41.

Hampson, I., Ewer, P. and Smith, M. (1994) 'Post-Fordism and workplace change: towards a critical research agenda', *Journal of Industrial Relations*, June: 231–56.

Handy, C. (1990) *The Age of Unreason*. Boston: Harvard Business School.

Herman, B. (1991) 'Competitive advantage through collaboration'. Paper presented to the Networking our Way to Competitiveness Seminar Series. April.

Hissey, I. (1994) 'Government funding for Network', *Network News*, Edition 2, Third Quarter.

Iles, P. A. (1996) 'International HRD', in J. Stewart and J. McGoldrick (eds), *Human Resource Development: Perspectives, Strategies and Practice*. London: Pitman. pp. 71–97.

Legge, K. (1989) 'Human resource management, a critical analysis,' in J. Storey (ed.), *New Perspectives on Human Resource Management*. London: Routledge. pp. 19–40.

Limerick, D. and Cunnington, B. (1993) *Managing the New Organization: a Blueprint for Networks and Strategic Alliances*. Australia: Business and Professional Publishing.

Mabey, C. and Salaman, G. (1995) *Strategic Human Resource Management*. Oxford: Blackwell.

NIES (1993) *Networking: What It Is and How To Do It. A Guide to Networking*. Australian Manufacturing Council, National Industry Extension Service.

Ogbonna, E. (1992) 'Organization culture and human resource management: dilemmas and contradictions', in P. Blyton and P. Turnbull (eds.), *Reassessing Human Resource Management*. London: Sage.

Payne, R. L. (1990) 'The concepts of culture and climate'. Working Paper 202, Manchester Business School.

Peters, T. and Waterman, H. Jr (1982) *In Search of Excellence: Lessons from America's Best Run Companies*. New York: Harper and Row.

Piore, M. and Sabel, C. (1984) T*he Second Industrial Divide*. New York: Basic Books.

Porter, B.L. and Parker, W.S. (1992) 'Culture change', *Human Resource Management*, 31 (1/2): 45–67.

Schein, E. (1985) *Organizational Culture and Leadership*. San Francisco: Jossey-Bass.

Smircich, L. (1983) 'Concepts of culture and organizational analysis', *Administrative Science Quarterly*, 28: 339–58.

Storey, J. (1992) *Developments in the Management of Human Resources*. Oxford: Blackwell.

Vecchio, R., Hearn, G. and Southey, G. (1996) *Organisational Behaviour* (2nd edn). Sydney: Harcourt Brace.

Waring, P. (1995) 'The paradox of prerogative in participative post-Fordist organizations'. Unpublished honours dissertation, University of Newcastle, NSW.

Whiteley, A. (1995) *Managing Change: a Core Values Approach*. Melbourne: Macmillan.

Wierner, Y. (1988) 'Forms of value systems: a focus on organizational effectiveness and cultural change and maintenance', *Academy of Management Review*, October: 536.

Wood, S. (1996) 'High commitment management and unionization in the UK', *Journal of International Industrial Relations*, 7 (1): 41–58.

Part IV

HRM PROVIDING CHOICES AND OPPORTUNITIES

A key issue to be considered when examining HRM from the employees' point of view is not only the degree to which they are able to choose to introduce and participate in HRM initiatives but also whether or not such initiatives provide greater opportunities for the recipients. The five chapters in this part of the book give the reader an insight into the way in which a range of very different HR initiatives offer both HR planners and those on the receiving end a variety of choices and opportunities, each of which is attended by a corresponding set of constraints and inhibitors.

Gunnigle and Morley examine the extent to which IR matters are integrated into strategic decision-making in greenfield sites. The chapter is premised on the idea that greenfield sites as wholly new, start-up operations offer management the greatest degree of discretion and choice and therefore the opportunity to introduce innovative working practices. To determine the level of integration they studied all greenfield sites established in manufacturing and internationally traded services in the Republic of Ireland in the period 1987–92. These numbered 53. Having discussed the method they used to measure integration, the authors report that integration was characterized as 'high' in one in five of the organizations, 'medium' in a little over half of the organizations and 'low' in a little under a third of the organizations. They conclude that the two factors which most determine the level of integration are ownership by a US parent and location in an advanced industrial sector. This suggests that there may be a number of extra-organizational factors which intervene to restrict the range of choices available to managers.

In contrast Mallon's chapter is a qualitative study of 22 individuals who have become 'portfolio' workers. Unusually the focus of her study is not on the experiences of those who have remained in 'downsized' organizations, but is focused on the motivations and experiences of those who have left an organization. In particular, her study aimed to discover the factors underpinning people's move into portfolio work, the kind of work in which they are engaged, their personal experiences of portfolio work and the nature of their relationship with employers. In other words, the central concerns of her study were the nature of the choice to become a portfolio worker (i.e. was it voluntary or not) and the opportunities it offered them. She reports that the majority of these portfolio workers are 'refugees'. That is, they left as a result of a variety of organizational changes (compulsory redundancy, change in culture, posts disappearing). They had little choice in becoming portfolio workers. The main low points these individuals experienced were the unpredictability and fall in their incomes, and the lack of respectability associated with being contract workers. The individuals had a mixture of relational and transactional links with their employers. The author argues that as traditional career paths break down, HR managers will have to increasingly learn how to manage the transition to portfolio work, including the consequences that this has for the psychological contract.

Iles, Wilson and Hicks-Clarke note that 'equal opportunities' is being increasingly replaced by notions of managing diversity. Central to this approach is the offer to business of the opportunity to gain competitive advantage by valuing the diversity amongst their employees and so maximizing the contribution of all organizational members to the achievement of strategic goals. But diversity needs to be actively managed if organizations are to fully realize the benefits and if their members are to be able to take advantage of the enhanced opportunities. The authors explore whether gender diversity has implications for organizational performance. Their research suggests that those organizations which give greater opportunities to women in management perform better than those who do not. However, they also demonstrate that there are a number of powerful blocks to increasing the proportion of women in management. Importantly, the authors identify the way in which organizational cultures can support and emphasize masculine values as opposed to both masculine and feminine values. HR managers must therefore carefully examine whether the values they design into and seek to disseminate via the organization's culture offer opportunities for all or restrict the advancement of particular sections of their workforce.

Preston and Hart examine the nature of organizational socialization for a group of graduate management trainees in a large retail organization, Taylors PLC, over a six-year period. The graduate training programme is a key opportunity for both the organization and the graduates. For the former it is an opportunity to begin to mould these key employees and for the latter it is an opportunity to learn about different aspects of the organization they have joined. The graduates were surveyed at three time points: (1) two weeks before joining the organization; (2) six months after joining; and (3) five to six years after joining. Graduates are an important group to study, partly because of their inexperience of employment and partly because of the resources devoted to graduate training programmes by organizations which operate these schemes. In studying organizational socialization the authors adopt the metaphor of a 'trail of clues'. They liken it to a mystery hunt in which the graduates must discover the clues before they can determine how to 'get on' in the organization. On the basis of their study they conclude that the planned events within the socialization programme are only part of the process by which newcomers come to know and understand an organization. Of considerable importance is the wider organizational context within which organizational socialization takes place. Within Taylors PLC cultural and structural changes led to conflicting signals and a failure to deliver parts of the programme. The implication is that the design of graduate training programmes has to be seen within a wider organizational context. These programmes cannot be developed in isolation of other organization-wide initiatives.

Beattie and McDougall also examine how people learn within organizations by focusing on learning within peer mentoring relationships. In particular they examine the impact of the overall HRM/HRD context on the nature of peer mentoring relationships within two public sector organizations. They are concerned with the central question of whether or not HR initiatives provide greater or fewer opportunities to learn. They conclude that whilst the HRD strategies in both organizations had contributed to a positive learning climate they nevertheless failed to meet the developmental needs of individuals. As a consequence, individuals engaged in informal learning with colleagues. Furthermore, whilst one of the organizations had created a formal structure the other had not. Yet more mutual learning was taking place in the organization where no formal structure existed. The authors suggest that the emphasis on one-way learning and line management supervision may have inhibited learning in the organization with the formal programme. Line management attitudes are therefore critical to the success of learning in peer mentoring relationships.

9

Strategic Integration and Industrial Relations in Greenfield Sites

Patrick Gunnigle and Michael Morley

An increased emphasis on the strategic significance of employee relations considerations in facilitating the achievement of business objectives is seen as a key characteristic of change in management approaches to industrial relations (Kochan et al., 1986; Guest, 1987; 1989; Storey, 1992). High levels of strategic integration are felt to contrast with the 'traditional pluralist' model which was essentially reactive in nature, with the result that industrial relations considerations were not a concern of strategic decision-makers, but rather an operational issue only given priority when problems arose (Armstrong, 1988; Purcell, 1987; 1989).

This chapter considers the extent of integration of industrial relations (IR) considerations in strategic decision-making in greenfield site companies. The perspective adopted is that greenfield sites afford management considerable strategic discretion in the area of industrial relations. Thus, it is reasonable to suggest that if managements are adopting more strategic approaches, this should be most evident in greenfield sites. While this chapter is based largely on a managerialist perspective, it addresses an issue of great significance for 'receiving end' human resource management (HRM), namely the impact of industrial relations considerations on the location and management of greenfield site companies.

Three broad research questions serve to structure the subsequent discussion:

- What measures can we use to evaluate strategic integration in industrial relations?
- To what extent does the research evidence in greenfield sites suggest that industrial relations considerations are strategically integrated in greenfield sites?
- What factors help explain variations in levels of strategic integration in industrial relations between greenfield site companies?

This chapter is based on a study of *all* greenfield site firms established in the manufacturing and internationally traded services sectors in the Republic of Ireland in the period 1987–92. The study population amounted to some 53 firms. Greenfield sites were defined as 'locations where an organization establishes a new facility in a start-up mode incorporating design of plant and recruitment of a new workforce'. The study excluded firms with fewer than 100 employees. The research was conducted using a methodologically pluralist approach involving: (a) qualitative semi-structured interviews with senior managers in all of the sites; (b) statistical analysis of a questionnaire-based survey completed by the senior manager responsible for personnel/HR in each site; (c) consideration of research findings by three HRM/IR 'expert' panels. These expert panels comprised managers, employees, and trade union representatives.

Ireland is considered a particularly appropriate testing site for the extent of strategic integration in industrial relations. It has a high level of inward investment and the Irish socio-political context provides a stark contrast to the US and the UK from where much of the contemporary literature on HRM emanates. In particular, the industrial relations system is characterized by widespread acceptance of the legitimacy of a strong trade union role in society and the adoption of centrally negotiated agreements on pay and other aspects of social and economic policy.

Towards acceptable measures of strategic integration

The integration of industrial relations considerations into strategic decision-making has been a recurrent theme in contemporary analyses of change in industrial relations management (Walton, 1985; Kochan et al., 1986; Guest, 1987; Storey, 1994; Beaumont, 1993; 1995). However, despite such analyses, the precise nature and extent of strategic integration of industrial relations considerations into top-level management decision-making remains unclear. The major reason for this lack of clarity is that strategic decision-making is a notoriously difficult area for researchers to analyse. Researchers often rely on individual proxy indicators of strategic integration, such as the role of the specialist personnel/industrial relations function in strategic decision-making (see, for example, Storey, 1992). This is a useful approach but requires the identification of an adequate *range* of robust indicators. Alternatively, researchers may rely on qualitative/intuitive analyses, particularly those focusing on the process of strategic decision-making (see, for example, Daft and Buenger, 1990).

In this study, rather than relying on a single indicator, four proxy measures were used. These measures comprised discrete variables considered indicative of strategic integration in industrial relations and were as follows:

Location   Assesses the impact of industrial relations considerations on the location of greenfield site facilities.
Formal strategy development   Addresses the extent of formal business strategy and HR/industrial relations strategy development in greenfield firms.
Business policy impact   Measures the impact of industrial relations considerations on business policy decisions at establishment level.
Role of personnel/industrial relations function   Assesses the incidence and role of a specialist personnel/industrial relations function.

The choice of variables and the construction of scales were heavily influenced by the theoretical literature on strategic integration (see, for example, Kochan et al., 1986; Marchington and Parker, 1990; Storey and Sisson, 1994; Roche and Turner, 1994). Each discrete indicator was evaluated on a low–medium–high (1–3) strategic integration scale. The results on each indicator were then aggregated to provide an overall *composite measure* of strategic integration on a similar scale range. The overall findings on levels of strategic integration in greenfield sites are outlined in Table 9.1.

The findings presented in Table 9.1 suggest that overall levels of strategic integration veer towards an average (medium) level. The mean score of 1.91 for the composite strategic integration measure is just below the average (i.e. score of 2). However, when one considers the four constituent indicators which comprise the overall composite measure, considerable variation is found. The highest scoring indicator (mean of 2.23) was that measuring the incidence and role of the specialist personnel/industrial relations function. The second highest scoring indicator was that measuring the level of formal strategy development (mean of 2.08). This indicator measured the extent of sophistication in the development of formal mission statements, corporate strategy and personnel/industrial relations strategy, and addressed the capacity of greenfield companies to engage in business strategy, and whether such capacity facilitates a more specific capacity to engage in personnel and industrial relations strategy (see Roche and Turner, 1994). In contrast, the lowest scoring variable (mean of 1.74) was that measuring the impact of personnel and industrial relations considerations on major business policy decisions. The variable measuring the impact of industrial relations on the decisions of where to locate a new greenfield site facility also scored below the average (mean of 1.87). The other key issue emerging from Table 9.1 is the generally high standard deviations (SDs), indicating considerable disparity in the nature and extent of strategic integration among the greenfield companies studied. This finding highlights the need for more qualitative analysis to help to explain the nature and causes of variation. While an in-depth review of such qualitative findings is beyond the scope of this chapter, the following discussion provides an overview of the research findings in each key area of strategic integration outlined in Table 9.1.

Location of greenfield sites

A pervasive theme in the contemporary literature on greenfield sites is the strategic significance of the decision on where to locate a greenfield facility (Lawler, 1978; Norman, 1983; Beaumont and Townley, 1985; Kochan et al., 1986). For example, Beaumont and Townley (1985) suggest that 'the importance of being removed from traditional manufacturing centres (i.e. conurbations)' is a strategic consideration for organizations establishing at greenfield sites. The literature also links the significance accorded to the decision on where to locate a greenfield site facility with managerial desires to establish styles of industrial relations which diverge significantly from practice

Table 9.1 *Description of variables used to construct composite indicator of strategic integration in industrial relations*

Variables	Variable description	Mean	SD	Alpha
Location	Findings coded on a 1–3 scale (low to high) as follows: 1 (low) industrial relations considerations not a significant factor in location decision; 2 (medium) industrial relations considerations one of range of factors significantly impacting on location decision; 3 (high) industrial relations considerations among the most significant factors impacting upon the location decision	1.87	0.59	N/A
Formal strategy development	Based on incidence of (i) formal mission statement; (ii) formal corporate strategy; (iii) formal personnel/industrial relations (P/IR) strategy, scored as follows: 1 (low) no formal strategy; 2 (medium) formal corporate strategy and mission statement but no written P/IR strategy; 3 (high) formal mission statement, corporate strategy and P/IR strategy	2.08	0.76	0.75 ($N = 3$)
Business policy impact	Impact of industrial relations on business policy decisions, scored on a 1–3 scale: 1 (low) P/IR considerations have little/no impact; 2 (medium) P/IR considerations have considerable impact; 3 (high) P/IR considerations have significant impact	1.74	0.65	N/A
Personnel/ industrial relations function	Based on five indicators: (i) incidence of specialist P/IR function; (ii) scale of P/IR function; (iii) participation of senior P/IR specialist in top management team; (iv) involvement of P/IR function in corporate strategy; (v) translation of P/IR strategy into work programmes and deadlines for P/IR function. Results aggregated into overall measure as follows: 1 (low) no specialist function; 2 (medium) P/IR function but small scale, no/little involvement in strategy; 3 (high) presence of significant P/IR function, major role in top team and in strategy development	2.23	0.87	0.88 ($N = 5$)
Strategic integration	Composite measure of strategic integration based on combination of the four variables above and minor recoding to aggregate scores on a low–medium–high scale (1–3)	1.91	0.69	0.69 ($N = 4$)

in 'traditional' firms operating in 'traditional' industrial locations (Whitaker, 1986).

Turning to the current study, the decision on where to locate the greenfield facility was demonstrably a strategic issue for senior management in the great majority of companies studied. The most important factors identified as impacting on the location decision were, in order of priority: (i) financial incentive package; (ii) labour availability and skills; (iii) access to the single European market (European Union); (iv) low labour costs; and (v) layout/configuration of the greenfield site facility.

The most revealing answers on this topic came from the foreign-owned firms. Here it emerged that industrial relations considerations *per se* did not feature as a significant factor impacting on the location decision. Does this mean that we can definitively say that industrial relations issues are not a consideration in influencing the location decisions of greenfield organizations? The authors believe not. During the case interviews, it soon became evident that *labour issues* were an important consideration in the decision of many foreign-owned companies to locate greenfield facilities in Ireland.

Of particular significance was the nature of the Irish labour market and, specifically, the availability of labour skills, as indicated in the following respondent commentaries among US firms:

> A major reason why we are here is the availability of a stable competent workforce who are better than what we can get in the US and has lower labour turnover. (Personnel Manager, US information processing company)

> We were very impressed by high education levels, particularly that of operators: we were having a hard time getting quality people with good conceptual skills in the US. Employee selection and skills isn't a problem here. We don't use as many [selection] tests in Ireland 'cause we don't need to. (Corporate Vice-President (Operations), US electronics firm)

It was also evident that, in seeking to improve their competitive position, issues such as labour costs, work practices and union status were also important considerations impacting on the location decision of foreign-owned companies. It was significant that the majority of companies studied (62 per cent), and over 70 per cent of US-owned companies, saw the availability of skilled labour as the central positive factor influencing the location of new start-up facilities in Ireland. Indeed, the interviews with senior management revealed that this was by far the most significant factor 'tipping the balance' in Ireland's favour. Some commentators might suggest that the financial incentive package remains a dominant factor. However, this study found that while the financial incentives were important (particularly low corporate taxation), there has been a considerable equalization of financial incentives between countries in recent years, so that mobile foreign investment can now get relatively similar packages in a number of countries.

An issue with obvious and strong industrial relations overtones affecting the location decision was the cost of labour. The attraction of Ireland as a low-wage-cost environment appeared to differ somewhat between European-owned and US-owned firms as well as between US-owned firms themselves. While five of the eight European-owned firms (63 per cent) saw low labour costs as a significant reason for locating in Ireland, this was the case in less than one-third of the US-owned firms. It is felt that this finding reflects both differences in comparative labour costs between countries (e.g. Germany and the US) and the differing cost structures (ratio of labour cost to total costs) of firms operating in different industrial sectors and adopting differing competitive strategies. Indeed, all of the European firms which saw low labour cost as a significant attraction in Ireland were (West) German-owned, and thus came from a high-labour-cost environment. The comments of a senior corporate manager and CEO of the Irish greenfield facility of one of these organizations are instructive:

> The decision to locate here was based on the following factors: (i) labour rates: we are a high-labour-cost company; they contribute 40 per cent of total costs; (ii) quality of labour; (iii) grants package and low corporate taxation. The personnel costs at [Irish regional location] are 45 per cent of Stuttgart costs while productivity is only 10 per cent below that in Germany. The attraction of Ireland remains its low wage cost and low (corporate) taxation. We are totally content with the work in Ireland. (Corporate MD, German engineering company)

It was interesting that the (Irish) Chief Executive concurred with the views of his (German) corporate MD:

> We [Irish greenfield facility] are a manufacturing facility only. We are seen as the cheap labour solution to German cost problems. (CEO, German engineering company)

It was apparent that the companies which were most concerned with ensuring low wage rates were those which came from a high-labour-cost environment and/or operated in highly competitive sectors where labour costs constituted a high proportion of total costs. As discussed above, most examples of the former category came from (West) Germany or the north-east United States, while the latter mostly operated in the information processing or subcontracted electronics sectors. The following comment again reflects the priorities of many of these firms:

> We located here because of lower costs and particularly [lower] labour costs. The cost of building facilities and employing people in Germany is very high. (General Manager, German engineering (auto parts) firm)

In contrast, a number of other firms, particularly those from the western and southern states in the US, felt that labour costs in Ireland were high, as evidenced from the following comments:

> This is the most expensive site in the corporation for labour: our other main manufacturing bases are in California and Taiwan. It's the labour quality and European base that has us here. (Industrial Relations Manager, US engineering firm)

It was also significant that firms which had an explicit policy of paying below the going rate for their sector chose to locate in more peripheral regional locations, to take advantage of pay rates which were felt to be lower than those

Table 9.2   *Impact of industrial relations considerations on location decision by ownership*

Nationality	Impact of IR on location decision (1–3)[1]	
	Mean	SD
USA	2.11	0.42
Europe	1.75	0.46
Asian	1.86	0.38
Irish	1.36	0.81
Overall mean	1.87	0.59

[1]   Scale: 1 = low, 2 = medium, 3 = high.

pertaining in more industrialized urban centres. This finding is important as it differs from the traditional argument that there are few regional variations in pay levels in Ireland because of its small scale and relative homogeneity in industrial and employment profile. A particular issue was the desire of 'low-pay' greenfield organizations to locate in rural areas or small provincial towns which provided them with a (more or less captive) labour pool because of the dearth of employment opportunities and the flight from agriculture.

In evaluating the aggregate evidence on the impact of industrial relations considerations on the location decision of greenfield site facilities, one finds a somewhat ambiguous picture. When one considers the impact of *broad* labour issues, it is clear that these had a significant impact on location decisions. However, when these are factored out and *only* direct industrial relations considerations are evaluated, the impact on location was considerably reduced. To establish a clearer picture it is useful to disaggregate the findings by ownership, as outlined in Table 9.2. This approach controls for indigenous organizations since, as was pointed out above, location decisions in the great majority of Irish companies were influenced by largely opportunistic and reactive considerations.

This evidence indicates that industrial relations considerations were an important factor influencing the location decision of many foreign-owned, and particularly US-owned, organizations establishing at greenfield sites in Ireland. Thus, in deference to Purcell's (1989) argument on strategic decision-making that industrial relations considerations are 'downstream' ones, the evidence presented here suggests that some industrial relations considerations are 'upstream' decisions in that they affect a key 'first-order' decision, namely that of location. Arguably, the reason for the significance of industrial relations considerations in impacting upon such a broad strategic decision is related to its impact on competitive positioning. For a large proportion of the greenfield organizations examined in this study, it appears that the route to competitive advantage was based on providing flexible products/services to customers at low cost. Many of the organizations studied operated as sub-contractors, and were thus required to meet the flexible demands of their customers, often on a 'just-in-time' basis. Such a scenario requires that these organizations deliver promptly, and at prescribed quality and cost levels, to their customers. Given such a competitive scenario, it is hardly surprising that industrial relations issues which impinge on competitive positioning (such as labour skills, wage costs and flexibility) were an important strategic concern for organizations locating at greenfield sites.

Formal strategy development

An important indicator of the level of strategic integration is the level of formal strategy development (Roche and Turner, 1994). The extent of formal strategy development in greenfield sites was initially explored through the interviews with management representatives. The issue of formal strategy development was further examined through the survey questionnaire and an analysis of published data, particularly annual reports, company handbooks and other company literature. The extent of formal strategy development was examined by exploring the incidence of: (i) a formal mission statement; (ii) a formal corporate strategy; and (iii) a formal personnel/industrial relations (P/IR) strategy. The findings indicate that over two-thirds of the greenfield companies studied had a formal mission statement and corporate strategy. However, the reverse is the case in relation to the incidence of a formal P/IR strategy. Here, just one-third of companies reported the incidence of formal P/IR strategy. Table 9.3 uses the overall measure of formal strategy development outlined earlier to assess the impact of ownership. The findings suggest that the level of formal strategy development was most advanced in US-owned companies. In contrast, indigenous greenfield organizations had the lowest levels of formal strategy development.

Turning to the issue of P/IR strategy, the evidence in the greenfield firms indicated that such formal strategies were particularly common in US firms. Interview data confirmed a strong preference among US-owned companies, particularly in the electronics/information technology sectors, to have explicit policies across a range of personnel and industrial relations areas. While almost 60 per cent of US companies had a written P/IR strategy, only 9 per cent of Irish companies had such a strategy. Japanese firms were likely to have broad mission statements, but less likely to develop these into explicit P/IR

Table 9.3   *Ownership and formal strategy development*

| Nationality | Extent of formal strategy development (1–3)[1] | |
	Mean	SD
USA	2.44	0.70
European	1.63	0.52
Asian	2.00	0.58
Irish	1.55	0.69
Overall mean	2.08	0.76

[1]   Scale: 1 = low, 2 = medium, 3 = high.

strategies. However, an interesting trend, identified during interviews with senior management in some organizations, was a growing disenchantment with the explicit commitments inherent in many P/IR policy statements. A number of these managers felt that, increasingly, organizations should avoid committing themselves in writing to specific P/IR policies, since these may inflate expectations and restrict management flexibility to initiate policy changes subsequently. This development may result, at least partially, from the trading difficulties encountered by some longer-established firms traditionally seen as the major Irish exponents of explicit 'soft' HRM policy commitments, such as Digital, Wang and Amdahl.

Impact of industrial relations considerations on business policy decisions

Alongside the issue of formal strategy development, the specific impact of industrial relations considerations on strategic decision-making at establishment level is another useful indicator of strategic integration in industrial relations. This study explored the impact of IR considerations on major business policy decisions in each of the companies studied.

The summary findings show that just over half the respondent firms indicated that IR considerations had a 'considerable' impact on major business policy decisions. However, 20 firms (38 per cent) reported that IR considerations had little influence on major business policy decisions, while at the other extreme only 6 firms (11 per cent) felt that IR considerations were 'very influential' in impacting on business policy decisions at establishment level. Overall, these findings suggest that IR considerations do not have a major impact on business policy decisions in greenfield site establishments.

In comparing these findings with the previous analysis on the extent of formal strategy development, a somewhat paradoxical picture emerges. It appears that while greenfield organizations have quite a high capacity for strategy (i.e. high level of formal strategy development), this does not result in IR considerations acting as a major influencing factor on business policy decisions at establishment level. Some of the possible reasons for this finding are discussed below.

There were some differences in the impact of IR considerations on business policy decisions when the data were disaggregated in terms of ownership (see Table 9.4). In particular, it appears that IR considerations had the greatest impact on business policy decisions among US and (to a lesser extent) European firms. The reasons for the difference between indigenous and US/European firms appear related to the relative maturity and scale of the organizations studied. As discussed earlier, most Irish greenfield companies were characterized by organic growth and were relatively 'small players' in their product market, acting as price-takers in supplying a few major customers. In many of these firms, the management team was quite small, and because of the market vulnerability of the firm, focused primarily on short-term financial survival, with particular emphasis on cost control and

Table 9.4   *Impact of industrial relations considerations on business policy decisions by ownership*

| Nationality | Impact of IR on business policy (1–3)[1] | |
	Mean	SD
USA	1.96	0.65
Europe	1.63	0.52
Asian	1.29	0.49
Irish	1.55	0.69
Overall mean	1.74	0.65

[1]   Scale: 1 = low, 2 = medium, 3 = high.

aggressive marketing. IR considerations were generally not perceived as a significant consideration in business policy decisions:

> Employee relations is not a strategic concern. Our task is to get product out the door. If we can grow the business then we may get breathing space to consider longer-term strategies including employee relations. (Operations Manager, Irish engineering company)

In contrast, most foreign-owned organizations tended to be larger in scale and more secure in their product market than their indigenous counterparts. Generally, the Irish facility was established as part of a broad business plan. The role of management at the Irish subsidiary, and specifically the responsibility of the personnel function (see next section), was to develop complementary personnel and industrial relations strategies effectively, to help to execute such business plans.

Role of the specialist personnel/industrial relations function

Probably the most widely used indicator of the impact of personnel/industrial relations considerations on strategic decision-making in organizations is the role of the specialist P/IR function (Tyson and Fell, 1986).

This study found that a significant majority of greenfield companies (72 per cent) had a specialist P/IR function. This figure is higher than comparative figures for established (brownfield) companies where studies have found lower functional presence (Shivanath, 1987; Brewster and Hegewisch, 1994). Indeed, the fact that over 7 out of every 10 greenfield companies had a specialist P/IR function appears quite high, given both the relative immaturity and smaller average size of greenfield companies. The presence of a specialist P/IR function in greenfield companies was largely related to ownership and size. Only 4 of the 11 Irish companies (36 per cent) had a specialist P/IR function, while the majority of US (79 per cent), Japanese (83 per cent), and other foreign companies (66 per cent) had a specialist P/IR function. However, none of the senior P/IR practitioners in the firms studied had a seat on the board of directors. The major reasons articulated by respondents for the absence of board membership were largely related to the fact that most firms with a specialist P/IR function were subsidiaries of larger, mostly for-eign-owned, corporations. Consequently, there was no potential for board-level involvement in the Irish operation, although at corporate level the P/IR function may indeed have been represented at (corporate) board level. The senior P/IR practitioner was part of the top management team in 76 per cent of the firms with a specialist P/IR function.

In terms of the role of the specialist P/IR function, the study findings, and particularly the interview data, suggest that product market position is a key factor impacting on the scale and nature of the P/IR function. Generally, organizations in highly price-competitive sectors tended towards 'lean' oper-ating structures and had either no or a very limited P/IR function. This was particularly the case among subcontracting suppliers, both indigenous and foreign-owned. On the other hand, it was generally the larger organizations in relatively strong product market positions which employed a large, well-resourced and influential P/IR function. This impact of product market position is illustrated in the contrast between, firstly, larger (more than 300 employees) establishments in relatively strong product market positions (high market share and high growth), and, secondly, smaller organizations (10–150 employees) operating in price-competitive subcontracted services and manu-facturing sectors.

Turning to the level of involvement of the P/IR function in the development of strategy, the picture is quite mixed. Only some 18 per cent of firms with a specialist P/IR function reported that the function was involved from the outset in strategy development. On the other hand, in the great majority of firms (61 per cent), the P/IR function was involved either in a consultative mode or in the implementation of strategy. A smaller but significant number of respondents (21 per cent) claimed that the P/IR function had no involve-ment in strategy development.

In summary, it appears that the general trend in relation to the nature of the P/IR function was that foreign-owned, and specifically US, companies were most likely to have a particular desired approach to industrial relations as generally manifested in an explicit P/IR strategy (see Table 9.5). In all but the smaller US-owned firms, a specialist P/IR function was vested with responsibility for the implementation of specific policies and practices to

Table 9.5   *Role of the personnel/industrial relations function by ownership*

| Nationality | Role of P/IR function (1–3)[1] | |
	Mean	SD
USA	2.56	0.75
European	1.88	0.83
Asian	2.43	0.79
Irish	1.54	0.82
Overall mean	1.23	0.87

[1] Scale: 1 = low, 2 = medium, 3 = high.

effect the desired industrial relations 'style'. The majority of indigenous organizations were less likely to have a particular desired P/IR approach and
related policies and practices, and tended to view industrial relations issues as
somewhat peripheral to the business and dealt with IR in a largely *ad hoc*
manner.

Explaining variations in strategic integration

The preceding discussion on the nature of strategic integration in greenfield
companies alluded to the impact of explanatory factors such as ownership
and product market performance. However, the basis for such relationships
was largely confined to simple cross-tabulations and intuitive knowledge
gained from the company visits, interviews and expert panel discussions.
While cross-tabulations and 'intuitive' insights are useful in highlighting possible associations between explanatory factors and variations in management
styles, they cannot be relied on to identify significant relationships, particularly where there is the possibility of numerous internal and external factors
impacting upon such relationships. This section seeks to identify the main
explanatory factors impacting upon variation in the extent of strategic integration in industrial relations in greenfield sites. To address adequately the
primary explanatory factors impacting upon variations in strategic integration, each of the integration measures was regressed on a range of
independent variables. This analysis is conducted to ensure that the relationships between the independent variables and variations in management styles
in industrial relations are not spurious. The construction of these independent
variables is summarized in Table 9.6.

The regression results with strategic integration as the dependent variable
are outlined in Table 9.6. In equation 1, strategic integration was regressed on
all the independent variables. Here we find that company size (beta =
0.36***), level of technological complexity (beta = 0.27**) and US ownership
(beta = 0.47***) are positively related to strategic integration (see table for
significance levels given by asterisks). The impact of size is not surprising and
concurs with much of the 'small-firm' literature which suggests that smaller
firms afford little strategic consideration to industrial relations considerations (see, for example, Curran, 1986; Curran and Stanworth, 1981). Location
in high-technology sectors has also been identified with more strategic
approaches to industrial relations (Guest, 1987; Yuen, 1990). The only other
variable which had a significant impact (beta = 0.3**) on strategic integration
was that measuring the location of the company's main market(s). This finding suggests that the more international a company's market is, the greater the
likelihood that it will adopt a strategic approach to industrial relations, and
vice versa. This finding is largely unsurprising and is in line with the business
strategy literature (Wheelen and Hunger, 1990).

In equation 2, strategic integration was regressed on all the independent
variables, *and* on composite measures of collectivism and individualism in

Table 9.6   *Explaining strategic integration in industrial relations*

Independent variables	Dependent variable: strategic integration	
	Equation 1	Equation 2
Structural		
Size	0.36**	0.06 (ns)
Manual	–0.18 (ns)	–0.16 (ns)
Gender	0.10 (ns)	0.18 (ns)
Temporary	–0.09 (ns)	0.16 (ns)
Sectoral		
Sector	–0.06 (ns)	–0.22*
Activity	0.08 (ns)	0.09 (ns)
Hi/lo tech	0.27**	0.13 (ns)
Economic		
Labour costs	–0.15 (ns)	–0.19 (ns)
Financial performance	–0.02 (ns)	–0.12 (ns)
Market		
Market	–0.30***	0.16 (ns)
Diverse	–0.12 (ns)	0.26**
Matrix	0.04 (ns)	0.12 (ns)
Ownership		
US	0.47***	0.15 (ns)
Irish	–0.13 (ns)	–0.14 (ns)
European	–0.00 (ns)	0.01 (ns)
Constant[1]	1.00***	0.8**
Collectivism		0.03 (ns)
Individualism		0.67***
R^2	0.50	0.52
F-ratio	14.0***	20.0***
N	53	53

* $P < 0.05$; ** $P = < 0.01$; *** $P = <0.001$; ns = not significant.
[1] Ownership was entered as a dummy variable with the Asian-coded companies taking the value of the constant. The coefficient reported for the constant is the unstandardized coefficient *B*.

industrial relations (see Appendix). Equation 2 indicates that the most significant and positive influence on levels of strategic integration is individualism (beta = 0.67***), accounting for 85 per cent of the reported variance in strategic integration. It is likely that the impact of the US-ownership dummy variable in equation 1 is replaced by individualism in equation 2, since it appears that US companies are associated with more individualist approaches to industrial relations compared with indigenous or other foreign-owned companies (see Gunnigle, 1995; Gunnigle et al., 1996). This finding suggests that companies adopting individualist industrial relations approaches are most likely to do so in a conscious and strategic mode. The only other independent variable exerting a significant impact on levels of strategic integration in equation 2 was sector. Here, presence in the manufacturing sector was negatively associated with levels of strategic integration (beta = –0.22*). However, as only 9 of the 53 greenfield companies operated in the services sector, one must be circumspect in interpreting the significance of this finding. Leaving aside this important caveat, these findings confirm a positive relationship between levels of individualism and strategic integration. Companies in the services sector were characterized by low levels of collectivism and high or medium levels of individualism. The most common category of service sector companies were those in the information/data processing sector. These were typically non-union and adopted other 'ideal-typical' characteristics of high individualism, most particularly the use of performance-related pay systems based on individual performance appraisals among *all* employee grades. This study also examined the impact of technological complexity as a separate independent variable. Much of the extant literature suggests that levels of technological complexity are positively associated with high strategic integration in industrial relations (Yuen, 1990; Turner, 1994). The findings identified a significant positive relationship between technological complexity and strategic integration. However, this impact was considerably less than that of ownership.

Reviewing the impact of a range of independent variables on levels of strategic integration in industrial relations, company ownership and specifically US ownership emerges as consistently the single most significant variable explaining variations. Apart from ownership, the only other variable which consistently exerted a significant impact on variations in management styles was location in advanced industrial sectors. Since a number of commentators have pointed to the potentially high levels of collinearity between location in advanced industrial sectors and US ownership, particular attention was paid to controlling for the impact of ownership and sectoral location in the analysis of the data (see also Beaumont and Harris, 1994; Roche and Turner, 1994). However, even after these controls, the study findings indicate that ownership rather than sectoral factors is most important in explaining variations in the extent of strategic integration in industrial relations. US ownership was the most significant variable positively impacting on levels of strategic integration.

In this chapter, company ownership is used as a proxy variable to analyse the impact of managerial values on variations in management styles in industrial relations. This approach is based on the expectation that the actual industrial relations approaches adopted in greenfield sites will closely reflect underlying managerial values associated with country of ownership (Beaumont, 1985; 1986; 1993; Beaumont and Townley, 1985; Whitaker, 1986; Poole, 1986). The study findings clearly point to the significance of US ownership in positively impacting on levels of strategic integration. In particular, it is apparent that US companies are most likely to avoid trade union recognition and also to adopt a more strategic and individualist approach to industrial relations management (see Gunnigle et al., 1996). Market location was also identified as exerting a significant impact on strategic location; levels of strategic integration were positively associated with companies which sold their goods or services on an international basis, and negatively associated with location in primarily domestic or local markets.

Discussion and conclusion

Drawing on the results emerging from the composite measure of strategic integration, the findings indicate that fewer than one in five (19 per cent) of the greenfield companies studied were characterized by high levels of strategic integration in industrial relations (see Table 9.7). Over half of the companies studied (53 per cent) were characterized by medium or average levels of strategic integration, while just under one-third of the companies (28 per cent) had low levels of strategic integration.

Table 9.7   *Levels of strategic integration in greenfield companies*

Level of strategic integration	Frequency	Percentage
High	10	18.9
Medium	28	52.8
Low	15	28.3
Total	53	100.0

The aggregate findings on both the composite strategic integration variable and the four constituent indicators are summarized in Table 9.8. Looking first at the composite measure of strategic integration, we find that this veered towards a medium or average level (mean of 1.91). However, there was considerable variation in relation to the four constituent indicators used to measure strategic integration. The highest-scoring indicators were those measuring the incidence and role of the specialist personnel/industrial relations function (mean of 2.23) and the level of formal strategy development (mean of 2.08). However, the study findings on the extent to which industrial relations considerations impacted on broader business policy decisions (mean of 1.74) and also decisions on the location of greenfield site facilities (mean of 1.87) indicated lower levels of strategic integration.

In attempting to explain these findings, it appears that when one looks at content issues, such as the presence of a well-resourced personnel/industrial relations function and the extent of formal strategy development, the results present quite a positive picture on the level of strategic integration of industrial relations considerations. However, when one examines more process-type issues, such as those measuring the impact of industrial relations considerations on business policy decisions, the results are much lower. Overall, it seems there is an increasing organizational acceptance that industrial relations policies and practices have a significant impact on strategic decision-making. However, the research evidence on greenfield sites suggests

Table 9.8   *Composite strategic integration measure and constituent indicators[1]*

Measure	Mean	SD
Location of greenfield site facility	1.87	0.59
Level of formal strategy development	2.08	0.76
Impact on business policy decisions	1.74	0.65
Role of specialist P/IR function	2.23	0.87
Composite measure of strategic integration	1.91	0.69

[1] Scale: 1 = low, 2 = medium, 3 = high individualism.

that this development is manifested more through institutional initiatives to formalize the industrial relations role and related strategies, than in industrial relations considerations impacting significantly on major business policy decisions at establishment level.

Turning to explanatory factors, company ownership and to a lesser extent industrial sector were most influential. Specifically, US ownership and location in advanced industrial sectors emerged as the most significant factors positively impacting on levels of strategic integration.

However, there is considerable disparity in the nature and extent of strategic integration among the greenfield companies studied. Therefore, the aggregate research evidence on the integration of industrial relations considerations into strategic decision-making in greenfield sites presents quite a mixed picture.

In evaluating the broader implications of this research for future work a number of issues worthy of further investigation emerge. As mentioned earlier, there have been few empirical attempts to investigate the impact of industrial relations considerations on strategic decision-making despite widespread references to this issue in the literature. This deficit is most probably related to the inherent difficulties in finding valid and reliable indicators of strategic integration. This study encountered similar problems. In addition to utilizing traditional measures such as the *role of the specialist personnel/industrial relations function* and the extent of *formal strategy development*, the study considered other indicators of the extent of strategic integration in industrial relations. These measures clearly need further empirical testing and refinement. Another interesting finding was the significant and positive relationship between the extent of strategic integration in industrial relations, levels of individualism and US ownership. These findings suggest that companies adopting individualist industrial relations styles are most likely to do so in a conscious and strategic vein. It is also likely that the converse of this conclusion also holds; namely, that companies whose industrial relations styles are more collectivist in character are also more likely to have developed these styles in a less strategic and more reactive fashion. What is unclear from this analysis is the line of causality and it is therefore difficult to conclude definitively which is the key influencing factor between levels of individualism and strategic integration. For example, it may be that greater strategic consideration of industrial relations leads to managements adopting more individualist industrial relations styles. Alternatively, it might be suggested that a management desire for more individualist and less collectivist styles leads to a greater strategic emphasis on developing policies and practices which help develop and sustain this approach. While a significant positive relationship between levels of strategic integration, individualism and US ownership is possibly the most important finding, more in-depth qualitative research is required to investigate the precise nature of these relationships.

Appendix: Measures of collectivism and individualism in industrial relations

Measures of collectivism

Trade union presence   Measured through an analysis of levels of trade union recognition and trade union density.

Pattern of trade union organization   Measured through an examination of the nature of trade union recognition and impact of trade unions on workplace industrial relations.

Role of trade unions and other employee representative bodies   Measured through an examination of role of trade unions and other employee representative bodies in management–employee communications/interactions.

Employer association membership and utilization   Measured through an examination of the extent to which greenfield companies are in membership of employer associations and of the patterns of utilization of employer association services.

Measures of individualism

Sophistication of the employment and socialization system   Measured through an evaluation of the degree of sophistication and relative emphasis on individualism in the management of human resource 'flows'.

Communications   Based on an analysis of the level, nature and sophistication of management–employee communications.

Performance-related pay   Measured through an analysis of the incidence of performance-related pay systems and the utilization of formal performance appraisals to aid performance-related pay decisions among manual/operative grades.

Employee involvement   Measured through an analysis of the extent to which management utilizes explicit techniques to facilitate employee involvement in decision-making.

Employee autonomy   Measured through an analysis of the extent to which management seek to facilitate/promote employee autonomy.

These indicators were combined to construct overall composite measures of both collectivism and individualism.

References

Armstrong, P. (1988) 'The personnel profession in the age of management accountancy', *Personnel Review,* 17 (1): 25–31.

Beaumont, P.B. (1985) 'New plant work practices', *Personnel Review,* 14 (5): 15–19.

Beaumont, P.B. (1986) 'Management opposition to union organisation: researching the indicators', *Employee Relations,* 8 (5): 31–8.

Beaumont, P.B. (1993) *Human Resource Management: Key Concepts and Skills.* London: Sage.

Beaumont, P.B. (1995) *The Future of Employment Relations.* London: Sage.

Beaumont, P.B. and Harris, R.I.D. (1994) 'Opposition to unions in the non-union sector in Britain', *International Journal of Human Resource Management,* 5 (2): 457–71.

Beaumont, P.B. and Townley, B. (1985) 'Greenfield sites, new plants and work practices', in Valerie Hammond (ed.), *Current Research in Management.* London: Frances Pinter.

Brewster, C. and Hegewisch, A. (1994) *Policy and Practice in European Human Resource Management: the Price Waterhouse Cranfield Survey.* London: Routledge.

Curran, J. (1986) *Bolton Fifteen Years On: a Review and Analysis of Small Business Research in Britain, 1971–1986.* London: Small Business Research Trust.

Curran, J. and Stanworth, J. (1981) 'Size of workplace and attitudes to industrial relations in the printing and electronics industries', *British Journal of Industrial Relations,* 19 (1): 14–25.

Daft, R.L. and Buenger, V. (1990) 'Hitching a ride on a fast train to nowhere', in J.W. Frederickson (ed.), *Perspectives on Strategic Management.* London: Harper and Row.

Guest, D. (1987) 'Human resource management and industrial relations', *Journal of Management Studies,* 24 (5): 503–21.

Guest, D. (1989) 'Human resource management: its implications for industrial relations and trade unions', in John Storey (ed.), *New Perspectives on Human Resource Management.* London: Routledge.

Gunnigle, P. (1995) 'Collectivism and the management of industrial relations in greenfield sites', *Human Resource Management Journal,* 5 (3): 24–40.

Gunnigle, P., Morley, M. and Turner, T. (1996) 'Challenging collectivist traditions: individualism and the management of industrial relations in greenfield sites'. Paper presented to the Irish Academy of Management Annual Conference, University College Cork.

Kochan, T. A., Katz, H.C. and McKersie, R.B. (1986) *The Transformation of American Industrial Relations,* New York: Basic Books.

Lawler, E.E. (1978) 'The new plant revolution', *Organisational Dynamics,* Winter: 3–12.

Marchington, M. and Parker, P. (1990) *Changing Patterns of Employee Relations.* Hemel Hempstead: Harvester Wheatsheaf.

Norman, D. (1983) 'How a new plant made Pilkington reflect on its IR structure', *Personnel Management,* January: 20–23.

Poole, M. (1986) 'Managerial strategies and styles in industrial relations: a comparative analysis', *Journal of General Management,* 12 (1): 40–53.

Purcell, J. (1987) 'Mapping management styles in employee relations', *Journal of Management Studies,* 24 (5): 533–48.

Purcell, J. (1989) 'The impact of corporate strategy on HRM', in J. Storey (ed.), *New Perspectives on Human Resource Management.* London: Routledge.

Roche, W.K. and Turner, T. (1994) 'Testing alternative models of human resource policy effects on trade union recognition in the Republic of Ireland', *International Journal of Human Resource Management,* 5 (3): 721–53.

Shivanath, G., (1987) 'Personnel practitioners: their role and status in Irish industry'. Unpublished MBS thesis, University of Limerick.

Storey, J. (1992) *Developments in the Management of Human Resources.* Oxford: Blackwell.

Storey, J. (1994) *Human Resource Management: a Critical Text.* London: Routledge.

Storey, J. and Sisson, K. (1994) *Managing Human Resources and Industrial Relations.* Buckingham: Open University Press.

Turner, T. (1994) 'Unionisation and human resource management in Irish companies', *Industrial Relations Journal,* 25 (1): 39–51.

Tyson, S. and Fell, A. (1986) *Evaluating the Personnel Function*. London: Hutchinson.

Walton, R.E. (1985) 'From control to commitment in the workplace', *Harvard Business Review*, March–April: 77–84.

Wheelen, T.L. and Hunger, J.D. (1990) *Strategic Management*. Reading, MA: Addison-Wesley.

Whitaker, A. (1986) 'Managerial strategy and industrial relations: a case study of plant relocation', *Journal of Management Studies*, 23 (6): 657–78.

Yuen, E.C. (1990) 'Human resource management in high and medium technology companies', *Personnel Review*, 19 (4): 36–46.

10

From Public Sector Employees to Portfolio Workers: Pioneers of New Careers?

Mary Mallon

Dramatic changes are being predicted in managerial career patterns. Expectations of steady, progressive and orderly movement up an organizational hierarchy are thought to be increasingly unrealistic as organizations downsize, delayer and restructure to deal with a turbulent environment and increasing competition (Kanter, 1989; Handy, 1994; Bridges, 1995). Instead individuals are being urged to manage their own career and specifically to concentrate on developing their own employability which will allow them to be less dependent on any one organization.

This chapter focuses on what is being heralded as a contemporary career transition – moving from a managerial position in an organizational hierarchy into the less structured and more uncertain world of building a career from a variety of working arrangements. This has been termed the 'portfolio' career (Handy, 1994; Herriot and Pemberton, 1995). Its defining features are independence from any one employer and the process of packaging and exercising one's skills in a variety of ways with different organizations. The notion was initially popularized by Handy:

> more and more individuals are behaving as professionals always have, charging fees not wages. They find they are 'going portfolio' or 'going plural'. 'Going portfolio' . . . means exchanging full-time employment for independence. The portfolio is a collection of different bits and pieces of work for different clients. The word 'job' now means a client. (1994: 175)

According to Ashforth and Saks any major change in the content or context of an individual's work (i.e. a work role transition) 'entails a reorientation of goals, attitudes, identity, behavioural routines, informal networks and many other large and small changes' (1995: 157). A study of career transitions may therefore potentially render more transparent the dynamic interaction between individuals, organizations and the ever changing social world. Individual career transitions are all the more interesting and important when, as in this case, they are thought to reflect macro level changes in career forms (Kanter, 1989).

At present we know little about the people who make the transition into 'portfolio' work. If current predictions that this will become a more common career pattern are correct then human resource managers will need to know more about such individuals in order to manage the relationship with them more effectively (Kanter, 1989; Handy, 1994; Bridges, 1995). By adopting a 'receiving end' perspective of HRM this chapter aims to provide an insight into the career world and the motivations and expectations of 22 former public sector managers who previously attached to the same organization and who have all 'gone portfolio'. It seeks to explore why they made this particular transition and the difference it has made in their relationship with employing organizations. In examining the issue of portfolio work the chapter begins by examining the nature of the 'managerial career' and the way in which it is changing, and then uses this discussion to inform the analysis of the research findings.

Managers in transition

The stability of managerial careers to date should not be over-stated. Empirical evidence about managerial job change shows that radical moves are frequent in terms of changes in status, employer or function (Nicholson and West, 1988). The same research suggests that such moves are uncommon in large bureaucracies. In a further study Inkson and Coe (1994) traced the job moves of 800 managers over the 13-year period between 1980 and 1992. Their results indicated that managers are changing jobs more frequently and that sideways and downwards moves are on the increase (upwards moves are decreasing). Furthermore, the reasons for managers changing jobs are themselves changing. Few now indicate personal choice or career and personal development as the reason for the change. Instead they report that increasingly job moves are imposed by the employer through organizational restructuring. However, other authors are convinced that there is a groundswell of opinion for a more reasonable balance between home and work and that managers are making decisions based on accommodating their myriad of personal needs (Bailyn, 1993; Hewitt, 1993; Marshall, 1995).

In terms of investigating what happens to managers who leave employment, voluntarily or not, the picture is opaque. When searching for managerial portfolio workers in the survey data, the question arises of where to look for them. Definitional difficulties and conflated categories bedevil the survey research which attempts to gauge the scale of increases in all forms of non-standard working (Industrial Relations Review and Report, 1994; Legge, 1995). Are we to consider people who go 'portfolio' as part-time, fixed-term, subcontractors, self-employed, or temporaries? These categories could all be implicated and yet all suggest widely differing images and types of work. Consequently the categories cannot safely be collapsed (Hyman, 1991), nor can their occupants be seen as homogeneous.[1]

Entrepreneurs or casual labour?

There is some evidence and much anecdotal conviction (Palmer, 1995) of a casualizing of managerial work as an increasing number of jobs are being created as temporary or contract posts. According to Stanworth and Stanworth, 'Casualisation involves a movement in the direction of insecure, short-term and irregular work, generally associated with the flexible, peripheral, non-standard or "atypical" workforce' (1995: 222). This potentially describes the working pattern of people who swap employment for any form of independence. The influential and much criticized flexible firm model suggested that the workforce could be seen as composing a core element of fully employed staff and a peripheral element of people with a range of less attached relationships to the organization providing numerical and financial flexibility (Atkinson and Meager, 1986; Pollert, 1991). There is a temptation to assume that those not in 'core' employment are those with less to offer in the labour market. However, increasingly those previously most embedded in secure and progressive employment find themselves occupying a position on the periphery by choice or circumstance. Indeed, Hutton (1995) suggests that insecurity increasingly characterizes middle class employment.

Managerial work, then, may be becoming more casualized but it may also be that it is becoming more entrepreneurial. Self-employment accounts for much of the rise in what can be termed 'non-standard' working. Self-employment, which comes in many guises and connotes a whole range of contracts and contexts, soared in the 1980s. For example between 1981 and 1989 the number of people self-employed grew by 57 per cent, from just over 2 million to nearly 3.5 million (Daly, 1991: 109). Despite difficulties with the ascription of self-employment, the trend is nevertheless compelling. As Savage et al. (1992) point out, there is some evidence that managers are increasingly considering a future career in self-employment. Whether they are actually doing so has yet to be established empirically. These writers speculate that the marginalized managers 'whose reliance on organization assets has proved insecure' (1992: 70) will be those who are most likely to seek self-employment.

In seeking to understand why people opt for self-employment, push and pull factors are implicated (Hakim, 1989; Bogenhold and Staber, 1991). Push is about necessity. People are propelled into self-employment through redundancy, unemployment and lack of success in labour markets. Pull is about searching for autonomy, independence and the opportunity for personal creativity. The weight of the discourse about the liberating benefits of self-employment is implicated in people's decisions (Burrows and Curran, 1991). The push/pull explanations were developed further by Granger et al. (1995), in exploring the rise in freelance working in the book publishing industry. Taking a more qualitative and historical perspective to try and understand the move to self-employment within the wider context of an individual's life, they proposed the existence of four self-employed career types:

Refugees The biggest group; are pushed to self-employment by labour market factors.
Missionaries Either have a positive orientation to entrepreneurial work or have taken the opportunity to regain some autonomy in their career.
Trade-offs Are seeking to balance work with other needs.

Converts   Come from all categories but are likely to start as refugees before converting.

Understanding the nature of career

As Granger et al. (1995) suggest, the move towards independence can best be understood in the context of exploring an individual's career. Career is an ideal vehicle to study change as it involves the individual in interaction with the organization within a changing social context (Arthur et al., 1989; Inkson, 1997).

However, defining careers is a problem. They can be studied from the organizational perspective as part of the process of managing the flow of people through the organization. This suggests that careers within organizations have structural properties which are manageable and as a consequence pays scant attention to people as individuals and so fails to consider the social processes by which career structures come into being. An individual-based perspective can be taken which examines the psychological and life stage profile of individuals with the implications for career choice. This view sees career as residing in the individuals and the various choices they make and thus it emphasizes human agency at the expense of recognizing structural constraints on the actions of individuals.

Some career commentators insist that everyone who works has a career (Arthur et al., 1989). Others believe that career should encompass paid as well as non-paid work, home life as much as work life (Mirvis and Hall, 1994). There are numerous typologies of career patterns (Driver, 1982; Gunz, 1989) and explanations for the various motivations which may lie behind an individual's career choices (Schein, 1978). However, the dominant view in popular discourse and HRM texts takes career to mean a linear, planned and orderly advancement through an organizational hierarchy or a rise through the ranks of a profession. It tends to be seen as a journey through intermediate stages, often within an internal labour market, to some terminal point (Nicholson and West, 1989). The stages of the journey are marked by observable badges of success such as enhanced job titles and larger salaries.

The 'bureaucratic' career

Kanter describes careers as we have traditionally understood them as 'bureaucratic' or 'corpocratic' careers:

> The bureaucratic career involves a sequence of positions in a formally defined hierarchy of other positions. 'Growth' is equated with promotion to a position of a higher rank that brings with it higher benefits, 'progress' means advancement within the hierarchy. Thus 'career' consists of formal movements from job to job . . . In the typical bureaucratic career, all the elements of career opportunity – responsibilities, challenges, influence, formal training and development, compensation – are all closely tied to rank in an organization . . . This pattern best describes the administrative/managerial careers in large oligopolistic corporations and the civil service in the mid twentieth century. (1989: 509)

This type of career has only ever described the working conditions of the minority. When we talk of threats to careers, it is this type of career which is implicated. Thus managers in bureaucracies who may have had the most to gain in traditional career patterns potentially now have the most to lose. However, this type of career is not without its restrictions and has long been satirized (Whyte, 1956) and criticized (Kanter, 1989; Scase and Goffee, 1989; Bridges, 1995; Hecksher, 1995). This model of careers has been judged to be a male model which does not meet the needs of women (or indeed of those men) who wish to combine family and career (Marshall, 1989; Bailyn, 1993). It can constrain, alienate and disappoint. But it is at the root of how we judge success in our society so threats to it are keenly felt.

Pahl, in his insightful book on the end of the century malaise and anxiety which appears to grip us, puts the collapse of the certainties of the traditional career at centre stage when he writes:

> take away the career and much more risk and uncertainty surround the idea of success. Without clearly marked out and structured ladders, it becomes less easy to prepare for advancement or to be sure that what one individual takes to be advancement has wider social acceptability. (1995: 2)

Recent studies reflect the difficulties we have as individuals and HR managers in accepting this. The impact of job loss, insecurity and collapsed promotion hopes is acknowledged to be considerable. Anxiety and insecurity are endemic (Pahl, 1995; Holbeche, 1995; Herriot and Pemberton, 1995). Job security remains what is prized. A recent IPD survey found that: 'Despite some fashionable rhetoric about "portfolio workers", most employees . . . continued to hold, perhaps as a forlorn hope, a relatively traditional expectation of continuing security of employment' (*People Management*, 1995: 17). It seems that the traditional career is far from dead in terms of preferred organizational approaches to career management (Guest and Davey, 1996).

One way to understand the continuing influence of this view is to see careers as social constructions, culturally embedded and reinforced by the language we use about them (Berger and Luckman, 1967). Gowler and Legge write that:

> just as language is both constituted by human agency yet at the same time is the medium of this constitution, so people construct careers through language by assigning meanings to their actions and use these constructs to interpret and express the experiences that provide the stimulus for such constructions. (1989: 439)

As the whole notion of career is intertwined with that of bureaucracy, the dominant organizational form of the century to date, it is to be expected that our constructions of careers will reflect its maxims and so notions of order, progress and rational planning are privileged in career debate.

Career patterns are learned and enacted by individuals over time and so come to acquire apparently structural properties (Evetts, 1992). Individuals entering a management career learn what they must do to acquire career success and what they can expect from the organization. Thus

individuals are renewing the organization's management structure through already
defined routes and paths. Individuals are obliged to follow such routes if they wish
to increase their chances of career success, that is if they wish to achieve promotion
in their careers. (1992: 9)

Viewing the bureaucratic career as a social construction warns against reification of the idea and alerts us to the essential duality of careers. They are just
as much about the apparently objective features of an individual's careers as
they are about the interpretations the individual puts on them and how those
interpretations spur individuals to action. This view was expressed as far
back as the 1930s:

A career consists objectively of a series of statuses and clearly defined offices . . .
subjectively a career is the moving perspective in which a person sees his life as a
whole and interprets the meaning of his various attributes, actions and things that
happen to him. (Hughes, cited in Barley, 1989: 46)

New careers

New thinking about careers focuses on the individual perspective. If the well-
known markers of the old career paths are to disappear then the internal,
subjective dimension comes to the fore. As Weick and Berlinger suggest in
their review of careers in putative self-designing organizations: 'in the absence
of . . . external markers, the objective career dissolves and in its place the subjective career becomes externalized and treated as a framework for career
growth' (1989: 321). It is suggested that we cannot rely on organizations to
manage our careers for us, we have to do it ourselves (Golzen and Garner,
1990). Furthermore, we must stop seeing a career as a succession of offices
and regard it as about all the events of our lives. Consequently, we need to
decouple our identity from our job (Weick and Berlinger, 1989). Careers need
to be viewed now as 'free form' (Leach and Chakiris, 1988), as 'boundaryless'
(Arthur, 1994; Mirvis and Hall, 1994), as requiring new ways of learning
(Defillippi and Arthur, 1994) and as a means of judging personal success
(Mirvis and Hall, 1994).

Kanter (1989) suggests that career forms are changing from the bureaucratic form (described above) to professional and entrepreneurial forms. The
professional form is based on what you offer as an individual, your portable
skills, knowledge and reputation along with a weaker link to the organization
and a stronger affiliation with one's craft. In the entrepreneurial form people
will find their careers shaped by the exercise and marketing of their own
skills and knowledge. Kanter (1989) argues that these career forms will
increasingly apply to people who have previously lived out their career in the
bureaucratic tradition.

Recognizing that many people will accept the independence implied by
these new career forms reluctantly, Kanter (1989) insists that this is something
we must get used to. Bridges (1995), warning us that we are witnessing the end
of the job, takes up the portfolio theme by suggesting that we look at our
career as a business by learning to trade, developing our reputation and

becoming more 'vendor minded'. In a similar vein Golzen and Garner suggest: 'in a career sense we are all self employed now' (1990: 160).

The psychological contract

At the heart of all these ideas concerning new career patterns and forms is the notion of reappraising the psychological contract between individual and organization, or as Rousseau puts it 'the reciprocal obligations between employee and employers' (1990: 389). Individuals are urged to change their expectations, to no longer seek job security and upward progress but to look for enhanced employability and personal development (Kanter, 1989; Bridges, 1995). As a consequence, these writers argue that organizations should concern themselves less with managing careers than with harnessing the talent and potential input of all members of the organization. This is taken further by other writers. For example, Waterman et al. propose the development of the 'career resilient' workforce who, they suggest (rather implausibly), are 'dedicated to the idea of continuous learning but also stand ready to reinvent themselves to keep pace with change; who take responsibility for their own career management and last but not least, who are committed to the company's success' (1994: 88). Waterman and his colleagues paint a picture of 'a workforce of loners, roaming corporate halls, factories and E-mail systems' (1994: 87) and insist that to minimize this effect, organizations as much as individuals must develop a covenant of shared responsibility for developing an individual's long-term employability even if that is to be exercised outside the firm. The literature on boundaryless organizations warns organizations that individuals operating in new ways can cause career effects and so the implications of new careers will not be borne by individuals alone. Just as individuals reproduce long-standing career paths by following the old rules and resources, so too they can be actively involved in changing them when, as groups of people, they find themselves, by choice or circumstance, relating to organizations in different ways and developing and exercising new competencies (Bird, 1994; Defillippi and Arthur, 1994).

Both parties are encouraged to forge 'new deals' more in keeping with the realities of the time, based on the various needs and wants of both parties (Herriot and Pemberton, 1996). The employment contract is predicted to become more transactional with individuals being urged to take a more instrumental approach to the relationship (Mirvis and Hall, 1994; Hecksher, 1995; Herriot and Pemberton, 1995). The old employment contract can be seen as relational, long term and built on an open ended relationship of mutual commitment and continuity. Transactional contracts are shorter term and based on monetizable exchanges with specified terms and low emotional investment (Rousseau, 1996: 91). At present there is no unequivocal evidence as to whether this has happened.

The research study

We know more about the changing career world of those who remain in paid employment, and there is increasing attention on the survivors of downsizing (Brockner et al., 1992). The literature may alert us to potential changes in career paths for managers and offer some explanations as to why individuals may leave organizations but we are still uncertain as to the motivations of organizationally rooted individuals leaving full-time contractual employment and not returning to it. A primary aim of the research was to overcome this deficiency by exploring the drivers to this career transition in individuals. Since little is currently known of people's experiences of this type of working the main research objectives were as follows:

- to discover the drivers encouraging people into portfolio work
- to determine the kind of work portfolios people develop
- to ascertain the highs and lows of this way of working
- to determine the nature of the new relationship with employers (i.e. whether it is transactional or relational).

In seeking to provide some initial answers to these questions this research responded to calls by writers such as Bailyn (1989) and Mirvis and Hall (1994) to study 'leading edge exemplars' of predicted changes in working practices because understanding those thought to be at the forefront of change is more likely to assist us in developing usable knowledge for the future than building incrementally on assumptions based on current norms. Individuals leaving organizations to develop their career across organizational boundaries appear to represent a break with tradition in the pursuit of a managerial career.

Research participants

The research participants were 22 individuals who had previously worked for a particular large public sector organization. They all had a career in the traditional sense, achieving a managerial position by the time of leaving, and are all now experiencing a more mixed portfolio of work and have retained some working connection with their former employer.

The organization is interesting because it provides an example of the previous 'job for life', managed approach to career development. In common with most of the public sector it has been subject to specific challenges to working practices, in particular the imposition of a more free-market, contract-based culture, arguably in direct opposition to some long-held beliefs about the nature and social purpose of the organization. This may well have impacted on individuals attitudes' towards the organization. This common background allowed for some potential coherence in the objective events and opportunities of their working lives.

A non-probability sampling frame was used to select the participants within the parameters discussed above. As the area of portfolio working is not yet adequately mapped it was necessary to identify people who might have information and insight into the phenomenon in question, rather than searching for generalizable individuals using highly pre-specified criteria. The initial contacts were supplied by a linked but independent part of the organization with a responsibility for career development. A letter was circulated to leavers known to the organization outlining the concept of portfolio working and individuals were asked to respond if it appeared to reflect their new working pattern. Sixteen people responded and the sample snowballed beyond this original group as interviewees suggested other people to interview.

The research design was rooted in an interpretative framework. It was based on in-depth, biographical interviews with individuals. These sought to explore the subjective meaning of this transition in their working lives. The centrality of personal interpretation of career events was acknowledged. It is important to recognize that behaviour and action are predicated on personal interpretation. So how individuals align themselves with and understand the events of their own career biographies will inform and affect their career decisions (Barley, 1989).

The research focus was therefore on the individual. The very nature of portfolio working implies that the individual will work with and for several organizations. The issue, then, is portable and, if current projections of an increase in this type of working arrangement are correct, more and more employers will be involved.

This chapter reports on the first stage of an ongoing investigation. The 22 participants were interviewed in depth and all interviews taped, transcribed and analysed. The categories evolved through an iterative process of data analysis and collection.

Research findings

In this section a profile of the participants is offered with a summary of their working patterns and a discussion of the drivers to this way of working. The highs and lows of portfolio working are identified and finally the new relationship with the organization is explored.

Introducing the portfolio workers

The interviewees – 7 men and 15 women – were all between the ages of 35 and 50. The majority were in their early to mid 40s. Two had previously been chief executives, the others had managed either a unit or a function. The majority had joined the organization early in their career. Only 2 people had been employed by the organization for less than 5 years, and half had been employed for over 10 years (with 5 people claiming over 20 years' service).

In terms of their period as portfolio workers, one person had 10 years, one person had just started whilst the others had commonly been independent for between 2 and 5 years. Two had returned to full-time employed work by the time the interview took place.

The 'portfolio' tag was familiar to most, largely through the work of Charles Handy. As one woman expressed it: 'the imprimatur of Handy rather legitimates for me what I am doing.' While this hints at a new sanctioned career identity in the making, all the participants (who were not fully employed), when asked about their current identity, styled themselves by the ready-made tag of management consultants.

Looking at their working patterns, many are engaged primarily in what could be termed 'extra pair of hands' consultancy. In other words they were brought in to assist on a particular project, to fill in for a managerial absence, or to do work which could potentially be done by 'core' staff. For some this is mixed with a more expert or process consultancy role (Schein, 1988). Most continue to work within the wider boundaries of their original organization, although a few have also branched out into other areas in the public sector. Very few have significant levels of work in the private sector.

The majority have, or have previously had, longer-term assignments spanning two or more days a week over several months. Others make do as best they can with the odd bit of work which comes their way. Only one felt he was too busy; most wanted more work or were concerned that current work would dry up and they would have no time to find other work while fulfilling their current contract. Only a minority of participants have a very varied working pattern. These individuals were combining part-time work (or job-share) at senior levels with other (linked) activities such as more or less successful consultancy, academic work and writing. All recognized dilemmas in accepting a mixed bag of work. As one participant stated:

> If I accept the possibility of a semi-permanent or part-time position, then my chances of consultancy work fade and I have to start the whole self-marketing process all over again when the employment contract ends.

The drivers to portfolio working

Two decisions are potentially implicated here: the decision to leave and the decision to stay independent from another employing organization. For some people there were two significant phases. For example, one woman resigned rather impetuously and drifted into portfolio working when she found it difficult to secure another post. For the majority, as they left their job they had already decided not to seek other permanent contractual employment. They had had some private work lined up or at least had made positive moves to secure it.

The reasons impelling them to portfolio work can be summarized using the categorization of self-employed career developed by Granger et al. (1995) and outlined earlier in the chapter. The *trade-offs* were the smallest category. Only one woman specifically left permanent work which had required long hours and foreign travel to spend more time with her young children. Only two people could be clearly classed as *missionaries*. Two women left senior posts (one was a chief executive) in which they were relatively happy and in which they had been successful because they felt they had gone as far in the organization as they wished and had no desire simply to trade one organization for another. Going independent for them was a route to ongoing personal and career development. A quarter of the interviewees felt that they had some inclination towards independence (two had run their own businesses) and some ascribed to themselves 'free-wheeling and creative' personalities and 'a rogue element' that had sat uneasily in the corporate world. But for the vast majority the actual trigger to leave was not about pursuing self-fulfilment, it was rather a response to organizational changes. Hence, by far the largest group could be termed *refugees*. Only two people were made compulsorily redundant. Several negotiated their own severance package when remaining with the organization became untenable for them. In some of these cases compulsory redundancy had been a possibility. Three people renegotiated their own employment contract as a commercial self-employed contract and carried out a very similar or in one case identical job in that way. Two did so because they found the organizational conditions unpalatable as an employee and felt they could regain some self-control and self-esteem as an independent. One was given a choice of continuing their job on a commercial basis or not at all. As all three were impelled to this state by organizational action we can include them as refugees.

For the 18 refugees the tales were of broken employment contracts with posts disappearing or being rendered unacceptably altered following reorganizations. They were also about broken psychological contracts, telling of shattered promotion and development hopes, of finding the increasing shift to a market culture unpalatable or of being treated in ways of which they did not dream the organization was capable. Some were bewildered that their face no longer seemed to fit and that their contribution no longer felt as welcome as once it had. In half the cases the appointment of a new boss was implicated. There was a palpable sense of betrayal and bitterness in some of the stories, with people talking about 'brutal endings', being 'frozen out', or 'sacrificed to structural neatness'. For a few people family needs and work clashed and the organization was unresponsive. One person was refused the opportunity to job-share:

> I had decided that I was never again going to get tied up with one employer, because it was such a slap in the face when I was supposedly . . . one of their real fast track people who was going to make it to the top.

However, the categories cannot be applied too rigidly as there is a complex interweaving of factors which may propel corporate flight (Rosin and Korabik, 1992). Other life factors hovered in the background for several interviewees. Although they were rarely cited as the actual trigger for leaving, they may well have been a feature which kept them out of the corporate world. Five people had recently experienced personal illness which had led to a reappraisal of what is important in life. For a further five there was family illness and death to be dealt with. There was a concern to preserve second marriages, disappointment at not being able to enjoy the infancy of a new baby.

In addition, wariness about further organizational enmeshment was a spur to staying outside conventional paid employment. Several were lured by the hope of financial success as an independent consultant. But for many, long servers in the organization, there was an additional fear that they would not fare well in an external labour market. In a sense independence seemed a safer option, but many embarked on this already assured of commercial contracts with their old organization.

Converting to portfolio working: the highs

Granger et al. (1995) suggest that initial refugees can become *converts*. It may be human nature to make the best of the circumstances in which one finds oneself, but once people had made the decision to go portfolio, or had it forced on them, several reasons were then advanced as to why it was a preferable way of working. In characterizing their new employment world the advantages expressed were about fun, independence, variety and integrity. And while they might not be as busy as they would wish at certain times there was a trade-off in terms of balance and quality of life. Most were delighted to discover a renewed vigour at work, a positive sense of enjoyment, even play. However, this was expressed conspiratorially, for example as: 'my big secret. It protects me inside against family and friends who think I have committed career suicide.'

There was a sense that, freed from the constraints of total immersion in the internal politics, they were able to offer a more honest, worthy and creative service to the organization. They talked of regaining some control and of the relative freedoms this offered. However, when asked about whether they would return to paid work, only three people gave an unequivocal 'no'.

Converting to portfolio working: the lows

The reasons propelling people to consider a return to the workplace were primarily material: earning enough money now and storing up against the future. There was only one example of 'downshifting' to express a considered move away from material considerations to those of quality of life. None were getting rich, but many were as well off as they had been in work. The issue was the unpredictability of income. Several talked about how their pension would be significantly enhanced if their last few working years could be spent back with the organization. More persistent worries were also voiced, particularly about reputation and status and how this period out of organizational hierarchies would be viewed by a future employer. Another problem for many was the isolation and sense of being disengaged from the wider working world, although some had developed networks that sustained them.

Several felt that portfolio working or management consultancy was not seen as a fully respectable thing to do, and was in fact seen as a cover for redundancy or unemployment (as Rainbird, 1991 suggests, this type of self-employment can be seen as disguised wage labour). Whilst they did not attribute this to themselves they worried that their own reputation would be dragged down by the ever increasing numbers pursuing this work because they could get no other. This is particularly important in considering if this way of working will become embedded as a viable career alternative. Clearly there is a long way to go and the 'psychic challenges' which Mirvis and Hall (1994) suggest pioneers will feel were well in evidence.

The new relationship: transactional or relational?

In seeking to answer this question the interviewees provide some mixed messages. The yearning for a more relational link with the organization had not faded. Commitment to its intrinsic goals and values tended to transcend the pain of broken employment and psychological contracts. Many talked of the benefits of longer-term contracts where one had a desk, a chair, a telephone and could plug into the daily life of the organization. Quite apart from the financial benefits of these arrangements, they were valued for the sense of belonging they afforded.

However, they also expressed the advantages of a more distant, transactional approach. One person valued it because:

> They had no control over my soul. My soul was mine. And I sold it when I wanted to. I sold my time and my commitment when I wanted to . . . a hired gun.

Another felt it was to his overall benefit in terms of securing future work:

> I think it [a transactional approach] is useful to somebody like me because I did not follow my own self-interests enough at work. I was much more interested in the overall project and wanted that to succeed . . . But now I am much more aware of audiences and it is not a matter of doing my own thing, it is also 'do the key people know what I have to offer?'

However, there was a good deal of ambivalence expressed. It may be a pleasure at times to do some work and walk away from the detail of seeing it through, but this also engendered much frustration. Overall, the sense of remaining free from the perils of organizational enmeshment was strong. Most were happy to leave behind the internal politics and the time wasting meetings. But this was not simply expressed negatively but as a positive advantage in the contribution that they could now make to employers. One person felt that in her dealings with individuals she was able to take a more robust approach than employees might feel able to do and thus was able to solve some lingering problems. Another thought that employers could use her as a confidential conduit:

> you see, for me, because I am known and because my integrity is known around the area, I am a useful consultant and people do use me knowing that they can say things to me in confidence and knowing that I will not pass through from person A to person B, but that the knowledge that I have can then enlighten the work that I do with them all.

The majority of people had some longer-term contracts with organizations, either lasting several months or involving a day or two each week. This had assisted people to develop a satisfying mix of relational and transactional arrangements as indicated by the following statement from a participant:

> I would feel extremely nervous about going back into any organization full-time but

the combination I have at the moment, I feel my need to belong. My affiliation needs are very well served by my being half-time, but I am really glad to get out there with the more creative and intuitive side of me which comes out much more in the book writing and in the consultancy.

Significantly many people felt that fellow portfolio workers had not yet come to terms with this new relationship:

I do get a bit cross with some of the consultants I network with who now think the organization owes them a living. I say yeah but you can't have your cake and eat it. If you want your freedom and independence there are compromises around that and the compromise situation is that if your current, even longer-term consultancy says well thank you and goodbye that is one of the downsides of it.

Some individuals had what one described as 'key exit minders'. This ensured a more positive attitude on leaving and enabled these people to take a measured view of the new relationship. They framed this in business terms, that as the organization put resources into training and socializing them previously it is a great waste to not capitalize on that now.

Sadly, there was little evidence that this happened significantly. For example, one person stated:

I get the best out of being a subcontractor because I still know the people there but on an official basis, they exploit you, expect time, don't do anything to help you and it is totally a one-way process and it is totally silly.

Although consultancy relationships can take many forms, publicly adopting the role of consultant in interaction with the organization tends to imply a transactional arrangement characterized more by formality, short-termism and economic exchange than the longer-term, mutually committed relational employment contract. In general people accept the implications of swapping a relational full-time contract for this arrangement.

However, there are dangers. Handy (1994), a leading proponent of the idea, worries about skills atrophying in isolation. Certainly some of the workers were getting less challenge in terms of work content from this type of role. The development they are engaged in is relatively narrow and feedback is limited. Their tactics and practice for development echoed those of the workplace. There were plenty of good intentions and some people talked about an annual planning process but most admitted to having difficulty finding the time although they were all happy to find the money to fund themselves. There was also a tendency to equate development with organized activity although a few people did have mentors and most used professional organizations to network and access courses. Most people were adamant that the organization had no responsibility for their ongoing development and most had very limited requirements of the organization, although there were pleas for induction and health and safety training to enable the individual to offer a safer, more effective and more culture-conscious service to the organization.

Other people were surprised at how little supervision there was of their work. The majority had absorbed the message of market forces. If you do a good job they will ask you back. But this assumes very rational activity on behalf of contract awarders. One woman recognized this, suggesting that it may simply be the comfort factor which leads to renewed contracts. In any case, it is a distant and uncertain feedback, allowing no room for improved performance and unsatisfactory for individuals and organizations. Some people specifically sought feedback, believing that to be their responsibility, but were often disappointed at the standard of it. A suggestion was made about organizations who have several such workers operating some form of supervision and regular meetings. Handy (1994) talks about how the support systems must develop if this way of working is to embed, but there was little sign of this. Some informal arrangements had emerged, often due to the enlightened attitude of individual managers.

A salutary point, perhaps, for HR managers and academics is that the function itself was not mentioned by the interviewees unprompted. Contracts are being issued by individual managers usually trading on past knowledge of individuals and their reputation and a fairly closed network. Work was awarded almost entirely through a network of contacts, with only a few instances of open tendering or cold marketing. Does this indicate a sort of return to patronage in the awarding of work? There was also an expressed view that organizations were poor at managing the transactional contract, indeed naïve in employing consultants such as themselves. It was their experience that outcomes were not clearly specified and that essential support mechanisms were not always in place and that either miracles or a very limited job of work were the requirements of them.

Conclusions

It may well be that only a minority of corporate employees, 'a small and self-conscious – or lucky – minority' (Pahl, 1995: 4) would ever embark on this type of work but it is significant that most of the people in this study have left organizations and launched themselves into a 'portfolio' working world as refugees from organizational changes in structure, culture and values. This appears to endorse those studies which argue that the push factors are the most significant. However, despite very real difficulties and drawbacks, most of the individuals are also making the best of it and finding either material success or enjoyment of the relative freedoms. Hence the idea of converting to 'portfolio' working is significant and hints at new ways of considering success in careers. This study does give some early indications that the discourse which surrounds new careers (i.e. self-managed and boundaryless) may be both constituted and reflected in the actions of individuals. It could be that if these early pioneers appear to thrive or even cope, then this type of transition may become more common for managers, whether that is by choice or circumstance.

HR managers are increasingly likely to find themselves considering how they will respond to workers who do not fit the model of permanent corporate employees. The changes may be slow and fitful but the existence in the workplace of people with a variety of work priorities is being heralded and noted more clearly than ever before. This is all the more significant when, among those who are forging new career paths, there are the erstwhile exemplars of the old career order, namely managers from bureaucracies. The idea of career as a joint project of organization and individual may be a way forward to review the new relationships which are developing with those on the so called 'periphery'. This links to the growing understanding of psychological contracts at work. Even those people who felt that their psychological contract with the organization had been violated were amenable to developing a revised relationship. While their new identity is generally subsumed under the notion of management consultant, there is evidence that many want a different relationship with organizations than that implies. There is scope for blurring of the distinctions between relational and transactional ways of approaching contracting.

It is often the role of the HR function to promote new ideas about staff management. The much vaunted notions of career self-management and a more flexible approach to contracting are relevant here. These ideas have consequences and the impact is not borne by individuals alone. The very fabric of the organization can be changed by having within its boundaries people who respond to it in different ways. The 'inside story' of the participants in this study serves to alert HR managers to the far-reaching human implications of the implementation of such corporate policies.

Notes

1 See *IRS Employment Trends* 565 for an overview of how the terms are used in various surveys and the extent to which very different working arrangements are often collapsed into one broad category, making it difficult to derive meaningful data.

References

Arthur, M.B. (1994) 'The boundaryless career: a new perspective for organizational inquiry', *Journal of Organizational Behaviour*, 15: 295–306.

Arthur, M.B., Hall, D.T. and Lawrence, B.S. (eds) (1989) *The Handbook of Career Theory*. Cambridge: Cambridge University Press.

Ashforth, B.E. and Saks, A.M. (1995) 'Work-role transitions: a longitudinal examination of the Nicholson model', *Journal of Occupational and Organizational Psychology*, 68: 157–75.

Atkinson, J. and Meager, N. (1986) 'New forms of work organization'. IMS Report 121, Institute of Management Studies, Brighton.

Bailyn, L. (1989) 'Understanding individual experiences at work: comment on the theory and practice of careers', in M.B. Arthur, D.T. Hall and B.S. Lawrence (eds), *The Handbook of Career Theory*. Cambridge: Cambridge University Press. pp. 477–89.

Bailyn, L. (1993) *Breaking the Mold: Women, Men and Time in the New Corporate World*. New York: Free Press.

Barley, S.R. (1989) 'Careers, identities and institutions', in M.B. Arthur, D.T. Hall and B.S. Lawrence (eds), *The Handbook of Career Theory*. Cambridge: Cambridge University Press. pp. 41–60.

Berger, P. and Luckmann, T. (1967) *The Social Construction of Reality*. Harmondsworth: Penguin.

Bird, A. (1994) 'Careers as repositories of knowledge: a new perspective on boundaryless careers', *Journal of Organisational Behaviour,* 15: 325–44.

Bogenhold, D. and Staber, U. (1991) 'The decline and rise of self-employment', *Work, Employment and Society,* 5: 223–39.

Bridges, W. (1995) *Job Shift: How To Prosper in a Workplace without Jobs.* London: Nicholas Brealey.

Brockner, J., Grover, S., Reed, T.G. and De Witt, R.L. (1992) 'Layoffs, job insecurity and survivors' work effort: evidence of an inverted-U relationship', *Academy of Management Journal,* 35: 413–25.

Burrows, R. and Curran, J. (1991) 'Not such a small business: reflections on the rhetoric, the reality and the future of the enterprise culture', in M. Cross and G. Payne (eds), *Work and the Enterprise Culture.* London: Falmer.

Daly, M. (1991) 'The 1980s, a decade of growth and enterprise: self-employment data from the Labour Force Survey', *Employment Gazette,* 99: 109–34.

Defillippi, R.J. and Arthur, M.B. (1994) 'The boundaryless career: a competency based perspective', *Journal of Organisational Behaviour,* 15: 307–24.

Driver, M.J. (1982) 'Career concepts – a new approach to career research', in R. Katz (ed.), *Career Issues in Human Resource Management.* Englewood Cliffs, NJ: Prentice-Hall.

Evetts, J. (1992) 'Dimensions of career: avoiding reification in the analysis of change', *Sociology,* 26: 1–21.

Golzen, G. and Garner, G. (1990) *Smart Moves.* Oxford: Blackwell.

Gowler, D. and Legge, K. (1989) 'Rhetoric in bureaucratic careers: managing the meaning of management success', in M.B. Arthur, D. T. Hall and B.S. Lawrence (eds), *The Handbook of Career Theory.* Cambridge: Cambridge University Press. pp. 437–53.

Granger, B., Stanworth, J. and Stanworth, C. (1995) 'Self-employment career dynamics: the case of "unemployment push" in UK book publishing', *Work, Employment and Society,* 9: 499–516.

Guest, D. and Davey, K.M. (1996) 'Don't write off the traditional career', *People Management,* 22 February: 22–5.

Gunz, H. (1989) 'The dual meaning of managerial careers: organisational and individual levels of analysis', *Journal of Management Studies,* 26: 225–50.

Hakim, C. (1989) 'New recruits to self-employment in the 1980s', *Employment Gazette,* June: 286–97.

Handy, C. (1994) *The Empty Raincoat: Making Sense of the Future.* London: Hutchinson.

Hecksher, C. (1995) *White Collar Blues: Management Loyalties in an Age of Corporate Restructuring.* New York: Basic Books.

Herriot, P. and Pemberton, C. (1995) *New Deals: the Revolution in Managerial Careers.* Chichester: Wiley.

Herriot, P. and Pemberton, C. (1996) 'Contracting careers', *Human Relations,* 49: 757–90.

Hewitt, P. (1993) *About Time: the Revolution in Work and Family Life.* London: IPPR/Rivers Oram Press.

Holbeche, L. (1995) 'Peering into the future of careers', *People Management,* 31 May: 26–31.

Hutton, W. (1995) *The State We're In.* London: Jonathan Cape.

Hyman, R. (1991) 'Plus ça change? The theory of production and the production of theory', in A. Pollert (ed.), *Farewell to Flexibility.* Oxford: Blackwell. pp. 259–83.

Industrial Relations Review and Report, (1994) 'Non standard working under review', *IRS Employment Trends* 565, August: 5–12.

Inkson, K. (1997) 'Organisation structure and the transformation of careers', in T. Clark (ed.), *Advancement in Organisation Behaviour.* Aldershot: Dartmouth.

Inkson, K. and Coe, T. (1994) 'Are career ladders disappearing?', *Management Auditing Journal,* 9: I–IX

Kanter, R.M. (1989) *When Giants Learn to Dance.* New York: Simon and Schuster.

Leach, J.L. and Chakiris, B.J. (1988) 'The future of work, careers and jobs', *Training and Development Journal,* April: 48–54.

Legge, K. (1995) *Human Resource Management: Rhetorics and Realities.* Basingstoke: Macmillan.

Marshall, J. (1989) 'Revisioning career concepts: a feminist invitation', in M.B. Arthur, D.T. Hall and B.S. Lawrence (eds), *The Handbook of Career Theory*. Cambridge: Cambridge University Press. pp. 275–91.

Marshall, J. (1995) *Women Managers Moving On: Exploring Career and Life Choices*. London: Routledge.

Mirvis, P. H. and Hall, D.T. (1994) 'Psychological success and the boundaryless career', *Journal of Organisational Behaviour*, 15: 365–80.

Nicholson, N. and West, M.A. (1988) *Managerial Job Change: Men and Women in Transition*. Cambridge: Cambridge University Press.

Nicholson, N. and West, M.A. (1989) 'Transitions, work histories and careers.' in M.B. Arthur, D. T. Hall and B. S. Lawrence (eds), *The Handbook of Career Theory*. Cambridge: Cambridge University Press. pp. 181–201.

Pahl, R. (1995) *After Success: Fin-de-Siècle Anxiety and Identity*. London: Polity.

Palmer, C. (1995) 'Management: white collar, black hole', *The Observer*, 12 February: 6.

Pollert, A. (ed.) (1991) *Farewell to Flexibility?* Oxford: Blackwell.

People Management (1995) Editorial, 21 December: 17.

Rainbird, H. (1991) 'The self-employed: small entrepreneurs or disguised wage labourers?', in A. Pollert (ed.), *Farewell to Flexibility*. Oxford: Blackwell. pp. 200–14.

Rosin, H.M. and Korabik, K. (1992) 'Corporate flight of women managers: moving from fiction to fact', *Women in Management Review*, 7: 31–5.

Rousseau, D.M. (1990) 'New hire perceptions of their own and their employer's obligations: a study of psychological contracts', *Journal of Organizational Behaviour*, 11: 389–400.

Rousseau, D.M. (1996) *Psychological Contracts in Organizations: Understanding Written and Unwritten Agreements*. Thousand Oaks, CA: Sage.

Savage, M., Barlow, J., Dickens, P. and Fielding, T. (1992) *Property, Bureaucracy and Culture: Middle Class Formation in Contemporary Britain*. London: Routledge.

Scase, R. and Goffee, R. (1989) *The Reluctant Manager: their Work and Lifestyles*. London: Unwin Hyman.

Schein, E. H. (1978) *Career Dynamics: Matching Individual and Organisational Needs*. Reading, MA: Addison-Wesley.

Schein, E. H. (1988) *Process Consultation,* vol. 1. Reading, MA: Addison-Wesley.

Stanworth, C. and Stanworth, J. (1995) 'The self employed without employees: autonomous or atypical?', *Industrial Relations Journal*, 26: 221–9.

Waterman, R.H., Waterman, J.A. and Collard, B.A. (1994) 'Towards the career resilient work-force', *Harvard Business Review*, July–August: 87–95.

Weick, K.E. and Berlinger, L.R. (1989) 'Career improvisation in self designing organisations', in M.B. Arthur, D.T. Hall and B.S. Lawrence (eds), *The Handbook of Career Theory*. Cambridge: Cambridge University Press. pp. 313–28.

Whyte, W.H. (1956) *The Organisation Man*. New York: Simon and Schuster.

11

Diversity Climates and Gendered Cultures: a Cross Sector Analysis

Paul Iles, Elisabeth Wilson and Deborah Hicks-Clarke

In recent years there has been a growing move to replace or complement the traditional 'discrimination, equal opportunity, positive action' paradigm in addressing issues of employment equity with an emerging 'managing diversity' paradigm. This has happened particularly in the United States in the 1980s, but also in Western Europe in the 1990s. It is argued that employee diversity can bring organizational and HR benefits to organizations if appropriately managed, such as more effective recruitment; retention and motivation of employees; more appropriate goods and services; better customer care; greater innovation and creativity; and more adaptability (e.g. Cox and Blake, 1991). However, the field is characterized by assertions, a lack of theoretical grounding, and a lack of empirical evidence for such claims. This chapter seeks to redress the balance, drawing in particular on our recent work in the area of gender and diversity at work. It seeks to utilize a variety of theoretical perspectives (the resource-based theory of the firm, requisite variety perspectives in systems theory, and organizational stakeholder theory) to present a theoretical basis for the benefits of diversity, especially gender diversity. It also presents recent empirical work which uses the *Wall Street Journal* rankings of women in management in leading US firms to analyse changes in the proportions of women in management and women in top management over the decade 1983–92, and to explore the relationships between these *Wall Street Journal* rankings and various measures of firm profitability and performance for the years 1992 and 1993. No previous research appears to have addressed the issue of whether the workforce diversity is in fact related to firm financial performance, one of the key tenets of the managing diversity paradigm.

The managing diversity framework, in its critique of previous approaches, highlights the key role played by organizational culture in realizing the claimed benefits of diversity. Hence this chapter will examine the barriers to realizing such benefits through the concept of 'gendered cultures', exploring male and female perceptions of organizational culture in several organizations in the north-west of Britain, using repertory grid analysis (Wilson, 1995). It also looks at specific aspects of culture through the concept of 'climate for diversity' and seeks to discover the determinants and consequences of diversity climates in several UK National Health Service trusts and through survey analysis. Specifically, it is hypothesized that the often-asserted benefits of diversity, especially in terms of gender, are more likely to be achieved and more likely to be effectively managed if a 'positive climate for diversity' is in place. Again, little previous research has addressed the issue of how best to *manage* diversity so as to realize its potential benefits. Our contention is that it is not so much diversity *per se*, but how effectively it is managed, that is the key to realizing its oft-proclaimed 'business benefits'.

Managing diversity in the USA and UK

As a new perspective on equal opportunity, 'managing diversity' has emerged in the 1980s in the USA and is likely to be also very influential in the UK. This perspective is often perceived as complementing, possibly even supplementing, previous approaches to employment equity based on anti-discrimination legislation, equal employment opportunity policies, and affirmative/positive action initiatives. These approaches, rooted as they are in the particular social and political agendas of the 1960s and 1970s, are increasingly seen by proponents of the diversity paradigm as outdated and unable to meet on their own the new challenges of the next millennium.

In the United States, the rise of the civil rights movement and the black rebellions of the 1960s led to a focus on 'white racism', especially as embodied in 'institutional racism' and the policies and practices of organizations. The major response was legislation, in the form of anti-discrimination and affirmative action legislation, and training white employees in 'racism awareness'. The 1970s and the rise of feminism saw gender emerge as a major focus, and the entry of women and black employees into formerly all-white, all-male sections of the workforce led to a concerted effort on harassment, whilst the rise of the gay movement led to sexual orientation also becoming a major issue. The increase in the numbers of categories receiving legislative protection (including age and military status), the increase in Asian and Hispanic migration transforming a primarily 'white oppressor, black victim' view of equality issues, and a white male backlash against forms of 'affirmative action' appear to have contributed to the popularity of the 'managing diversity' paradigm.

It is noticeable that the UK appears to have followed the USA in its approach to equality issues, modelling its legislation in part on US practice, if stopping short of full-blooded 'affirmative action' in favour of certain permitted 'positive actions' in recruitment and training. In addition it has mirrored the US in including gender and disability issues alongside race and ethnicity ones in its legislation, and in recent debate over such categories as age, sexual orientation and religion (a legislative category in Northern Ireland). It might therefore be expected that 'managing diversity' will become an increasingly important paradigm in the UK also. However, in the rest of the European Union race and ethnicity issues have never received comparable attention to gender, except in the Netherlands, perhaps because of different conceptions of citizenship. Whereas managing diversity has become of interest to organizations in continental Europe, it is seen as more related to transnational diversity and the need to build transnational teams and organizations, rather than to issues of 'domestic diversity'.

There is an interesting parallel here with the reception of human resource management (HRM) in the UK from the USA. HRM appeared to develop in the 1980s in the USA as a critique of existing models of management which failed to give issues of employee relations the strategic importance afforded them in Germany and Japan, for example (e.g. Boxall, 1996). In the UK, it was immediately contrasted with 'personnel administration', which was seen as reactive, not strategic, short-term, and focused on lower levels of employees. HRM in contrast was portrayed as proactive, strategic, long-term, and oriented towards managers in particular. Managing diversity has also been seen as a paradigmatic shift from equal opportunity. In its own self-description it often depicts itself as taking a longer-term, more proactive, more central, more strategic and more top management oriented view of equality issues than the perspective often associated with equal opportunities (Wilson and Iles, 1996). Similarly UK critics of the managing diversity approach, like UK critics of HRM, often accuse it of adopting a managerialist, individualistic and unitary view of organizations, downplaying conflicts, tensions, competing views and power differentials in its stress on the 'benefits' of managing diversity. For example, Vince (1996) contend that it offers a power-free perspective on equalities, emphasizing a consistency between mission and HRM and 'taking the politics out', so creating mechanisms for denial and control, silencing conflicts and differences. HRM in the UK has also often been seen as individualizing employment relations. However, just as in the UK, an inordinate amount of time seems to have been spent in conceptual arguments at the expense of empirical evidence (e.g. to what extent are UK organizations adopting employment practices that can be described as HRM, and what is their impact, especially on employees?). There is a pressing need to address empirical, not just conceptual, issues in diversity. This chapter seeks to do this, exploring three issues: what are the 'business benefits' of diversity? What practices prevent organizations and employees from realizing them? What steps can organizations take to remove the barriers to harnessing the potential benefits of diversity?

Managing diversity as a business issue

What has given great impetus to the managing diversity model has been the increasing realization that valuing differences makes business sense and can be a source of competitive advantage. As Copeland puts it, 'those who view diversity among employees as a source of richness and strength . . . can help bring a wide range of benefits to their organizations' (1988: 52). Such a perspective is reflected in recent texts which stress the 'diversity advantage'

(Fernandez, 1993) and the need to utilize 'women as a management strategy' (Rosener, 1995). However, diversity needs to be actively *managed*, it is claimed, if its benefits are to be realized. Many managers may be prevented from doing this effectively because of the prejudices and stereotypes they currently hold. For example, managers in general may express the view that women and minority managers need to adopt the dominant culture if they are to succeed in organizations. A focus on culture highlights one key contention of diversity proponents: that many traditional equity models, in their focus on numbers and targets, may have neglected less quantitative and more subtle aspects of how to measure equal opportunity 'success'. In some such approaches, dominant organizational cultures and climates were left unchallenged and taken for granted as long as the numbers worked out. As a result, many women and members of minority groups may have felt that they needed to deny or downplay crucial aspects of their identity in order to gain access, stay and 'succeed' – success being judged by dominant cultural criteria. Hence a focus on organizational cultures and climates becomes a key element of a diversity approach, and is a key focus of the research described in this chapter. For example, Thomas (1991) has tried to move from a solely race and gender emphasis towards employee self-realization in a diverse environment, and to a recognition that 'diversity' encompasses sexual orientation, personal background and functional experience as well as other 'visible differences', with several leading American corporations enthusiastically taking up this banner.

Such diversity initiatives in the USA have often accompanied affirmative action efforts, and may also accompany other initiatives like minority or women support groups and networks, special training programmes for women and minorities, and training for the supervision of women and minorities, such as Xerox Corporation's Balanced Workforce Strategy (Copeland, 1988: 48). In this company, commitment to affirmative action was seen as the first and most important step to workforce diversity, emphasizing behavioural expectations rather than consciousness raising. Minority and women's employee support groups were encouraged, and diversity goals set for upper-level jobs.

Thomas (1991) points out that many leading US companies have moved beyond their 1970s focus on numbers, recruitment, equal employment, and affirmative action towards creating an environment where every employee can use his or her potential in a climate which values and celebrates differences. In some companies equal opportunity initiatives have been retained to focus on legal issues, affirmative action initiatives preserved to focus on systemic change, and valuing differences programmes introduced to focus on personal and group development. Affirmative action is seen as holding the different circles of equal opportunity and valuing differences together, with appropriate policies and procedures. In other companies like Avon, with its stress on reflecting its customer base in its workforce, disillusion with affirmative action in the 1970s has caused a refocusing around how decisions are made, rather than around numbers and targets *per se* (Thomas, 1991).

It is likely that in the UK as well as in the USA 'managing diversity' will grow in importance, as it will be argued to make good business sense. Already it appears that many formerly 'equal opportunity' jobs and courses have been relabelled, and the Equal Opportunities Commission has begun to stress the 'business case' for equal opportunities, not only the ethical, moral or political case for it as a basic human right. As in the USA, the focus is likely to move from discrimination *per se* to the full utilization of all potential resources in the organization and towards issues of enhanced mobility rather than access. It is likely to be an attractive concept, embracing a broader range of issues and groups than those traditionally encompassed by equal opportunity and positive action approaches. It is also more likely to focus on organizational culture and management style than previous approaches. This is both the basis of its appeal and the source of its problems and limitations.

Theoretical frameworks

Few studies have examined the firm- or organizational-level outcomes of managerial diversity; yet conceptual arguments for expecting positive benefits can be found from general major theoretical streams in strategic management and organization theory. One major strand derives from the *resource-based theory* of competitive advantage (e.g. Barney, 1991; Grant, 1991; Kiernan, 1993). In contrast to other perspectives stressing the role of industry structure, this perspective stresses the key role played by the firm's unique resource base and distinctive internal capabilities, including those embodied in its human resources. Robins and Wiersema (1995) have shown that the ability to build distinctive capabilities and resources and exploit them whilst addressing gaps in resources seems to pay off in terms of return on investment. Recent conceptualizations of strategic management emphasizing the importance of 'core competences' (e.g. Hamel and Prahalad, 1994) also highlight the key role of leveraging unique resources and distinctive capabilities – especially if hard to imitate – in the search for competitive advantage. Employee and management capabilities are seen as first-level resources that are sustainable and hard to imitate, and therefore a key to competitive advantage. Since women managers appear to be at least as effective as male managers (Powell, 1993), firms that employ more women managers appear to be making more effective appraisal and utilization of a critical resource, and not limiting their recruitment and selection decisions to half the workforce. Firms employing more women managers appear to have been more effective in recruiting capable managers from the available talent pool. In addition the ability to manage gender diversity effectively may also be a key capability.

Some attention to this issue has been given in the HRM literature (e.g. Boxall, 1996; Wright et al., 1994) especially in the work of Kamoche (1994; 1996). Most work in strategic HRM has been dominated by the 'matching' mode which sees competitive advantage accruing from 'fitting' the firm's HR strategy to the firm's competitive strategy, life cycle stage and structure. In these models, HRM practices, including diversity management practices, should support and reinforce the firm's generic strategies or strategic type; HRM systems must be both internally integrated with each other and externally integrated with corporate strategy. This model has been criticized for its implicit unitarism and its reliance on an over-simple model of strategy, as well as having limited empirical support in its favour. The resource-based view is seen as having in contrast greater historical sensitivity and a greater sensitivity to process, as well as providing a conceptual basis for '"theorizing" the contribution of HR strategy that does not rely solely on the reactive notions of the matching model' (Boxall, 1996: 66). Firms may enjoy 'human capital advantage' through recruiting, retaining and developing talent drawn from diverse backgrounds through training and development; they may also enjoy 'human process advantage' through encouraging learning, co-operation and innovation. Innovative diversity management strategies may thus, if durable and hard to imitate, contribute to sustained competitive advantage by helping in retaining and developing staff from diverse backgrounds who do not leave or under-perform because of the firm's reneging on its side of the diversity contract or because of a lack of trust or commitment by the organization to diversity. Some see the contribution of human resources to competitive advantage as lying less in HR practices, since these are too common, well known and mobile to constitute a valuable form of advantage, and more in the nature of the human capital itself in the form of employee knowledge, skills and abilities. It is likely that both sources can make a contribution to strategic advantage. The knowledge of how to combine, implement and fine-tune effective diversity management practices may not be widely understood or perfectly translatable to other contexts. Whether innovative diversity management practices are indeed valuable in generating and sustaining competitive advantage, as the resource-capability perspective suggests, deserves further research (Kamoche and Mueller, 1995).

Requisite variety theory, derived from systems theory, suggests that the internal environment of a system must be at least as 'complex' as its external environment. This also supports the contention that increasingly diverse external environments call for increasingly diverse internal environments (Iles, 1995). Internal diversity may, as we have seen, lead to a greater diversity of perspectives and more creative, synergistic problem-solving. *Stakeholder management theory* also supports the view that gender diversity may lead to firm-led benefits, as more diverse workforces may be more responsive to diverse stakeholder groups. For Freeman, 'Organizations with high stakeholder management capabilities allocate resources in a manner consistent with stakeholder concerns' (1984: 80). Such firms may be more effective, as they can better serve diverse stakeholder groups, and firms with high levels of gender diversity may be in a better position to connect with diverse employees, customers and other constituencies, a view explicitly taken in some feminist treatments (e.g. Wicks et al., 1994). Therefore, resource-based theories of competitive advantage, requisite variety theories and stakeholder management theories all support the view that employee and management diversity can enhance organizational performance in dynamic, diverse and complex environments. However, little evidence exists for the proposition that gender, race or cultural diversity can impact positively on organizational-level performance measures. Recent research suggests that this may be the case for gender diversity in management, though admittedly consultancy based. Katzenbach et al. (1995) in their study of company change efforts, for example, assert that human resources have been under-utilized, particularly women and especially women middle-level managers highly attuned to change. Jelinek and Adler (1985) found that women expatriates were seen as particularly good at developing interpersonal relations and co-operative alliances, whilst Rosener (1995) argues that firms fully utilizing the diverse talents of women managers are in a position to gain competitive advantage. What is required, however, is more systematic work that addresses the issue of whether firm financial performance is indeed linked to gender diversity, which is one of the strands of our recent research initiatives.

Gendered cultures in UK organizations

If the theoretical arguments and exploratory research evidence reported earlier are valid, then increased gender diversity in management is likely to confer significant firm-level benefits. Yet within the UK, despite women forming over 43 per cent of the workforce (Hanna, 1991), even fewer women are in management or top management positions than in the US (12 per cent and 1–2 per cent in 1988, according to Davidson and Cooper, 1992). Why should such horizontal and vertical segregation persist, given the apparent cost of restricting the full utilization of human resources in this way? A variety of explanations have been offered, ranging from deficit theories positing female deficiency in intellect, personality, ambition or leadership skills to structural explanations focusing on the blocks and barriers faced by women, whether societal, educational or organizational (e.g. restricted training and development, career paths, biased selection methods, etc.). Domestic responsibilities and the structuring of family relationships are also often cited. Recent US surveys (e.g. Fisher, 1992; Biley and Manoocherhri, 1995) show that men are not comfortable with women in senior management positions. Other arguments emphasize choice: women may choose not to enter management or pursue a career in it because they perceive the cost of surmounting the perceived barriers to be too high, and because they wish not to behave in the 'male style' apparently necessary for managerial success (Marshall, 1994). This hypothesis clearly identifies the issue of *organizational culture* as a critical factor in explaining barriers causing under-representation in management. Only rarely, however (e.g. Cockburn, 1991; Maddock and Parkin, 1993), has organizational culture been studied from a gender perspective in terms of how gendered aspects of culture are anchored, embedded, produced, reproduced and sustained. A specific aim of the research described here is to explore how the principles of organizational culture support and reproduce its gendered aspects.

In order to address this issue, three organizations in the north of England, chosen to represent both public and private sectors, have been studied using repertory grid interviews with male and female managers (Stewart et al., 1981), supplemented by workshop sessions (Schein, 1992) and documentary evidence. In all three cases, both general and gendered aspects of the organizational culture have been explored, with a focus on managerial success and how people progressed in the company in terms of promotion and career development. All organizations had an equal opportunities policy, but commitment to it and the extent of its implementation varied from extensive to negligible. The assumption guiding the research was that cultures are integrally cast in terms of gender (Hearn et al., 1989). As Acker (1990) states, 'To say that an organization, or any other analytic unit, is gendered means that advantage and disadvantage, exploitation and control, action and emotion, meaning and identity, are patterned through and in terms of a distinction between male and female, masculine and feminine.' The extent to which these features are evident in the case study organizations is discussed below.

Westco

Westco is a privatized public utility. To rise to middle management, the Westco employee needs a background in one of the main divisions, all traditional male enclaves. Above this level, managerial qualifications and experience gained elsewhere are important. Vision, analytical ability and problem-solving are put above leadership and 'man management' (*sic*). Being presentable and articulate is associated with success, as is working long hours and the ability to play organizational politics. Alongside espoused company values of competitiveness and entrepreneurial behaviour, there is a risk-averse attitude to decision-making. Both physical artifacts and behaviour indicate a time orientation towards the past when the company faced few competitors, there was a traditional, predominantly white male culture, and women were kept in their place, principally in the lower levels and in support services. Recently some women managers have risen to higher positions or been appointed from outside. Both male and female managers identified that female managers were often ignored in meetings, and pointed to gendered assumptions and stereotypes reinforcing myths about women's unsuitability for entry into the main (traditionally male) divisions of the company. Golf, an unofficial men's club, and a paternalistic 'protective' culture (e.g. in relation to women swearing) also tended to exclude women from participating, with little commitment to equal opportunities. Two younger male managers referred to hostility towards women managers stemming from changes to maternity regulations.

Whilst top management overtly championed a more participative and democratic style, manifestations of a 'macho' management style abounded. Gender as an organizing principle was evident when comparing the main case study organization, shaped by white male heterosexist assumptions, with Servco, one of its successful subsidiaries. This subsidiary was principally staffed and directed by women, and provided a service only marginally related to Westco's core business. In Servco mistakes were seen as a way to learn, a high value was put on communication, a positive attitude was demanded, and all staff regardless of job role were expected to contribute actively to the improvement of the service. Its culture was much more future oriented and expressive, though some staff saw it as resembling a compulsory holiday-camp.

NHS Trust

The NHS Trust (hereafter the Trust) is headed by a dynamic woman Chief Executive. It has been a consistently good performer with reference to the NHS Patient's Charter standards. Whilst the case study was under way three out of five executive directors were women, and women were well represented among the managers. To see this in context, the NHS nationally consists of 75 per cent female employees (NHS Management Executive, 1992).

Desired managerial characteristics identified by respondents were a mixture of personal attributes, relevant experience, managerial skills and what might be termed a 'managerial outlook'. First and foremost one needed a pleasant personality to succeed. One male manager said that he had noticed throughout his career in the NHS that a stress was put on being a 'nice person'. Other personal attributes identified included drive and ambition, closely related to having a dynamic personality, a strong character, being assertive, confident, tough, able to withstand pressure, and articulate. Also mentioned were honesty and personal presentation. In discussing everyday managerial skills there was a heavy emphasis towards 'people skills'; most often mentioned were participatory, facilitative and collaborative skills. A high premium was put on communication skills and on having an open and informal style of management. This is perhaps best illustrated by the personal style of the Chief Executive, whom everyone refers to as 'Sarah'. The communications strategy included monthly meetings throughout the Trust, at different locations and places, where current Trust plans are presented to staff by Sarah and her team, and any member of staff can ask a question. The required managerial outlook involves being corporate in outlook, allied to commitment and vision. Political awareness and the constructive use of power and conflict were valued, as were proactivity and innovative behaviour. To summarize the desired managerial characteristics, there seems to be an active mixture of the strong and the nice, analogous in some ways to the androgynous style of management described by Bem (1975).

Within the Trust, gender does not seem to be a particularly significant issue. There are pockets of male chauvinism, such as pinups in one department, and calling women 'love', but these are not felt to be seriously detrimental to women. Although no significant difference was evident between male and female respondents in relation to what they saw as a successful manager in the

NHS, gender has been an issue in relation to promotions. As one of the founder members of Opportunity 2000, the initiative to improve the quantity and quality of women's contribution in the workplace (Opportunity 2000, 1995), the NHS has set up a national Women's Unit to give positive encouragement to the promotion of women. The Trust already had a number of competent women just below Board level, and on incorporation the new management team had a majority of women. The male managers said that at this time it was well known in the NHS that there was no point applying for certain posts if you were a man. However, whilst they alleged that unsuitable female directors had been appointed elsewhere, they were full of praise for the competence of their own female managerial colleagues. Perhaps because of this good record in promoting women, the Trust may be tempted into complacency. Whilst the predominance of women managers is accepted within the Trust, outside it may be denigrated as 'petticoat management', and this may indicate its vulnerability within the larger culture of the NHS (Alimo-Metcalfe, 1991). The mostly male consultants formed a subculture largely resistant to the changes taking place around them.

Leisure Services Department

The Leisure Services Department has four main divisions: Museums and Arts, Libraries, Service Development and Direct Services. The last includes a number of manual services for which the council won competitive tenders, such as highways and grounds maintenance. There is a common commitment to enhancing the leisure activities and artistic enjoyment of the inhabitants of the area, and the department is proud both of the quality of its front-line staff in all divisions and its ability to balance a budget of over £20 million down to the last £60.

In exploring desirable managerial characteristics, a much less coherent picture emerged than is the case for Westco and the Trust. This appeared to be related to the diversity between divisions. On a personal level, to be successful a manager needed to be dynamic, committed and of smart appearance (the last mentioned much more by women). Tension existed between promoting internally and recruiting outsiders. The latter were welcomed for their fresh ideas, but increasingly retrenchment and redeployment made external recruitment all but impossible. Qualifications, both professional and managerial, were helpful but not necessary to rise to the top; of more value were outside professional links. Valued managerial skills included interpersonal skills, being good at organization and holding your own in debates. Caring for staff was mentioned less often. To get to the top, important features identified included being innovatory and politically aware, necessitating building relationships with councillors. Corporate understanding and working long hours were also identified as requisites for success.

As in Westco, the day-to-day processing of gender in Leisure Services included verbal put-downs of women, gender stereotyping, and clashes of management style between the directive and the participative. Women managers felt constrained by their gender, despite a strong equal opportunities commitment by the council as a whole. Of more consequence is the gendering of divisions. Roper (1994) observes that even within a department certain sections and activities can be perceived as male and female. Museums and Arts is seen as the 'arty farty' lot, indecisive and over-consultative. It is definitely female, and this colours the view by outsiders of the competent male deputy, who is not quite 'one of the boys'. Libraries has an overwhelmingly female staff, but is now headed up by a new keen male Assistant Director who has won funding as the UK partner in a leading EU information project. Perceived as traditionally female, its image is now more indeterminate. Both of these divisions can be contrasted with the others, which view themselves as being involved with more down-to-earth concerns, and which are alleged to have more robust, even macho, management styles; their gender is seen as male. These contradictions and tensions were held in check by the former Director, universally liked and respected and recently promoted, and the department was (1996) awaiting a new appointment.

To summarize, in both Westco and Leisure Services there is internal conflict about management style. Gender is a key organizing principle, keeping some people (mostly women) in their place, constraining the behaviour of both men and women, and thus limiting a diversity of contribution to their respective organizations. Servo's small size and overwhelmingly female staff make evaluation more difficult. Only in the Trust did there seem to be a true valuing of people for what they could deliver, regardless of gender, and this was seen to be an exception within the NHS. Gendered cultures, embedded in individual organizational cultures, are therefore a key obstacle to enabling a diverse workforce, to realize its potential.

What do climates for diversity deliver for the individual?

In the research reported here, we were interested in examining 'climates for diversity'; in other words, exploring the degree to which there was a climate in which human resource diversity was valued and in which employees from diverse backgrounds felt valued and included. We were particularly interested in the National Health Service, as traditionally this has employed many women and may be an area where women are making significant career progress. With the coming of trust status to the vast majority of health care organizations in Britain, changes in the culture of the NHS have been noted. For example, Maddock and Parkin (1993) have asserted that a 'smart macho' culture is now present in the NHS, one which may inhibit women in particular from achieving high status. Such a culture, they argue, demands long hours from its workers so that a new breed of manager is growing, usually a single young man.

Drawing on Kossek and Zonia's (1993) research on diversity climates in American universities, we developed a model with three main factors as likely determinants of diversity climates: (a) demographic mix, in terms of diversity; (b) organizational justice, both distributive and procedural justice (Iles and Robertson, 1995); (c) commitment by the organization to employees, especially in terms of diversity.

We then selected three hypothesized outcomes of a climate for diversity for employees: (a) individual career achievement (including career commitment, career satisfaction and career aspirations/plans); (b) satisfaction with job and supervisor; (c) commitment to the organization by employees.

One hypothesis selected for analysis was that if a positive climate for diversity was present in an organization, then both men and women will feel more committed in terms of their jobs and careers. We also hypothesized that managers in organizations with stronger positive climates for diversity would be more accepting of diversity and diversity initiatives, and also that women will generally be more positive towards diversity and diversity initiatives than men. Women may, however, consider that they have fewer opportunities than men in their organizations. However, in organizations where diversity is valued, white men may have more understanding of the problems that minorities and women have, compared with other organizations.

A study of two NHS trusts

Two NHS trusts in the north-west of Britain were surveyed in the first phase of the research ($n = 116$ employees). The questionnaire was given to managers as they are the ones who are held to influence climate in an organization, as Schnieder et al. (1994) have pointed out. Research has shown (Cox, 1994) that managers' commitment to diversity is also crucial to organizational acceptance of diversity and to developing a positive climate for diversity.

Both trusts served the local community, but were in different environments. Trust A ($n = 56$) was in a town which had a large elderly community, and Trust B was in the middle of a city which had experienced severe economic problems. Trust A had become a centre of excellence for certain types of medicine, and outside health authorities would use their services. Trust A was the main hospital in the area, whereas in the case of Trust B several hospitals were in the vicinity. It was considered that both trusts were similar in a number of ways, as both had casualty wards, both served the local community, and both were relatively large organizations.

The questionnaire used was devised in order to assess climate for diversity and explore individual and organizational outcomes. Measures used were largely Likert scale items, although some closed questions were also used in order to find out 'facts' about individuals and their knowledge of benefits in their own organizations. The scales selected measured each concept in the model: outcomes (individual career achievement, job/supervisor satisfaction, career commitment) and diversity climate indicators (demographic mix, benefits and procedures, organizational justice). Closed questions were used for demographic mix and commitment by the organization. Attitude scales were used for other indicators and outcomes: organizational justice, individual career achievement (with scales measuring career commitment, career satisfaction and career aspirations/plans), job/supervisor satisfaction and commitment to the organization by employees. Individual career achievement was made up of four parts: career commitment (from the work of Blau, 1985 on career satisfaction), a Likert-style scale to measure career future satisfaction (Scarpello and Campbell, 1980); career aspirations/plans measured by a Likert-style scale (Gould, 1979); and newly created items. Career planning had items drawn from the work of Gould (1979) and newly created items.

Kossek and Zonia's (1993) attitude measures of organizational support for diversity initiatives were included in the questionnaire as measuring individual attitudes to diversity. It was hypothesized that in organizations with a more positive climate for diversity, all managers will score more highly on the Kossek and Zonia measures.

The data were input on to a data base in the Statistics Package for Social Scientists (SPSS) and analysed by variable, and also by gender and management level. The replies to the questionnaire were not evenly balanced, so there were not the same number of replies for each category. Favourable alpha scores were recorded for all scale measurements (a typical alpha score was 0.7).

A positive correlation was shown between organizational justice and individual career achievement, satisfaction with job and supervisor and commitment to the organization. However, little correlation was shown between commitment by the organization and the outcomes. It could be that as the NHS employs women, women managers are either used to seeing women in managerial positions or perhaps felt they had to answer in a way which suggested women had to change as much as men in the organization. Follow-up interviews may be able to explore these possibilities.

Determinants of diversity climates

Organizational justice   In Trust A, managers overall were more positive about organizational justice being present. However, a difference between men and women was noted; women were neutral about the presence of organizational justice in their trust, whereas men believed it to be present. In Trust B, there seems to be very little difference; overall both men and women were both neutral about its presence. However, in both organizations the mean score increased at each higher management level. This suggests that those who are higher in terms of management level in both instances believe there to be more organizational justice present than those on a lower management rung.

Commitment by the organization   Commitment by the organization in terms of policies and knowledge of those policies was stronger in Trust B than in Trust A. Trust B had a slightly higher mean response in support for diversity initiatives (scale mean 15.7) compared with Trust A (scale mean 14.6). For support for minorities and women, both organizations recorded the same mean score. Women in both organizations were slightly more positive towards diversity and diversity initiatives than men were.

Outcomes for diversity climates

Individual career achievement   Men were more positive about their individual career achievement than were women. There was, however, only one significant difference in career future satisfaction, where women's mean was 4.1 compared with men's of 4.6. In both organizations, as the level of management increased then so did the individual career achievement score. In Trust A men scored slightly higher than women. In Trust B, women scored slightly higher than men. Generally, the level of individual career achievement reported was higher in B than in A.

Satisfaction with current supervisor and job   In both organizations employees were generally satisfied with their current job and supervisor. However, men were slightly more satisfied with their current supervisor and jobs than women.

Organizational commitment   Organizational commitment increased with management level. This was more distinct in Trust A, where mean item score increased from 4.95 at junior level to 6.09 at senior level. An increase was also present in Trust B, but less dramatic. In Trust A, male managers were more committed than female managers: females were committed and males strongly committed to the organization. In Trust B, both male and female managers were equally committed to the organization. Women in Trust A were not as committed to the organization, their jobs or their careers as were those female managers in Trust B.

Both organizations appear to have positive climates for diversity to some extent. In Trust A organizational justice is more highly perceived to be present than in Trust B. However, demographic mix and commitment by the organization are better represented in Trust B.

One hypothesis, that women would be more committed to diversity and diversity initiatives than men, was borne out by the research, though not as much as we had expected. One important finding is that opinions and perceptions of the organization change with management levels and with organizational affiliation.

More research needs to address the issue of climate for diversity, and its link with the hypothesized outcomes. There does seem to be some difference between men's and women's experience of climate for diversity. We plan as the next stage of the research to interview managers in the organization in order to explore further their understanding of diversity climates.

Conclusions and implications for policy

Organizations will increasingly need to address the issue of diversity as their workforces, customer bases and stakeholder groups become increasingly diverse on many dimensions. The resource-based theory of competitive advantage, requisite variety theory, and stakeholder theory, as well as empirical research on small-group performance and top-team strategies, all suggest that diversity can confer significant organization-level advantages on organizations able to capitalize on them. The research discussed in this chapter relating women in management to firm financial performance certainly suggests this is the case for gender; research on other dimensions of diversity remains to be done. Research discussed here, however, also demonstrates the continuing blocks and barriers faced by women in management. These blocks and barriers are often inherent in the culture of the organization in terms of taken-for-granted assumptions about managerial effectiveness and 'success recipes' for what makes an effective manager.

However, though the research and theoretical perspectives discussed suggest that gender and other aspects of diversity may confer 'business benefits', a number of qualifications to this argument must be raised. In the first place, we think it mistaken to stress solely the 'business case' for diversity if it implies the neglect of other justifications based on treating equal opportunity as a basic human right. The 1980s attachment of the equal opportunities case to the anticipated 'demographic downturn' and the de-emphasizing of political and ethical arguments in favour of 'business' ones should lead us to express some caution in this area. Secondly, the concept of diversity is useful both tactically in engaging white men who otherwise may feel excluded from an equal opportunities discourse, and strategically in focusing not just on numbers but on management styles and organization cultures. However, the focus on diversity goals can lead to a neglect of equality goals. Thirdly, diversity in itself is unlikely to confer organizational benefits: it is more likely to do so if organizations adopt appropriate strategies towards it and organizational members develop appropriate skills to manage it (Iles, 1995). Finally, important among these skills and strategies will be the ability to question, re-evaluate and change, where necessary, taken-for-granted assumptions of management, organization and effectiveness, given the gendered nature of all three. Procedural and legislative changes (for example, introducing formal selection and promotion procedures that promise bias-free, objective selection and assessment) may be necessary, but they are not sufficient. Illegal and unfair discriminatory practices may still continue, but remain masked by reference to an apparently technical objective and scientific rhetoric (Iles and Robertson, 1995). This chapter suggests that an interrogation of often deep, hidden cultural assumptions about what constitutes success and effectiveness – questions that address both the accepted 'theory of the firm' and the 'theory of management' – may be necessary if the potential benefits and advantages of diversity are to be realized, both for organizations and for organizational members. In particular, our exploratory research on 'climates for diversity' suggests that it is an important facet of organizational culture which may well impact on individual performance and the experience of employees. Showing commitment to diversity in terms of policies and practices in all the HRM areas such as recruitment, selection, training, appraisal and career development, as well as in terms of grievances and discipline, may well be necessary to generate such a climate. Further, this should be carried out in such a way that it not only meets criteria of 'distributive justices (where outcomes are felt to be fair) but also criteria of 'procedural justice' (where the procedures used to make HRM decisions are also seen as fair and just). The perception of these attributes, judging from our research, varies with management level and with gender, supporting our contention that organizational cultures are gendered. Such findings give even more support to the need to get the 'inside story' on HRM and explore how individuals in different categories and at different levels actually experience the impact of HRM policies, and what significance this has for career and organizational attitudes and behaviour.

References

Acker, J. (1996) 'Hierarchies, jobs, bodies: a theory of gendered organization', *Gender and Society*, 4 (2): 139–58.

Alimo-Metcalfe, B. (1991) 'What a waste! Women in the National Health Service', *Women in Management Review*, 6 (5): 68–83.

Barney, J. (1991) 'Firm resources and sustained competitive advantage', *Journal of Management*, 17: 99–120.

Bem, S.L. (1975) 'Sex role adaptability: one consequence of psychological androgeny', *Journal of Consulting and Clinical Psychology*, 3: 634–43

Biley, S. and Manoocherhri, G. (1995) 'Breaking the glass ceiling', *American Business Review*, 13 (June): 33–40.

Blau, G. (1985) 'The measurement and prediction of career commitment', *Journal of Occupational Psychology*, 56: 277–88.

Boxall P, (1996) 'The strategic HRM debate and the resource-based view of the firm', *Human Resource Management Journal*, 6 (3): 59–75.

Cockburn, Cynthia (1991) *In the Way of Women: Men's Resistance to Sex Equality in Organizations*. London: Macmillan.

Copeland, L. (1988) 'Valuing diversity: making the most of cultural differences at the workplace', *Personnel*, June, 55–60.

Corporate Yellow Book, vol. 9. New York: Leadership Directories Inc.

Cox, T. (1994) *Cultural Diversity in Organizations: Theory and Practice'*. San Francisco: Barrett-Koehler.

Cox, T. and Blake, S. (1991) 'Managing cultural diversity: implications for organizationnal competitiveness', *Academy of Management Executive*, 5: 45–56.

Davidson, Marilyn and Cooper, Cary (1992) *Shattering the Glass Ceiling: the Woman Manager*. London: Paul Chapman.

Fernandez, J. (1993) *The Diversity Advantage*. Lexington, MA: Lexington Books.

Fisher, A.B. (1992) 'When will women get to the top?', *Fortune*, 21 September: 44–56.

Freeman, R.E. (1984) *Strategic Management: a Stakeholder Approach*. Marshfield, MA: Pitman Publishing.

Gould, S. (1979) 'Characteristics of career planners in upwardly mobile occupations', *Academy of Management Journal*, 22: 539–50.

Grant, R.M. (1991) 'The resource-based theory of competitive advantage: implications for strategy formulation', *California Management Review*, 33: 114–35.

Hamel, G. and Prahalad, C.K. (1994) *Competing for the Future: Breakthrough Strategies for Seizing Control of your Industry and Creating the Markets of Tomorrow*. Boston: Harvard Business School Press.

Hanna, Lynn (1991): 'Just the job?', *The Guardian*, 22 October: 20.

Iles, P.A. (1995) 'Learning to work with difference', *Personnel Review*, 24 (6): 44–60.

Iles, P. and Robertson, P. (1995) 'Impact of personnel selection on candidates', in N. Anderson and P. Herriot (eds), *Assessment and Selection in Organizations*. Chichester: Wiley.

Jelinek, M. and Adler, N.J. (1988) 'Women: world class managers in global competition', *Academy of Management Executive*, 2: 11–19.

Kamoche, K. (1994) 'A critique and proposed reformulation of strategic human resource management', *Human Resource Management Journal*, 414: 29–43.

Kamoche, K. (1996) 'Strategic human resource management within a resource capability view of the firm', *Journal of Management Studies*, 33 (2): 213–33.

Kamoche, K. and Mueller F. (1995) 'Human resources and competitive advantage: an appropriability-learning perspective'. Paper presented at the Conference on Strategic Human Resource Management, Nottingham Trent University, December.

Kandola, R. (1993) 'Managing diversity, keynote address to British Psychological Society Occupational Psychology Conference, Brighton.

Kandola, R. and Fullerton, J. (1994) *Managing the Mosaic*. London: Institute of Personnel and Development.

Katzenbach, J.R., Beckett, F., Dichter, S., Fergen, M., Gragman, C., Hope, Q. and Ling, R. (1995) *Real Change Leaders: How You Can Create Growth and High Performance at Your Company*, New York Times Books, Random House.

Kiernan, M.J. (1993) 'The new strategic architecture: learning to compete in the twenty-first century'. *Academy of Management Executive*, 7 (February): 7–21.

Kossek, E. and Zonia, S. (1993) 'Assessing diversity climate: a field study of reactions to employer efforts to promote diversity', *Journal of Organisational Behaviour*, 14: 61–81.

Maddock, S. and Parkin, D. (1993) 'Gender cultures: women's choices and strategies at work', *Women in Management Review*, 8 (2): 3–9.

Marshall, Judi (1994) 'Why women leave management jobs', in M. Tanton (ed.), *Women in Management: a Developing Presence*. Chichester: Wiley.

NHS Management Executive (1992) *Women in the NHS: an implementation guide to Opportunity 2000*. London: Department of Health.

Opportunity 2000 (1995) *Opportunity 2000 Information Pack*. London: Business in the Community.

Powell, G. (1993) *Women in Management*. London: Sage.

Robins, R. and Wiersema, M.F. (1995) 'A resource-based approach to the multibusiness firm: empirical analysis of portfolio interrelationships and corporate financial performance', *Strategic Management Journal*, 16: 277–99.

Roper, M. (1994) *Masculinity and the British Organizational Man since 1945*. Oxford: Oxford University Press.

Rosener, J.B. (1995) *America's Competitive Secrets: Utilizing Women as a Management Strategy*. New York: Oxford University Press.

Scarpello, V. and Campbell, J. (1980) 'Job satisfaction and the fit between individual needs and organisational rewards', *Journal of Occupational Psychology*, 56: 315–28.

Schein, E. (1992) *Organizational Culture and Leadership* (2nd edn). San Francisco: Jossey-Bass.

Schneider, B. (1972) 'Organizational climate: individual preferences and organizational Realities', *Journal of Applied Psychology*, 56 (3): 211–17.

Schneider, B. and Bartlett, C.J. (1968) 'Individual difference and organizational climate: 1. The research plan and questionnaire development', *Personnel Psychology*, 21: 323–33.

Schneider, B., Wheeler, J.K. and Cox, J.F. (1992) 'A passion for service: using content analysis to explicate service themes', *Journal of Applied Psychology*, 77 (5): 705–16.

Schneider, B. Gunnarson, S.K. and Niles-Jolly, D. (1994) 'Creating the climate and culture of success', *Organizational Dynamics*, 23 (1): 17–29.

Schneider, N. and Hall, D.T. (1972) 'Towards specifying the concept of work climate: a study of Roman Catholic diocesan priests', *Journal of Applied Psychology*, 56 (6): 447–55.

Stewart, V., Stewart, A. and Fonda, N. (1981) *Business Applications of Repertory Grid*. London: McGraw-Hill.

Thomas, R.R. (1991) *Beyond Race and Gender*. New York: AMACOM.

Vince, R. (1996) Conference paper at the British Academy of Management Annual Conference, September.

Walker, B. (1994) 'Valiuing differences: the concept and a model', in C. Mabey and P.A. Iles (eds), *Managing Learning*, London: Sage.

Wicks, A.C., Gilbert, D.R. Jr and Freeman, R.E. (1994) 'A feminist reinterpretation of the stakeholder concept', *Business Ethics Quarterly*, 4: 475–97.

Wilson, E. (1995) 'The constraints of gendered culture'. Presentation to Standing Conference on Organizational Symbolism, Turku, Finland, June.

Wilson, E. and Iles, P.A. (1995) 'HRD and the management of diversity', in J. McGoldrick, and J. Stewart (eds), HRD: *Strategies, Issues and Perspectives*, London: Pitman.

Wright, P.M., McMahon, G.C. and McWilliams, A. (1994) 'Human resources and sustained competitive advantage: a resource based perspective', *International Journal of Human Resource Management*, 5 (2): 301–26.

12

A Trail of Clues for Graduate Trainees

Diane Preston and Cathy Hart

> There have been so many changes in this one year that I have worked here. It's been great to witness. They are being far too ambitious though, they are going far too quickly. Trying to change a culture, which is what they have done, in the space of a year, is too fast, it's not been gradual enough.

Learning about the organization and what is expected in terms of one's allocated role within it (organizational socialization) is a crucial lesson for any employee. Understanding both the formal and informal sides of the organization determines the individual's survival within it. It is necessary to know what is expected in terms of the task – job content and performance – but also in terms of the process, the interpersonal relationships and the social rules which constitute the organizational culture. In order to ascertain the nature and clarity of the information about the organization given at different stages in the socialization process from a 'receiving end' perspective, this chapter explores the experiences of a group of newcomers at Taylors PLC, a large retailing organization within the UK. The newcomers are all graduate management trainees who participate in a year-long training programme in one of Taylors's stores before moving on to a junior management position within the company.

Graduates were chosen as the focus of the study for two main reasons. Firstly, since the employment of graduates represents a major investment in managers of the future for any company, it is likely that the employer will expend time and effort in ensuring that the clues about what is expected are there for this group of employees and that they understand them as intended. Secondly, graduates are individuals who have little or no experience of the employing organization and often of employment generally. Because of this, they 'lack both a framework within which to interpret events and a set of previous job successes and failures to moderate the impact of present ones' (Arnold, 1986: 17). This should make for a receptive audience in terms of the organizational socialization clues laid down by the employer.

The chapter is structured as follows. It begins by developing the notion of organization socialization as a trail of clues for new employees to discover and understand. The context of the study is then outlined, followed by a discussion of the results.

Organizational socialization as a trail of clues

Organizational socialization can be envisaged as the employer leaving a trail
of clues for employees to understand and use in finding their way through the
organization. Recruitment criteria, job descriptions, appraisal guidelines,
management competencies and promotion prerequisites are all examples of
the types of clues laid down by senior management (usually through the
HRM department) which denote to the employee what it takes to get on in
the organization. These clues can be seen as processional, occurring at different stages of the employment cycle as employees progress through the
company. The trail of clues may be flimsy in that it is constructed in accordance with what senior management might *believe* is important or helpful to
those seeking guidance. Moreover, it may be planned without due recognition
of the multi-faceted nature of the organizational socialization process. It may
also be that different individuals may require different maps; in other words,
the number and types of clues and their degree of explicitness may need to
vary according to who the person is and what stage of their career within the
organization they are at.

A prominent theme within the literature on organizational socialization has
been the different tactics which could be used by employers to influence newcomers' thinking. Schein (1968), for example, refers to this as a process by
which beliefs are 'unfrozen' and 'refrozen'. Wanous (1990) has summarized
the main organizational socialization strategies described in the literature.
These include, among others, overt indoctrination programmes and other,
more subtle, 'seduction' techniques designed to 'unhinge' the newcomer from
previously held beliefs and values. Such strategies not only appear to demand
a great deal of thought and cunning on behalf of the managers responsible for
organizational socialization but also concentrate on changes in the individual
without sufficient acknowledgement of the organizational context in which
they take place. They imply that clues about what is expected will result in
attitudinal and behavioural change rather like a mechanical process that is
merely done to newcomers (Preston, 1991).

Furthermore, in much of the literature there appears to be an implicit
assumption that such clues will be understood by everyone in the same way
(Preston, 1993). In contrast, this chapter will argue that organizational socialization is a complex and ongoing process which is experienced differently by
individual employees. Other authors within this area (e.g. Louis, 1980; Fisher,
1985; Collin, 1986) do acknowledge the more complex side of organizational
socialization and particularly the part that newcomers play in terms of efforts
to make sense of their environment. The role of the immediate line manager
and/or mentor, for example, has received much attention and is discussed
later in relation to Taylors. Several factors could account for the different perceptions described by employees participating in the same organizational
socialization programme. The subsequent discussion relating to the research
findings presented in this chapter highlights the importance of a number of
unplanned clues around the graduate training programme at Taylors. These

appear to account for some of the differing experiences described by graduates in the study.

Another theme within the literature on organizational socialization is the idea that there are a series of stages through which the new employee passes. Typically three stages are identified: the 'anticipatory' stage (before an employee starts working for an organization); the 'entry' stage (when they begin working for an organization); and the 'accommodation' stage (after the first few months or years of employment where early experiences help to formulate and cement their impressions). Earlier stage models (for example, Buchanan, 1974; Porter et al., 1975; Schein, 1978) have been criticized for implying that the newcomer has to complete one stage before another and that variables and influences at each stage are discrete (Fisher, 1986; Bauer and Green, 1994; Mabey et al., 1996). The research design behind the Taylors study (described in detail below) is based on the three-stage concept but assumes that organizational socialization is an overall and cumulative process. Importantly, the series of clues is assumed to be a trail of understanding; each piece of paper does not need to be collected and assimilated before the next distinct piece can be acquired.

Accepting that organizational socialization is an ongoing process raises another important methodological issue: that is, at what point(s) in time the impressions of newcomers should be examined. More recent work (for example, Allen and Meyer, 1990; Bauer and Green, 1994; Mabey et al., 1996) seeks to tackle this problem by adopting a longitudinal perspective. This, it is argued, presents a more realistic view of organizational socialization in that it is a process which takes place throughout an individual's employment (Van Maanen and Schein, 1979). The difficulties of capturing a genuine picture of graduates' experiences and the factors which might affect them are discussed in detail by Mabey et al. (1996) who point out that taking a snapshot of graduates' perceptions at any stage of organizational socialization is difficult because there is no knowledge of what happened before and after, or about the ongoing factors which may have influenced responses. The authors provide a helpful discussion of these difficulties and sought to minimize their impact by conducting a six-year longitudinal study in which the same group of graduates were surveyed at three points in time: (1) two weeks before entering employment; (2) six months into it; and (3) five or six years later. However, owing to limitations of access and time it was not possible to pursue a longitudinal approach within the realms of the present study.

The context: Taylors PLC

> You can see it, the level of anxiety and the responsibility levels. It's like the department managers are walking around with a huge burden on their shoulders and they can't off-load it any more, so they'll take that with them and go and hide in a corner. They would sit together every lunch time, but they don't do that now.

In recent years, Taylors has seen radical attempts at change in terms of both structure and culture. A number of HRM initiatives have been introduced based upon a general theme of redefining the role of a manager within the company. A business process re-engineering exercise was taking place at head office at the time of the study, for example. In addition, a major organizational change programme had begun 18 months earlier in which employees from all stores participated in an extensive training course concentrating on team building, empowerment and communication skills. As a result of this managers within Taylors were beginning to be rewarded for evidence of teamwork within their stores whereas, previously, appraisal criteria had been solely concerned with store profit levels. Such initiatives have required a certain amount of 'relaying' of clues for employees within the company including graduate management trainees.

A few years before the study Taylors had produced a management document entitled a 'Strategy for fast-stream graduates'. This had laid down the guidelines for the new set of clues for graduates about the role of management within the organization. The document recommended a more demanding recruitment and training schedule; specifically, that training should increase the emphasis on the development of management skills (through fewer technical workbooks and different types of projects) and that the overall assessment of graduate trainees should be more rigorous. A key aim of the present study was to assess whether graduates within the company had recognized that these new clues had been put into place.

As we shall discuss later, the findings of the present study suggest that the overall changes taking place within Taylors have indeed had implications for graduates' understanding of the organization. The restructuring and changes to the graduate training programme have apparently created what Louis (1980) termed 'surprises' for graduates. That is, for some graduates, actual experiences did not align with anticipations. It appeared that the organizational socialization clues provided by the graduate training programme were being interpreted in a much wider context. There seemed to be a series of apparently unanticipated clues provided by factors *around* the programme which Taylors had been slow to provide or strengthen in the midst of organizational change. This supports the contention in the organizational socialization literature that there needs to be a greater focus on the overall process of sense-making for graduates. As Mabey suggested, 'future attitudes and actions in the company are likely to be shaped less by prospective expectations and more by retrospective processes of self justification' (1986: 30). In other words, it is not enough to concentrate on the design and placing of clues upfront; it is equally important to monitor how the clues are interpreted by individuals in the light of their own experience. In this context, it was the authors' intention to look beyond the design of the training programme itself and to present the more general impressions of Taylors formed by individuals who either had participated or were currently participating in the graduate training programme. We had been asked by staff within the Corporate Resourcing Department at Taylors to find out what graduates thought of the newly designed training programme. From this basis, it was also possible to explore the different stages of the organizational socialization process and the factors which appeared to influence them in the Taylors context.

The study: research methods

As described above, a common theme within the organizational socialization literature is that the process consists of various stages (what Nicholson, 1987 has referred to as the transition cycle) beginning with individuals' expectations about entering the organization through to where the employee begins to feel settled and aware of what is expected of them. Nicholson and Arnold suggest that in general 'it is true to say that organizations confidently expend most resources at the earliest of these stages . . . and pay least attention to the later stages' (1989a: 24). This study sought to establish whether this was the case within Taylors. Essentially it sought to answer the question: were the expectations built by Taylors's high-profile graduate recruitment campaign sustained through the few years of employment? As mentioned earlier, the study consisted of three parts based on the three-stage theory of organizational socialization. In the first part of the study all those graduates about to join the company were contacted. The purpose of this part of the study was to ascertain the levels of expectations created by Taylors's recruitment process. The questionnaire sent to this group asked for opinions on the recruitment and selection process they had been through and why they had applied to this particular organization. Of the 50 questionnaires distributed, 44 were returned (an 88 per cent response rate). In the second part of the study a sample of graduates (30) across all geographical areas were interviewed regarding their perceptions of recruitment but also about their experiences of the newly designed graduate training programme at Taylors. This enabled us to interview a widely located group of graduates whose experiences of the training programme itself were pertinent in their minds and to establish whether, about a year on, their perceptions of the training specifically and working for Taylors in general had been altered. All graduates in this second sample had just completed the new training programme which had been redesigned to reflect the new type of management skills being encouraged in the company. The main difference in the new programme was a de-emphasis on technical knowledge assessed by workbooks and tests and a change in the style of in-store projects undertaken. These new projects tested graduates on powers of analysis and application rather than, as before, testing technical knowledge of different areas of store management. The interviews from this second stage were transcribed and themes arising from them were used to design a second questionnaire. In the third and final part of the study a second questionnaire was sent to all graduates who had joined (and were still working for) the company over the last five years. This enabled us to survey the views of graduates at later stages of organizational socialization. Of the 202 questionnaires distributed, 105 were returned (52 per cent response rate).

Findings from the study: the set of clues about graduates

In this section we outline some of the results of the study. The discussion is organized in terms of the three stages identified earlier: anticipatory (prior to arrival), entry (during the graduate training programme, the first 12 to 18 months), and accommodation (the first five years of employment in the organization).

Anticipatory

The first part of our study concentrated on the expectations graduates had before arriving at Taylors and what appeared to have influenced this. We were particularly concerned to discover if the graduates felt that they had had enough information about the job they were going to be doing and the training programme they were about to embark upon. When asked what had most attracted them to apply to Taylors, the majority replied 'likely future career prospects' (73 per cent) and 'the graduate training scheme' (66 per cent). The next two most popular reasons were that Taylors was one of the largest UK retailers (50 per cent) and the image of the company (52 per cent).

The clues provided at the recruitment stage intended to attract graduates to Taylors had apparently worked: 30 per cent of respondents said it was their only job application, 16 per cent said it was their first choice and another 30 per cent said it was in the top five of the companies they had considered. Asked where they had learnt about Taylors as an employer, 59 per cent said the graduate brochure, 39 per cent through a personal contact and others from across a range of graduate careers publications. Almost half (41 per cent) of respondents said that the information they had received from Taylors had made them more motivated to apply, whilst 52 per cent felt their motivation level had been about the same, the main reasons given for this being that their motivation to apply had been very high to start with. Almost all had found the supplied information helpful although, in terms of providing enough detail about more specific elements, respondents were a little more reticent. A significant minority thought that they had *not* had enough information about the training programme (32 per cent), career prospects (39 per cent), pay and conditions (39 per cent) and their specific role within the company (45 per cent). It is interesting that, despite a relatively high percentage of graduates stating that not enough information had been provided about career prospects and the graduate training programme at Taylors, these still remained their main reasons for wanting to work there.

In sum, the expectations of the graduates about to start work with Taylors were high. Taylors benefited from being an extremely well-known organization and from having a reputation within the industry for providing excellent training for graduates. The graduate brochure appeared to have played an important part in shaping applicants' anticipations and the very positive impressions of the recruitment and selection process itself had built high expectations. Taylors had apparently made efforts to provide an honest view of the job of a graduate trainee but some of the clues provided may have been somewhat blurred. It is clearly important that graduates begin on the right trail within a new organization; over-inflated expectations may cause later clues to be misread or overlooked.

Entry

Having built up certain expectations of being an employee within Taylors, graduates found the next important set of clues waiting for them on arrival – at their first training store. Questions in the interviews and survey were put to graduates who had worked within Taylors for varying periods (anything between five months and five years) to encourage them to think back to those factors which they remembered as being significant on entry; that is, in the first few days of employment within a Taylors store. Responses to the question regarding graduates' first impressions of training stores showed that, generally, graduates seemed happy with locations (only 19 per cent found it 'disappointing') and a relatively friendly environment. Many had, however (as ascertained from comments in the interviews and written on returned questionnaires), been expecting closer support from management level during their training than was actually experienced. Several trainees expressed the view that managers seemed unaware that they were due to arrive, what their role was to be and the demands put upon graduates to complete the training within the required period. For example, one trainee said:

> The first day I was a little bit distressed because I turned up and I was supposed to see the personnel manager. She wasn't here, it was her day off. So I asked to see the store manager; he wasn't here, it was his day off. They had known for months that I was coming to the store, so I didn't really have a great start.

The issue of how much support was available appeared to vary according to the training store. A little under half (43 per cent) of the interviewees, for example, said that they had found their store managers to be supportive and encouraging. Other managers were perceived to be too busy and unapproachable. One graduate commented: 'I don't know if store managers see trainees as a resource or a hindrance.'

Similarly, only 38 per cent of graduates in the survey felt that their departmental managers (middle management within a store) had given a high level of support. This is surprising considering that they may have experienced similar problems during their own training. One interviewee suggested that, instead of trying to improve the situation for other trainees, they appeared ready to perpetuate the attitude of 'we never got any time for it so you are not going to be given time for it. We did it at home; we all passed, you all pass.'

As outlined earlier, the underlying theme of the recent culture change initiatives in Taylors had been that managers should be involved in encouraging their employees to work as a team and empowering them to take more responsibility for the day-to-day running of the store. This ethos was also

meant to be reflected in the changes made to the graduate management training programme in terms of not only the types of project undertaken by
trainees but also the level of support received from store managers. This
required a major change in attitude and behaviour for most store managers
within Taylors as the concern – and basis of reward – had always been the
profit levels of the store. Part of a store manager's extended responsibilities
was to play a direct part in the individual graduate trainees' training programme – a role model providing vital clues as to what 'manager' meant in a
Taylors context.

Another intended clue to help graduates was the provision of an assigned
mentor for each trainee. Findings from the survey, however, showed that
about a quarter (23 per cent) of respondents had received no support from
mentors and only a fifth (20 per cent) of those who had been assigned a
mentor thought that the level of support they had received had been high.
This would appear to be a significant omission in the training programme in
that the literature on mentoring suggests it to be a significant learning tool for
graduates (see, for example, Kram, 1985). One graduate at Taylors felt that
the mentoring aspect might be more important than the specifics of the training programme itself:

> There should be regular meetings with mentors to discuss trainees' needs and con-
> cerns rather than constantly testing theoretical knowledge and ability to boot lick.

There is also evidence in the literature to suggest that having an assigned
mentor as opposed to *not* having one can result in positive career progression
for the graduate (Fagenson, 1989; Scandura, 1992). Mentors potentially offer
vital clues to the graduate in terms of understanding their work (Ostroff and
Kozlowki, 1992) and accelerating the organizational socialization process.
Certainly, when asked in the interviews about how the training programme
could be improved, several graduates at Taylors suggested 'official mentors
should be assigned in each department' or 'appoint a mentor for each trainee
at store and at district level'.

It was the other trainees within Taylors who appeared to offer the most
support (67 per cent of respondents thought peer support had been high)
whether from within the same store or at other stores. The 'insight days' and
training courses (where provided), as another planned part of the graduate
training programme, gave an opportunity for graduates to share experiences:

> What gets you through is when you go to these training centres and talk to the other
> trainee managers and you realize it's not the world that is just against you, it's like
> that for everyone.

Area and district offices personnel were perceived to offer the least support
(only 8 per cent and 16 per cent of graduates respectively felt they had
received a high level of support), mainly through unfulfilled promises.

> You would ring up for advice and get, yes, we'll sort it out. We met a personnel offi-
> cer for trainee managers, she said we'll fighting for your training time. She
> turned up in our store to ask if there were any problems and that was the last we
> saw of her.

Accommodation

An integral part of the training scheme was intended to be that graduates should receive ongoing support from store managers and district personnel in the form of, for example, assessment of work and training courses run at district offices. However, this link in the trainee managers' overall development appeared to have been overlooked in the case of some individuals. District managers also scored very low in the survey on the amount of support they had given trainees in the study; only 14 per cent said that support from this source had been high. One respondent, for example, commented that 'on completing the training programme I would have liked more support, perhaps meeting with district personnel to discuss subsequent development and progression.' Almost half of respondents (47 per cent) cited insight days (training days provided by district offices) as a method of training in the programme as 'very relevant' or 'relevant' but, importantly, some 42 per cent responded that they had not actually been given the opportunity to attend them as part of their training programme.

Several studies (Arnold, 1986; Nicholson and Arnold, 1989b, for example) have identified common factors in the successful content and design of jobs for graduates such as social support, a degree of autonomy, and clear feedback in order to increase their likelihood of staying with the company. This is because such factors help to increase the graduates' sense of usefulness and capability. Whilst additional, ongoing support mechanisms (in the form of people or training) had been planned into the Taylors' programme by head office personnel, findings from the study indicated that they were often not in place in the stores. Some aspects of the work itself had also been unanticipated by some trainees.

> You are put on the shop floor just to replenish and you think I am being paid this much money just to replenish, probably 50 per cent of the training scheme is just you replenishing on the shop floor.

This was seen by some respondents as indicative of the lack of support or understanding of the graduate training programme demonstrated by some store managers (see above). The majority of respondents had experienced periods of being used as 'shelf fillers' and in this sense they had felt under-utilized. Many had anticipated this to some degree in order to learn the practicalities and help out during busy periods, but for some it was felt to be excessive.

> They've spent so much money, they've recruited you, obviously gone to a lot of trouble to actually interview you, assess you, are paying a lot of money to put you through the training scheme. You think at times, why are they just using me as a pair of hands? Why can't they let me use my knowledge and ideas?

The still evident overriding concern with cost savings (old cultural values) within Taylors was given as the rationale for this behaviour by some graduates.

> I object to working until 10.15 p.m. on a Friday night, being told I am working efficiently, not being criticized for the way in which I organized myself, but then being expected to be in at 6.00 a.m. the next day. I can't fight the culture. It isn't the shifts you have to work it is the length of time.

and

> Basically they are just screwing the hours down in the store, they think of X number of reasons to take hours out of the store, and you find more and more that you are doing a member of staff's job. You are not managing to your full potential or capacity. It's all cost cutting.

Importantly, in the survey results, the majority (89 per cent) of respondents said that they had assumed that the job would 'involve managing others, not doing the job myself'. Moreover, 18 per cent said they had not assumed that the job would be 'practical'. Clearly, entering the company as graduates, there may have been some illusions about being given a management job straight away; however, most respondents did appear to see the necessity and benefit of shop floor work experience. Asked what they thought were the most relevant parts of the training scheme, 66 per cent said 'on-the-job experience' and 78 per cent thought 'running a department'. The dissatisfaction seemed to be concerned less with working on the shop floor than doing what many viewed as menial jobs. Another interviewee said:

> It's important to consider whether shop floor work is suitable for graduates at all. Even with the attempts at a change of culture and the greater emphasis placed on 'professional' management in the departments, the basic truth and overriding aim is to 'fill up the shop'. This takes up most of the working day (and far beyond). Is this an attractive proposition for a graduate?

In sum, whilst changes had been made to the graduate training programme in order to present clues about the new demands of a store manager within Taylors, these were apparently being contradicted by the heavy demands of day-to-day trading and prevalent attitudes about what was important for trainee or junior managers to be doing.

The structure of the training programme and how it all fitted together in practice was another planned part of its intended effectiveness. For many trainees, the structure would have been acceptable if they had been able to follow it. It was often the case, however, that the pressures of the business interrupted their training. Some graduates felt that it was part of the (intended) supportive role of the store manager to monitor trainees' hours and create time for them to complete their training. One interviewee said, 'trainee managers are exploited and, unless the store manager is sympathetic, times can be very hard.' For several the long hours of work meant that training often had to be carried out in their own time:

> If somebody had said that you are going to be doing 12 hours a day, you probably won't get any training and you are going to have to do all of your training in your own time after a 12-hour day, I don't think many people would take the job.

As mentioned earlier, one of the main problems seemed to be that store managers were not aware of the part they were supposed to play in the training or had apparently not received enough information about the programme or the changes made to it the year before:

> After we grumbled, the managers were told by district training how quickly they

had to do things and were given the dates of the exams. They were very surprised. From then on they said you write your own schedule and you need to go on a certain department you do it, and for the next three months I could plan my week as I wanted, it was brilliant.

This again suggested a lack of communication between management at head office (who designed the graduate training programme), store and district levels – a fatal flaw in terms of the continuity of the trail of clues. Another frequent complaint was that graduates felt unhappy about the amount of time allocated to the assessment of their training. After working extended hours and fighting for training time in order to complete the workbooks and projects, some graduates found that the finished documents appeared to be ignored:

Having spent two weeks on projects before the panel nobody actually looked at them. Nobody followed them up. I could have done nothing, none of them.

Timing appeared to be a critical factor in the effectiveness of the assessment. A few of the trainees found that the dates of assessments frequently moved around. This gave an impression of a lack of urgency. The survey findings indicated that 27 per cent of respondents had felt dissatisfied with the assessment of their training workbooks and 34 per cent with the assessment of projects which were both intended to form a vital part of the new training programme.

However, one of the worries of some trainees was that insisting on taking time out to complete training books and projects might be viewed negatively by senior management. One said:

There are certain trainees I know who did fight for their time, and who did get more time allocated to them, but I feel that perhaps they jeopardized their position within the team, or they upset too many people.

To summarize, the management training programme at Taylors formed the core of the organizational socialization process for new graduates within the company. Aspects of the training had been changed in order to provide clues for graduates about the type of cultural values that were beginning to be promoted within the organization. The descriptions given by graduates in the study suggested that their experiences varied, indicating that the trail of clues lacked consistency. There appeared to be communication problems between both individuals (graduates and managers) and sites (stores, district and head office personnel) within Taylors at the time of the study.

Conclusions

This chapter has described the organizational socialization process for graduate trainees within a large retailing organization and considered the various factors which appear to have an effect on their understanding of the organization and their role within it. This chapter has adopted a 'receiving end' perspective in that the primary focus has been on graduates' descriptions of their experiences within Taylors, with a particular emphasis on the two-sided nature of the organizational socialization process. The experiences of graduates at Taylors appear to confirm previous findings in the literature that planned organizational socialization events (or clues) are just *some* of the critical incidents (Grundy and Rousseau, 1994) which are mediated by newcomers in their efforts to understand the organization. These findings indicate that equal attention must be given to, firstly, the design of an organizational socialization programme and, secondly, the wider organizational context in which organizational socialization takes place.

As with all case study research, the findings must be bounded within a context which in this instance was an organization where many change initiatives were taking place. Perhaps a result of this state of transition within the organization was that not all aspects of the newly designed graduate training programme were in place at the time of the study; this certainly seemed to be one of the main factors underlying the differing perceptions of graduate trainees across Taylors. Because the planned communication links between different parts of the organization were not in place, the provision of support and feedback from store managers and elsewhere was a significant missing clue for many graduates. Expectations of both the organization and the graduate training programme had been very high and these gaps in the trail of clues often meant that essential messages of recognition, reassurance and achievement were missing in many instances. As the organizational socialization process progresses (that is, newcomers move from the entry to the accommodation stage) an inconsistent trail of clues causes confusion and uncertainty for those seeking direction. Data from the study suggested that, as a group of new, young employees, the graduates had been attracted to, and believed in, the values of the new organizational culture which Taylors was attempting to promote. The difficulty seemed to be that traditional cultural values were still evident within the company. Their continuing presence had direct implications for the graduate training programme (e.g. the lack of time given to trainees by managers, no establishment of a mentoring system, lack of district training events, and so forth).

It can be argued that one of the key roles of the HRM function is to help the newcomer by providing an infrastructure of support (represented in this chapter as a trail of clues) to be used by the individual trainee. It is not possible to control the presentation of all clues given the impact and influence of organizational events (in Taylors, for example, extremely busy trading periods and structural changes). As a group of employees, graduates are likely to be particularly proactive in searching for clues to help them comprehend their world of work. The present and other case studies of organizational socialization suggest that employers must not only focus on the provision of clues to new and potential employees, but also acknowledge newcomers' interpretations of the clues they provide and the effects these can have on later commitment to, and views of, the organization for which they work.

References

Allen, N.J. and Meyer, J.P. (1990) 'Organizational socialization: a longitudinal analysis of newcomers' commitment and role orientation', *Academy of Management Journal*, 33: 847–58.

Arnold, J. (1986) 'Getting started: how graduates adjust to employment', *Personnel Review*, 15 (1): 16–20.

Bauer, T.N. and Green, S.G. (1994) 'Effect of newcomer involvement in work-related activities: a longitudinal study of socialization', *Journal of Applied Psychology*, 79 (2): 211–23.

Buchanan, B. (1974) 'Building organizational commitment: the socialization of managers in work organizations', *Administrative Science Quarterly*, 18: 533–46.

Collin, A. (1986) 'Career development: the significance of the subjective career', *Personnel Review*, 15 (2): 22–29.

Fagenson, E.A. (1989) 'The mentor advantage: perceived career/job experience of protégés vs. non-protégés', *Journal of Organizational Behaviour*, 10 (4): 309–21.

Fisher, C.D. (1985) 'Social support and adjustment to work: a longitudinal study', *Journal of Management*, 11: 39–53.

Fisher, C.D. (1986) 'Organizational socialization: an integrative review', in G.R. Ferris and K. M. Rowland (eds), *Research in Personnel and Human Resources Management*, vol. 4. Greenwich, CT: JAI. pp. 101–45.

Grundy, L.K. and Rousseau, D.M. (1994) 'Critical incidents in communicating culture to newcomers: the meaning is the message', *Human Relations Journal*, 47 (9): 1063–88.

Kram, K.E. (1985) *Mentoring at Work: Developmental Relationships in Organizational Life*. Glenfield, IL: Scott, Foresman.

Louis, M.R. (1980) 'Surprise and sense making: what newcomers experience in entering unfamiliar organizational settings', *Administrative Science Quarterly*, 25 (2): 226–51.

Mabey, C. (1986) *Graduates into Industry*. Aldershot: Gower.

Mabey, C., Clark, T. and Daniels, K. (1996) 'A six year longitudinal study of graduate expectations: the implications for graduate recruitment and selection strategies', *International Journal of Selection and Assessment*, 4 (3): 139–50.

Nicholson, N. (1987) 'The transition cycle: a conceptual framework for the analysis of change and human resource management', in J. Ferris and K.M. Rowland (eds), *Personnel and Human Resources Management*, vol 15. Greenwich, CT: JAI.

Nicholson, N. and Arnold, J. (1989a) 'Graduate entry and adjustment to corporate life', *Personnel Review*, 18 (3): 23–35.

Nicholson, N. and Arnold, J. (1989b) 'Graduate early experience in a multi-national corporation', *Personnel Review*, 18 (4): 3–14.

Ostroff, C. and Kozlowski, S.W.J. (1992) 'Organizational socialization as a learning process: the role of information acquisition', *Personnel Psychology*, 45: 849–74.

Porter, L.W., Lawler, E.E. and Hackman, J.R. (1975) *Behaviour in Organizations*. New York: McGraw-Hill.

Preston, D. (1991) 'Making sense of organizational culture: the role of management development in organizational socialization'. Doctoral thesis, Department of Management Learning, University of Lancaster.

Preston, D. (1993) 'Learning the organization: contradictions and confusions for new managers', *Human Resource Management Journal*, 4 (1).

Scandura, T.A. (1992) 'Mentorship and career mobility: an empirical investigation', *Journal of Vocational Behaviour*, 13: 169–74.

Schein, E.H. (1968) 'Socializing individuals into organizational roles', reprinted in B.M. Staw (ed.) (1983), *Psychological Foundations of Organizational Behaviour*, 2nd edn. Glenfield, IL: Scott, Foresman.

Schein, E.H. (1978) *Career Dynamics: Matching Individual and Organizational Needs*. Reading, MA: Addison-Wesley.

Van Maanen, J. and Schein, E.H. (1979) 'Towards a theory of organizational socialization', in B. M. Staw (ed.) *Research in Organizational Behaviour*, vol. 1. Greenwich, CT: JAI.

Wanous, J.P. (1990) *Organizational Entry: Recruitment, Selection and Socialization of Newcomers*. Reading, MA: Addison-Wesley.

13

Inside or Outside HRM?
Locating Lateral Learning in Two
Voluntary Sector Organizations

Rona S. Beattie and Marilyn McDougall

Discussions concerning the nature of human resource management (HRM) are increasingly stressing the importance of the contribution of training and development to individual and organizational performance (Keep, 1989; Storey, 1992; Storey and Sisson, 1993). As to descriptions of human resource development (HRD), the view is growing that training and development is perhaps the pivotal element of HRM (Garavan et al., 1995; Mabey and Salaman, 1995), although Stewart and McGoldrick (1996) view the relationship more in terms of a nexus.

To date, however, evidence suggests that there has been limited adoption in the UK of HRD as a key HRM value (Storey, 1992; Ashton and Felstead, 1995). This is highlighted by Storey (1992: 111) who argues that the level of training and development activity is the key litmus test of whether HRM has become established in the UK. He proposes that organizations which train are more likely to have other complementary HRM practices to protect this investment. However, his findings show that few UK companies would pass this test. Indeed, there is still little evidence of a transformation of training activity at the company level (Ashton and Felstead, 1995: 248), although Investors in People perhaps presents an opportunity for the personnel and development function to raise its profile (Marchington and Wilkinson, 1996).

Whilst acknowledging that, as with HRM, there is no universally accepted definition of HRD, Stewart and McGoldrick (1996) offer a tentative philosophy where HRD encompasses activities and processes which are intended to have impact on organizational and individual learning. The scope of HRD therefore includes close links with strategy and practice as well as with the functional world of training and development. For these writers HRD is 'fundamentally about change' (1996: 2), being concerned with the whole organization and the whole person.

Recent research into HRD in the UK has tended to concentrate on studies at national and corporate levels (Keep, 1989; Rainbird, 1994; Ashton and Felstead, 1995) and is generally written from a managerial perspective. However, the importance of learning in the workplace is highlighted by the concepts of the learning organization (Pedler et al., 1991), albeit a concept needing considerably more empirical study, and the management of learning (Mabey and Iles, 1994a). Important contributions such as the learning cycle (Kolb et al., 1974) and learning styles (Honey and Mumford, 1986) have been made with regard to how individuals learn. However, since these studies focus on learning purely from a behavioural perspective they do not explore the relationship between individual learning and the organizational context. This is an area which has largely been neglected .

The role of line managers in driving and delivering human resource policies has been extensively highlighted (Garavan et al., 1995; Keep, 1989; Legge, 1995; Storey, 1995). Yet the limited empirical work to date exploring line management's contribution to HRM, and in particular to HRD, has found little evidence of this normative value being achieved in reality. Compared with other European countries there has been very limited devolvement of training and development responsibilities in the UK (Brewster and Hegewisch, 1994). Perhaps a key reason for this is that line managers find the staff development role particularly difficult to adopt (Bevan and Hayday, 1994; IPD, 1995). The role of line managers in learning is an issue which is worthy of further study.

The current climate of organizational and social change makes learning a key component in individual and organizational effectiveness. It has been suggested, however (McCalman and Paton, 1992), that attention to people issues can become obscured, in times of change, by matters like organization restructuring, shifting management roles and the contribution of technology. Such factors can result in negative outcomes in terms of discontinuity and the destruction of familiar social structures and relationships (Huczynski and Buchanan, 1991). In addition, delayering causes conditions in which there is reduced access to opportunities for coaching from line managers and for traditional mentoring (Coulson-Thomas and Coe, 1991; Storey, 1993; McDougall and Briley, 1994). With regard to the gender division of labour, there is limited availability of senior women managers as role models and mentors to their junior colleagues (NEDO, 1991; Scottish Office, 1993). These circumstances highlight the importance of creating conditions in which individuals can acquire the skills, knowledge and attitudes to cope with circumstances of change in their organizations and in society, and to be supported in this process. The question arises as to whether or not these conditions always require to be formally structured.

The previous discussion indicates that there are a number of important issues with regard to learning in organizations which have been overlooked. The first issue is whether training and development activities are fully able to meet the ever changing demands on the personal competency of individuals. A second issue concerns whether learning must always be managed formally by organizations as part of the HRM/HRD strategy, or whether it happens just as effectively in informal and natural ways. Another issue is the extent to which line managers are equipped and willing to accept the devolvement of HRM responsibilities, particularly with regard to employee development. A final issue highlights the nature of the relationship between HRM and HRD and in particular whether HRM is a necessary precondition for HRD.

To date, much of the literature in the field of HRM and HRD is either normative (written mainly by those in consultancy roles) or conceptual (written by academics). While there have been a few attempts to integrate the conceptual with the normative in the generalist HRM literature (e.g. Storey, 1992; Sisson, 1994), there are even fewer in the more specialized field of HRD (e.g. Mabey and Iles, 1994b). This chapter contributes to redressing the imbalance of studies which explore HRM from normative, managerialist and industrial relations perspectives, by adopting an empirical and individual perspective focusing on developmental relationships. The specific focus of this chapter is on one particular type of relationship – peer mentoring.

Through data from two case studies, this chapter now examines the interaction between peer mentoring relationships and the organizational context, particularly exploring the effect of HRM/HRD strategy and practices on these lateral learning relationships. It also explores the role of the line manager in lateral learning, and the extent to which the establishment of a formal strategy for peer mentoring influences such learning relationships.

Peer mentoring

It has been argued that the *lack* of the hierarchical dimension between peers makes it easier to achieve the communication, mutual support, and collaboration essential for effective learning to take place (Kram and Isabella, 1985; Smith, 1990). Indeed colleagues have been identified as being a key source of motivation (Evenden and Anderson, 1992). The importance of lateral relationships is highlighted by the growing interest in organic structures (Claydon, 1994) where horizontal ties between peers are replacing vertical ties as channels of activity and communication (Kanter, 1989). Where this is occurring the importance of peers to the developmental role in career management may be greater (Germain and Heath, 1991; Holbeche, 1995).

Although there have been a limited number of studies into peer relationships (see, for example, Kram and Isabella, 1985; Mumford, 1993; Conway, 1994) it continues to be recognized that this is an under-researched area (Beattie and McDougall, 1994; Mumford, 1993). The issues of organizational and social change mentioned above highlight the need for an approach to learning which helps overcome the constraints created by circumstances such as restructuring, especially delayering, and the lack of women in management. These trends make more urgent the task to understand this phenomenon. Learning between peers is one such approach.

A variety of frameworks of peer learning have been presented. Stokes (1994) identifies a work focus for learning where peers from different organizational functions act as 'internal consultants' to each other, sharing their knowledge and skill. Conway (1994) presents a personal focus where 'peer pals' provide support, encouragement and counselling to each other. Kram and Isabella (1985), perhaps the seminal writers in this field, along with Mumford (1993), develop frameworks which include both these foci. Kram and Isabella identify from their empirical work three types of peer relationships: information peer, where the emphasis is on information sharing; collegial peer, where the emphasis is on career planning, job-related feedback and friendship; and special peer, where the emphasis is on providing confirmation, emotional support, personal feedback and friendship. They highlight the special attribute of peer relationships as mutuality between partners, a distinctive feature that distinguishes this form of learning from other types of development. Mumford also identifies three types of peer relationships: networking and sharing information; discussing problems; and emotional support.

In the discussion which follows we use a framework which has emanated from previous work by the authors into the nature and practice of peer mentoring relationships (see Beattie and McDougall, 1995; McDougall and Beattie, 1995a). This initial study was conducted by interviewing 14 pairs of peer mentors in a range of organizations. We define peer mentoring as 'a process where there is mutual involvement in encouraging and enhancing learning and development between two peers, where peers are people of similar hierarchical status or who perceive themselves as equals' (Beattie and McDougall, 1995).

On the basis of this research we developed a threefold typology of peer mentoring relationships. This is illustrated in Figure 13.1. This typology resulted from our exploration of respondents' reflections on the nature of their learning from these relationships, and the behaviours involved. The research found that peer mentoring provides an important focus for support and learning of individuals, particularly at times of organizational change (McDougall and Beattie, 1995b). Following content analysis of interview data it became evident that there were different types of learning relationships between peers determined by two criteria, which are shown as dimensions in the typology in Figure 13.1. These are the extent to which *work* and/or *personal* issues were important as the vehicles for learning. In the former, the primary focus for learning was job-related issues dealing with work problems such as decanting a hospital ward. With the latter, the main focus for learning related to matters concerning the individual personally, within and without the immediate work context such as balancing career and family. When the data were analysed further, these different learning relationships were found to be typified by different combinations of the following behaviours:

- *communicative behaviours* which included discussion, listening and questioning, collaborating and summing up
- *affective behaviours* which involved helping, supporting, encouraging, reaffirming, understanding, and calming
- *cognitive behaviours* which involved explaining, advising, accessing and sharing information, playing devil's advocate, exchanging, developing and bouncing ideas with the partner

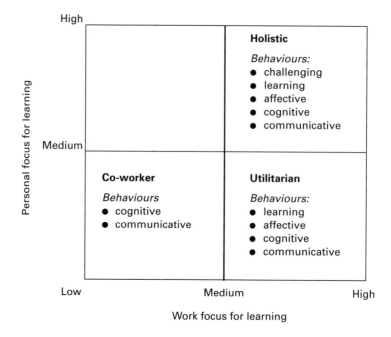

Figure 13.1   *Typology of peer mentoring relationships*

- *learning behaviours* which were facilitating, reflecting, taking on different perspectives from the peer mentor, coaching, modelling on the partner
- *challenging behaviours* which involved criticizing constructively, disagreeing, providing a good discipline for progress.

On the basis of this analysis we developed a classification of peer development relationships to reflect the differences in emphases between work and personal foci for learning and the different behaviours represented within them. We termed these different types of peer relationships co-workers, utilitarian peer mentors and holistic peer mentors.

Co-workers   These had a low work focus for learning and a low personal focus for learning. Here the partners were colleagues where day-to-day issues of work and – to a lesser extent – personal life were discussed, but to no great depth. Key elements were information exchange and that both parties were experiencing similar problems in their jobs. Their experience centred on communicative and cognitive behaviours only and this is probably explained by the primarily work focused nature of the relationship. There was limited learning in this type of relationship, and it is therefore questionable whether this is an example of peer mentoring.

Utilitarian peer mentors These had a medium to high work focus for learning and low to medium personal focus for learning. Behaviours involved were communicative, affective, cognitive and learning. The qualities valued as important attributes were trust, friendship, support, having a sense of humour, and knowing where you are with the partner. Learning was often based on mutual work interests, and the different professional perspectives often brought to the relationship were highly valued. These relationships also fostered a degree of involvement such that limited personal issues were also the subject of discussion and learning.

Holistic peer mentors These were medium to high for both the work and personal aspects of learning. In all cases these were relationships where the development of the whole person – at work and personally – was the domain of conversations and actions regarding learning. Relationships had often existed for several years, and for over half of this group the original issue in common had changed although the relationship had been sustained. While holistic peer mentors also used communicative, affective, cognitive and learning behaviours, this was the only category in which challenging behaviours were present. This included the partner being critical in a constructive manner by 'providing a critique even if it was uncomfortable'. In this type of relationship the attributes valued were trust, support, sense of humour and friendship as in utilitarian peer mentoring, and in addition included being able to express personal or professional vulnerability, and having a partner who listened and was interested in the whole person, who was not judgemental, and was not in competition.

Research methods

The main aim of the present study was to explore the practice of peer mentoring and its relationship, if any, with the overall HRM/HRD context in which it is to be found. Specifically we sought to:

- explore the impact of organizational change and HRM and HRD policy and practice on developmental relationships between colleagues
- explore the incidence and nature of peer mentoring relationships and the needs being met by them
- explore the impact of peer mentoring on the organization with particular emphasis on the benefits, problems and any other issues arising from its introduction
- consider the appropriateness of a formal strategy and structure for peer mentoring in organizations.

In order to achieve these objectives a case study methodology was used since primarily the research was an empirical enquiry investigating a contemporary phenomenon within its real-life context (Yin, 1989). More specifically an explanatory case study approach was adopted which aimed to explain the causal links in real-life interventions too complex for other methods. This approach was deemed appropriate as there was no control over behavioural events which were contemporary rather than historical.

The two case studies presented have a number of important similarities and one important difference. Both are in the same sector with similar structures, objectives and ethos. Both encourage and provide opportunities for learning. The difference is in terms of the formal recognition of lateral relationships. In one organization, called Stepping Stones in Scotland, a Peer Supervision and Support Group (PSSG) for managers has been established as a response to delayering. In the other organization, called Richmond Fellowship Scotland, lateral relationships are recognized only informally. It was felt these cases would provide an interesting vehicle through which to explore the effect of formal organizational mechanisms on peer mentoring.

To collect the data within the two organizations we used both question-naires and semi-structured interviews. A questionnaire was distributed at the outset of the study to the target population – managers and professionals. The purpose of this initial questionnaire was to investigate who, in this group, identified with our definition of peer mentoring and had a peer mentor in their current organization. We achieved a response rate of 65 per cent ($n = 26$) in Richmond Fellowship Scotland and 70 per cent ($n = 22$) in Stepping Stones.

As to the proportion of respondents who said they had a colleague in the organization where they encouraged and enhanced each other's learning, responses in the two case study organizations were fairly close, at 62 per cent ($n = 16$) in Richmond Fellowship Scotland and 70 per cent ($n = 15$) in Stepping Stones in Scotland.

The semi-structured interview was chosen as an appropriate means by which to maintain individual confidentiality and yet explore in depth the perceptions of organizational factors influencing learning, and individuals' experiences of peer mentoring. In Richmond Fellowship Scotland, all of those in peer mentoring relationships were interviewed, involving eight part-nerships, and of these the gender split was two-thirds female/female and one-third male/female. This was a similar distribution to previous research conducted by the authors when most individuals identifying with this concept were women (Beattie and McDougall, 1995). In Stepping Stones in Scotland, the focus for interviews and analysis was the PSSG of centre managers who were all women.

During the interviews we explored key HRM and HRD issues, in particu-lar those relating to organizational structures, the encouragement of learning within the organization; the line manager's role in learning, and experience of access to training and development opportunities; organizational change issues, particularly the extent of change and its impact on individuals; the nature of the peer mentoring relationship (e.g. the criteria for choice of peer mentor); needs met by the relationship; and the extent to which this relation-ship was influenced by formal organizational structures and initiatives.

To improve our understanding of the interaction between the partners, the critical incident technique was used during interviews. Respondents were asked to recount a specific situation where they had learned from their Peer Mentor and to describe the behaviours, feelings and thoughts within the incident. The use of this technique, in conjunction with the semi-structured interviews of both partners, enabled us to develop a more expansive picture of the peer mentoring relationships.

In addition, semi-structured interviews were also conducted with the Training Manager in each organization to explore contextual issues such as HRM and HRD policy and practice relating to structure and staffing; organizational change; and awareness of peer mentoring practice.

We now turn to consider the findings from this research.

Findings

Organizational context

As mentioned earlier, both of the organizations are in the voluntary sector. Richmond Fellowship Scotland is in the field of community mental health, providing supported accommodation for individuals leaving psychiatric hospitals and returning to the community; and providing support also for individuals living independently in their own homes. It is the larger of the two organizations with 180 employees, and the majority of employees are located in 23 projects in different parts of Scotland. Stepping Stones in Scotland is smaller with 60 employees, and works in partnership with young families in disadvantaged communities, providing learning and growing opportunities for young children and adults. This is carried out through a total of six community-based projects in various parts of Glasgow. Both of the organizations are similar in that they have a small head office function with the majority of staff located in the various projects.

Both organizations had undergone transformational change in the past few years, and an important external driving force for change in both cases was legislation such as Care in the Community. Richmond Fellowship Scotland has grown rapidly from 4 to 23 projects, has diversified its client group, and has undergone a major philosophical change. Stepping Stones in Scotland has been greatly affected by uncertainties of funding. This together with new legislation has required the organization to be registered and to be inspected annually, and has meant new methods of working, the need for more professionalism, and greater devolvement of management. In both cases staff expressed concerns that change caused by these various factors could change the ethos of the organization so that aspects originally valued could be lost.

The development of the work of Stepping Stones in Scotland, together with the need to increase effectiveness, had highlighted the need to initiate change internally, and as part of this, delayering had been undertaken at a senior level. The Development Officer (DO) role, previously located in the structure between the Centre Managers and the Director, was removed. This role was replaced in the form of lateral supervision by the establishment of a Peer Supervision and Support Group (PSSG) for the six family centre managers.

Strategies of HRM and HRD

HRM strategy was fairly underdeveloped in both organizations, although both had recently developed policies and procedures in response to current changes. In both cases people management activities were described as personnel rather than HRM and in Stepping Stones in Scotland this was described as being a role in transition from its previous 'underdeveloped' status. The locus of responsibility for personnel issues lay with senior operational managers in both cases, and while this may suggest an HRM approach, the reality was that personnel matters tended to be treated administratively rather than strategically.

As to HRD, both organizations had developed a training strategy designed to support the organization's business plan over the next few years, and both had recently made appointments in the area of training: in Richmond Fellowship Scotland this was a Training Officer to support the Training Manager, and in Stepping Stones in Scotland it was the first appointment of a Training Manager. Both organizations offered a range of topics provided by training staff and external providers. Both have provided initial management training and give access to external courses and conferences, although this is constrained by the availability of funding, particularly in Stepping Stones in Scotland. There has been no history in either organization of formal traditional mentoring.

All the respondents in both organizations indicated that learning was encouraged. The scale of formal learning opportunities was greater in Richmond Fellowship Scotland, and a concern was expressed by one respondent that there had been so much training it could be difficult to consolidate learning. One respondent in this organization described herself as feeling 'very nourished' by the training she had received, whilst another felt that management acknowledged that staff were the organization's key resource and therefore the need for development was recognized. A spin-off of formal training identified by the respondents in Richmond Fellowship Scotland was the opportunity to 'learn through networking in training sessions'. Learning from each other in training was seen as being actively encouraged by the Training Manager in Richmond Fellowship Scotland and indeed several peer mentoring relationships had been established from meeting at training events.

In Stepping Stones in Scotland, all of the respondents indicated that learning was encouraged and various opportunities were mentioned from the formally organized management training provided recently, through learning opportunities emerging from the job, to opportunities to participate in teams undertaking specific tasks such as training needs analysis.

Lateral structures: formal or informal?

In Stepping Stones in Scotland, with the advent of the PSSG a formal structure for lateral relationships had been developed. The nature of peer supervision was outlined by the Director and Training Manager at a training meeting as:

- a formal meeting between two peers to talk about work
- a sounding board or listening device for proposals of work
- an acknowledgement of or praise for work done
- an opportunity for teasing out of ideas/options
- an opportunity for challenging, honesty, constructive criticism.

These were very similar to the processes and benefits of peer mentoring identified in previous research (McDougall and Beattie, 1995b).

While the most senior management of the organization had intended that this would result in various one-to-one mutual supervisory relationships being created, they had left the detail of the mechanics of this to be decided by the group. On the day, this had proved to be problematic and was almost 'a case of drawing names out of a hat'. In the end the group had decided to base the supervision arrangements on the basis of how they were sitting round the table – with each individual supervising the person on their left and in turn being supervised by the person on their right.

It was identified that peer meetings should be held on a bimonthly basis and that a record of discussion should be made in terms of area of work, discussion/options, and agreed action. It was decided that any difficulties relating to supervision would be aired at peer group support meetings and it was acknowledged that there must be respect between peers. It was also agreed that issues raised at these meetings should be treated on a confidential basis.

In this case, while an organizational structure with a focus on peer relationships had been put in place through the PSSG, mixed feelings and some confusion were reported from this initiative. The point was made by one respondent that a previous PSSG had been very successful and a key element was the existence of trust in the group. This respondent felt there was currently a lack of trust and mutual respect. It was recognized by managers that this structure was an attempt to be more cost effective. However, it was difficult to make these relationships work if partners had different views or 'pictures of management'. There was some benefit, however, in discussing issues with colleagues who understood exactly what the job entailed.

While all of those in this group said they learned from colleagues, there was only one pair of peer mentors where partners identified each other. Three of the Centre Managers identified 'their supervisor' in the PSSG structure although this was not reciprocated. One did not identify with individual developmental relationships favouring group learning.

Learning between peers was described by one respondent as 'a natural thing', that as with any relationship, some people hit it off and some did not.

The view expressed was that it would therefore be difficult for any organization to pair people off and it would also be difficult to monitor progress. One respondent highlighted that the supervision relationship with the peer resulting from the current structure could become a peer mentoring relationship. It would, however, require some considerable time.

This process was in its early stages: it had been in existence for only five months. However, various managers indicated a constraint was the lack of authority of their peer to make decisions on which respondents required an answer, and one manager felt that there was a lack of feedback on what she was doing – that 'praise, which is a vital part of learning, is missing.'

In Richmond Fellowship Scotland, the majority of respondents felt that the organization should have a role in supporting peer mentoring, because of the wide range of benefits accruing from such relationships, particularly the dissemination of good practice and the comfort of knowing that other managers are facing the same problems. The type of organizational support suggested included raising awareness of the potential benefits from peer mentoring; researching the current peer mentoring relationships to gain a better understanding of how they work; and providing opportunities, time and space for people to meet. There had been discussion about the possibility of introducing peer group supervision such as that in Stepping Stones in Scotland. However, this had not taken off, perhaps because previous attempts at peer support groups for project managers had degenerated into griping sessions rather than a forum for learning. It was also recognized that the style of training adopted by the organization involved encouraging people to work and learn together: 'the training role is distributed throughout the organization.'

The view was also expressed that peer mentoring would happen regardless of any organization's actions. These individuals felt that the development of peer mentoring relationships were dependent on trust and/or luck: 'it either happens or it doesn't'. It was felt that such relationships could lose their value if they became formal: a 'positive thing about peer mentoring is the fact it's informal, flexible, happens when *you* want. Formality would limit the impact.'

Line manager's role in development

As in many social care organizations, the role of 'supervision' in Richmond Fellowship Scotland is that of supporting, managing and developing staff. Supervision in this sector is not the monitoring and control role of other sectors, but rather 'good supervision is a function of effective leadership. It is the platform for training and staff development, and the stem on which the flower of good practice is nurtured' (Gilbert and Scragg, 1992: 184). The Training Manager expressed some concern that some staff may not view supervision as developmental, particularly those who had recently moved from the more bureaucratic culture of the National Health Service. However, the vast majority of respondents talked very positively about supervision and the developmental potential it offered. It may be that these supervision practices contribute to the positive learning ethos in this case.

Respondents felt that their line manager was encouraging of their learning, and that much of this development occurred through supervision, as well as informally day to day. Line managers were described as looking for opportunities to develop their staff, as well as allowing staff to carry out more innovative work to facilitate their development. Some indicated that their line manager encouraged them to form developmental relationships with colleagues, and indeed some of these line managers had peer mentors themselves. This case provides a positive example of the powerful influence that line managers can play in driving key HRD values and practices. Only three of the staff interviewed indicated that their line manager was not particularly positive about their learning. Of these, two shared the same line manager and had formed a peer mentoring relationship partly in response to the lack of development coming from this manager.

Learning and development between peers

In both case studies, peer mentoring relationships had been established as a result of working together in a project or in close proximity to one another, sharing a task or opinion, or being involved either in attending or in developing training.

All of the pairs of peer mentoring relationships demonstrated learning over a range of work-related issues with personal issues being of less importance, and were at an early stage of establishment with duration ranging from less than a year to three years. This was consistent with previous findings (McDougall and Beattie, 1995a) and they therefore could be classified as utilitarian in the typology given earlier.

Holistic peer mentoring relationships have been found previously to be of longer duration where significant matters of both work and personal nature were discussed. Currently, none of the relationships in this study were of this type and this may be explained by their relatively short duration to date. It could be hypothesized that a number of these relationships will eventually become holistic in nature.

The managers in Stepping Stones in Scotland, apart from the one peer mentoring partnership, were only involved in information exchange and seeking help with current job-related problems. They did not engage in *mutual* learning with a partner, and so could be classified not as utilitarian peer mentors but rather as co-workers.

This study confirmed previous research: that trust, honesty, and being able to have an open relationship were key qualities in a peer mentor. A clear trend was that the relationship was built on a combination of similar and different qualities which were complementary: 'we're a good balance.' Important similarities included sharing a similar philosophy or values, while important differences included offering another perspective, or having different ideas, backgrounds or experience. Such differences were described as providing 'a forum for learning – she asks me about nursing and drugs, I'll ask her about social work, benefits, welfare rights.' Other differences mentioned included taking a long-term or a short-term view, and where one partner was viewed as a reflector whilst the other was a doer. It was also acknowledged and valued that peer mentors did not always agree. This was viewed positively, with neither party taking offence.

Learning in these utilitarian peer mentoring relationships involved a range of behaviours including questioning, discussing issues, suggesting other ways of looking at things and sharing experiences. Sometimes it was 'difficult to separate who's learned what – it's bounced between us as mutual learning.' In this study, learning about management was highlighted as important, particularly regarding the supervision, support and management of staff, perhaps reflecting that these were issues which interviewees could not discuss with their own team, and indeed may also be reluctant to raise with their line manager. Attitudinal learning was also reported which involved becoming more patient and calm, and learning to adapt to the new philosophy of the organization. One interviewee reported that her peer mentor had helped her become more assertive and that she had learned 'to be clear and concise about what I want from the organization and staff as a manager.' Other learning benefits mentioned to a lesser extent included career development, communication skills particularly regarding the use of language, and role modelling.

Needs met by this relationship related to being able to be perfectly honest about work issues and to know 'it's a non-risk situation.' The most significant needs were gaining support and reassurance from the peer mentor; having a sounding board; confidence building; having someone to let off steam with and utilize as a stress release; and mutual problem-solving and enhanced self-awareness. The range and importance of issues discussed varied: 'everything from being brassed off to having a tricky problem to work out.'

Peer mentoring therefore met a wide and diverse range of needs, although one interviewee summed up her continual need for this type of relationship by stating that 'I've always looked for a peer mentor in a job.' Others reported that the attraction of having a peer mentor was the fact that it was an informal relationship, welcoming the fact that they did *not* have responsibility for each other, that this was a relationship that people entered willingly.

The benefits of peer mentoring are as shown in Table 13.1. The top four benefits are similar in both organizations, namely having a sounding board, a different perspective, a supportive partner and a confidante. The first three of these correlate with benefits identified for utilitarian peer mentors in previous research (McDougall and Beattie, 1995a). The benefit of having a confidante was associated with holistic peer mentoring relationships in this previous work and this embraced both personal and work-related matters. However, in this study, the confidante role focused on work-related issues only.

Few problems were mentioned, and this is consistent with previous research (McDougall and Beattie, 1995a). This is perhaps an indicator of the empowering nature of peer mentoring which reduces or minimizes the problems associated with more structured learning interventions. The main issue raised in Richmond Fellowship Scotland was the geographic dispersal of the

Table 13.1 *Benefits of peer mentoring*

Rank	Richmond Fellowship Scotland	Stepping Stones in Scotland
1	Sounding board	{ Sounding board / Supportive partner
2	Different perspective	
3	Supportive partner	Confidante
4	Confidante	Different perspective
5	Confidence building	Mutual learning
6	Motivational	Networking
7	Mutual learning	Stress management
8	Stress management	Confidence building
9	Friendship	Motivational
10	Networking	Friendship

workforce which made it difficult for staff to meet and have the opportunity to develop such relationships. However, the provision of training courses or other centrally organized meetings provided a forum for such relationships to become established. In Stepping Stones in Scotland a potential problem was mentioned in terms of the danger of fragmentation within the PSSG if a close peer mentoring relationship became apparent in the group, though it was felt by peer mentoring partners that they would be sensitive enough to prevent this happening.

Conclusions

While HRM strategy in the two case study organizations was relatively under-developed, HRD had a higher strategic profile since it was perceived as providing a key competitive edge. It was clear that HRD rather than HRM was central to the delivery of corporate strategy, providing endorsement of Mabey and Salaman's view that the skills, knowledge and attitudes engendered by a firm's training and development activities are 'pivotal to its human resource strategy, for on these depend the appropriateness and end efficacy of personal competency, without which no strategy – however elegantly fashioned and meticulously planned – can succeed' (1995: 177). In these cases, then, HRM was not a precondition for effective HRD.

The case study organizations were undergoing transformational change and, while the formal HRD strategy had contributed to a positive learning climate, it did not meet fully the support and developmental needs of individuals. As a consequence of their experience of change, individuals engaged in informal learning with colleagues, and had established peer mentoring relationships. There was evidence that HRD policies had made an indirect impact on these relationships, however, through various interventions such as heightening awareness to learning through formal developmental opportunities; providing opportunities to meet and establish relationships through formal training courses; and creating an organizational ethos which encouraged individuals to learn from one another.

There was an important difference between the cases with regard to strategies towards peer relationships, with one organization having created a formal structure in this regard whilst in the other these relationships evolved naturally. A key finding was that there was more evidence of mutual learning where no formal structure existed. This could be explained in various ways. It may be that the particular design of the formalized approach used, with its emphasis on one-way supervision, mitigated against a two-way learning relationship. A further explanation could relate to the inhibiting effect on learning of the line management function, identified in previous studies (McDougall and Beattie, 1995a), which in this case had been imposed on peer relationships. In the case with no formal structure, it was evident that there was no support for the creation of a formal structure for peer mentoring and, in particular, respondents were opposed to the idea of the organization matching partners. However, respondents felt the organization could provide some support, particularly in terms of an appropriate environment for such relationships to flourish. This would include heightened awareness and understanding of such relationships; provision of time and space for peer mentors to meet; recognition of the value of such relationships; and the continuation of the positive learning ethos present in the organization. It seems that while HRD can play an important role in creating an ethos which encourages peer learning relationships, the appropriate place for peer mentoring relationships is actually *outside* the formal HRM and HRD strategies. This supports the results of a study of 120 MBA managers by Mabey and Iles (1994a). They found that compared with assigned mentors, informal mentors were not only more widespread but also seen as more useful and influential in career terms.

Unlike in other sectors, the particular practice of supervision in the field of social care has emphasized line manager responsibilities for development. However, even in such positive conditions, individuals still sought alternative sources of learning to support them through the changes characteristic of the late 1990s. Whilst managers in other sectors could learn from these management practices, it is clear that the devolvement of HRD to line managers is not the panacea suggested by much of the normative literature.

This study found that there were a number of important external and internal variables which contribute to the development of peer mentoring relationships, and these are shown in Figure 13.2. External influencing factors include organizational change issues, HRD policy and practice, whether there is a formal or an informal approach to lateral relationships, and line management attitudes to learning. Internal factors relate to commonalities between partners such as shared values and philosophy, and complementary differences such as having a different perspective, experience and/or background; mutual trust and respect were critical elements. The most important benefits of peer mentoring relationships identified in this study were those of

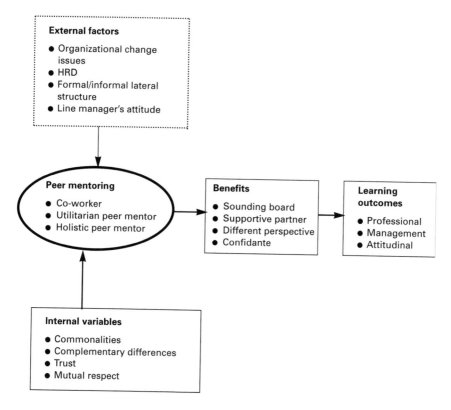

Figure 13.2   *Factors infuencing peer mentoring*

having a sounding board, a different perspective, a supportive partner, and a confidante. Outcomes included different types of learning – professional, managerial and attitudinal – and of particular importance is the finding that informal strategies for learning make a powerful contribution to the support and development of individuals undergoing change.

References

Ashton, D. and Felstead, A. (1995) 'Training and Development', in J Storey (ed.), *Human Resource Management: a Critical Text.* London: Routledge.

Beattie, R.S. and McDougall, M.F. (1994) 'Peer mentoring: a development strategy for the 1990s and beyond'. Paper presented at the Research Conference on Mentoring, Sheffield Business School/European Mentoring Centre.

Beattie, R.S. and McDougall, M.F. (1995) 'Peer mentoring: the issues and outcomes of non-hierarchical developmental relationships'. Paper presented to the British Academy of Management Annual Conference, Sheffield.

Bevan, S. and Hayday, S. (1994) *Towing the Line: Helping Managers to Manage People.* Brighton: University of Sussex, Institute of Manpower Studies.

Brewster, C. and Hegewisch, A. (eds) (1994) *Policy and Practice in European Human Resource Management: the Price Waterhouse Cranfield Survey.* London: Routledge.

Claydon, T. (1994) 'Human resource management and the USA', in I. Beardwell and L. Holden (eds), *Human Resource Management: a Contemporary Perspective.* London: Pitman.

Coulson-Thomas, C.J. and Coe, T. (1991) *The Flat Organisation: Philosophy and Practice.* Corby: BIM.

Conway, C. (1994) 'Mentoring managers in organisations', *Training and Development*, December.

Evenden, R. and Anderson, G.C. (1992) *Management Skills: Making the Most of People.* Wokingham: Addison-Wesley.

Garavan, T., Costine, P. and Heraty, N. (1995) 'The emergence of strategic human resource development', *Journal of European Industrial Training*, 19: 4–10.

Germain, C.A. and Heath, C.E. (1991) 'Career development 2000', *Training and Development,* May: 12–14.

Gilbert, P. and Scragg, T. (1992) *Managing to Care: the Management of Services for People with Learning Difficulties.* Reed/Community Care.

Holbeche, L. (1995) 'Peering into the future of careers', *People Management*, 31 May: 26–8.

Honey, P. and Mumford, A. (1986) *The Manual of Learning Styles.* Maidenhead: Peter Honey.

Huczynski, A. and Buchanan, D. (1991) *Organizational Behaviour.* Cambridge: Prentice-Hall.

IPD (1995) *Personnel and the Line Manager: Developing the New Relationship.* Wimbledon: Institute of Personnel and Development.

Kanter, R. (1989) 'The new managerial work', *Harvard Business Review*, November–December: 80–92.

Keep, E. (1989) 'Corporate training strategies: the vital component?', in J. Storey (ed.), *New Perspectives in Human Resource Management.* London: Routledge.

Kolb, D.A., Rubin, I.M. and McIntyre, J.M. (1974) *Organizational Psychology: an Experiential Approach.* Englewood Cliffs, NJ: Prentice-Hall.

Kram, K. and Isabella, L. (1985) 'Alternatives to mentoring', *Academy of Management Journal*, 28 (1).

Legge, K. (1989) 'Human resource management: a critical analysis', in J. Storey (ed.), *New Perspectives on Human Resource Management.* London: Routledge.

Legge, K. (1995) 'HRM: rhetoric, reality and hidden agendas', in J. Storey (ed.), *Human Resource Management: a Critical Text.* London: Routledge.

McCalman, J. and Paton, R. A. (1992) *Change Management: a Guide to Effective Implementation.* London: Paul Chapman.

McDougall, M. and Beattie, R. (1995a) 'Peer mentoring in practice: organisational and individual factors influencing non-hierarchical developmental relationships'. Paper presented to the Australian and New Zealand Academy of Management Annual Conference, Queensland.

McDougall, M. and Beattie, R. (1995b) 'Peer mentoring to support organizational transformation'. Paper presented to the Scottish Conference on Organizational Transformation, University of Strathclyde/AMED, Glasgow.

McDougall, M. and Briley, S. (1994) *Developing Women Managers: Current Issues and Good Practice.* Edinburgh: HMSO.

Mabey, C. and Iles, P. (1994a) *Managing Learning.* London: OU/Routledge.

Mabey, C. and Iles, P. (1994b) 'Career development practices in the UK: a participant perspective', in C. Mabey and P. Iles (eds), *Managing Learning.* London: OU/Routledge.

Mabey, C. and Salaman, G. (1995) *Strategic Human Resource Management.* Oxford: Blackwell.

Marchington, M. and Wilkinson, A. (1996) *Core Personnel and Development.* London: IPD.

Mumford, A. (1993) *How Managers Can Develop Managers.* Aldershot: Gower.

NEDO (1991) *Women Managers: the Untapped Resource.* London: Kogan Page.

Pedler, M., Burgoyne, J. and Boydell, T. (1991) *The Learning Company.* Maidenhead: McGraw-Hill.

Rainbird, H. (1994) 'The changing role of the training function: a test for the integration of human resource and business strategies', *Human Resource Management Journal*, 5.

Scottish Office (1993) *Employment Trends.* Edinburgh: HMSO.

Sisson, K. (ed.) (1994) *Personnel Management: a Comprehensive Guide to Theory and Practice* (2nd edn). Oxford: Blackwell.

Smith, B. (1990), 'Mutual mentoring on projects', *The Journal of Management Development*, 9.

Stewart, J. and McGoldrick, J. (eds) (1996) *Human Resource Development: Perspectives, Strategies and Practice*. London: Pitman.

Stokes, S.L. (1994) 'Networking with a human face: mentoring as a career strategy', *Information Systems Management,* Summer.

Storey, J. (1992) *Developments in the Management of Human Resources.* Oxford: Blackwell.

Storey, J. (1993), 'How new-style management is taking hold', *Personnel Management,* January.

Storey, J. (1995) 'Human resource management: still marching on, or marching out?', in J. Storey (ed.), *Human Resource Management: a Critical Text.* London: Routledge.

Storey, J. and Sisson, K. (1993) *Managing Human Resources and Industrial Relations.* Buckingham: Open University Press.

Yin, R.K. (1989) *Case Study Research: Design and Methods.* Newbury Park, CA: Sage.

Part V

CONCLUSION

14

Getting the Story Straight

Christopher Mabey, Timothy Clark and Denise Skinner

Put simply, this book sets out to answer three questions. First, a decade or so from its arrival, is HRM delivering on its promises? Second, if it is delivering, are the changes in workplace policies and practices truly strategic in nature? Third, if and where changes are occurring in the name of HRM, who is benefiting? In order to find answers we have chosen to consult exclusively those on the receiving end of HRM. For the reasons we outlined in the Introduction we believe this to be a more credible source than those with a vested interest in sustaining the rhetoric of HRM on the one hand, and those who will always be ideologically suspicious of managerial strategies on the other.

Is HRM delivering on its promises?

On the first question concerning the promise of HRM we have to conclude, on the evidence of this volume, that many of its prized goals (more satisfied customers, more empowered workers, more trusting employment relationships, more unified culture, greater workforce creativity and commitment) remain unproven at best, and unfulfilled at worst. Having said this, the heralded outcomes in these accounts are, almost without exception, unrealistically high. The predicted benefits of the HR interventions described, fuelled by the initiators and often 'bought into' by the participants, are not attained because they expect too much in too short a timescale. This comes as no surprise. As Martin, Beaumont and Staines note in their analysis of attempts to change the culture of a Scottish local authority, 'Managers as consumers and consultants as producers of such programmes are frequently observed to consciously or unconsciously collude in applying packaged solutions to complex problems.' The lure of an HR strategy that promises to simultaneously improve productivity and resolve deep-seated pockets of resistance is difficult for any senior manager to resist, especially when he is attempting to manoeuvre himself and the authority into a favourable political light prior to local government reorganization. But, even for the rank and file staff, the offer of greater discretion, more responsibility and the necessary training to support them in their new roles is equally seductive.

In many of the preceding accounts, the early stages of the HR initiatives were accompanied by such optimism from all quarters of the organization. In some instances this optimism was well founded, as with the shop floor view of QM at a car components manufacturing plant Glover and Fitzgerald Moore) which was that: 'management . . . had not contravened the explicit or implicit promises that they had made to the workforce. They had developed a fragile new relationship between management and shop floor which, at least at the time of the study, was welcomed.' Gunnigle and Morley, in their study of industrial relations at greenfield sites, found that two factors, US ownership and location in advanced industrial sectors, had a significantly positive impact on levels of strategic integration. This suggests that the ability of HRM to deliver on its promises may be in part related to national and industry culture, with some cultures more receptive to the central ideas of HRM than others.

However, these 'successes' are more the exception than the rule. More typical was the finding reported by Connell and Ryan on their network of five organizations in Australia. Here, differences in perception between managers and employees emerged and remained over the period of the study despite the stated intention of the culture change programme which was to integrate management with the shop floor. The research found that management could, by changing its own behaviour, effect change in areas of perceived leadership, communication and participation which in turn positively impacted on job performance and quality. But when it came to people's core values, as demonstrated in aspects such as commitment and workplace relationships, these were more resistant to the programme and did not change. In other cases, the outcomes were even more bruising. In her study of the main drivers underpinning staff moving to portfolio work, Mallon describes the largest category as 'refugees'. These were individuals who had been forced to leave the organization for a variety of reasons (e.g. compulsory redundancy, job disappeared owing to restructuring, etc.). For these people HRM had definitely not delivered on its promises. They were the human debris created by a variety of HR initiatives. This was indicated by their accounts of how they felt which were replete with phrases such as 'betrayal', 'bitterness', 'brutal endings' and 'sacrifice'. Many seemed bewildered that their contribution was no longer valued by their former organization. Hence their move into portfolio work had not been easy.

Are the HR interventions strategic in nature?

This leads us to the second question of whether all the talk about, and changes in the name of, HRM reported in this volume actually amount to a distinctively *strategic* approach to the deployment and development of people. Or, to address Beaumont's pertinent question: 'Does the above imply that a coherent human resource management strategy, which is closely linked to the nature of larger competitive strategy, will emerge via a learning curve?' (1994: 6). Against this stringent yardstick, the evidence is mixed. Certainly, the preceding chapters offer many examples of management *setting out* to use HR policies and practices to achieve strategic outcomes like greater flexibility and improved productivity. For example, Rees was able to point to improved levels of trust together with a greater degree of grass-roots involvement in problem-solving and influence over quality, as a result of the HR strategies adopted (under the guise of quality management) in three of the four organizations he surveyed. Likewise, Glover and Fitzgerald-Moore found that at the plant where a holistic and developmental approach had been incorporated into the QM strategy (comprising job re-design, extensive TQM training, a payment system linked to quality and skill acquisition and the negotiation of TW contracts with the unions), the outcomes were regarded as beneficial by employees, who had previously experienced many years of boring, monotonous work.

The supposed hallmarks of strategic HRM are vertical integration, between business and HR strategies, and horizontal integration, between the sub-elements of the HR measures themselves. While the preceding chapters generally represent organizations attempting to manage their human resources in a more enlightened manner, we have to question – on the evidence presented – how many exhibit these hallmarks. For instance Beattie and McDougall report that the training strategies developed and implemented in the two organizations they studied led to greater learning opportunities for employees and a generally positive learning climate. However, they also note that whilst learning was encouraged formal learning strategies were insufficient to meet fully the developmental needs of individuals.

In the Kelly and Monks chapter, performance-related pay (PRP) was clearly perceived by the architect of the scheme as supporting the strategic thrust of the organization and as an effective way of promoting the desired values and behaviours. Unfortunately this view was not entirely shared by those affected by the scheme. In terms of the HR package on offer, the individual is a consumer in the sense that s/he can choose not to 'buy in', accepting the penalties this incurs. In this case a significant proportion of the group did not share the HR Director's view that the reward was worth striving for or that the measures in place would enable a fair distribution to take place. Preston and Hart also highlight the importance of integrating the various aspects of HR strategy so that they are mutually reinforcing. Whilst the graduate training programmes they examined provided critical information to newcomers about different aspects of the organization and in particular the nature of the management role, these images (or what the authors significantly refer to as 'clues') were not reinforced by the wider organizational context. Taylors, a retailer and the focal organization in their study, had been undergoing a major organizational change which placed greater emphasis on team building. The research shows a number of inconsistencies in the images conveyed to newcomers with the consequence that the participants in the graduate training programme were receiving contradictory signals.

So the collective picture seems to be of organizations being more aware of the distinctive benefits of HRM, more astute at planning multi-faceted HR interventions, but still struggling to realize the potential of HRM that is both truly strategic in business terms and synergistic at a practice level.

Who is benefiting?

So finally, who benefits? Of course, this question begs others. Like, it depends who you ask and what criteria you apply. It was for this reason that the early chapter by Legge was included on evaluating the experience of HRM. Her references to some glaring instances of unwittingly poor and/or cynical HRM, where the only beneficiaries were the instigators, serve to remind us how the high expectations of more enlightened people deployment can soon be crushed – either by the vicissitudes of a harsh market place or by the ineptitudes of a self-seeking management. However, all is not gloom and doom. In our view some of the accounts in this volume 'pass' the *utilitarianism* test, with the majority of participants in a given HR change benefiting in a way which outweighs the costs to the minority.

For instance, Rees notes, in relation to the four cases he studied, that the structure of authority was not radically changed by the HR initiatives ushered in under the banner of QM. While 'detailed control' at the point of production or service delivery passed to employees, management increased their grip on 'general control'. He concludes that the introduction of QM at these sites has led to 'a reorganization of control, whereby an organizationally specific mix of contingent factors leads to a particular balance between control and consent'. In other words, there has been a step forward (rather than a radical overhaul) in the negotiated order that all parties could take some satisfaction from.

The same could be said of the new working practices and approach to training in the company described by Heyes. Here the intention was to extend management control through the formalization of practices which had previously been subject to informal negotiation. Workers felt demoralized and devalued and reacted in a way that allowed them to regain a measure of control over the terms on which their skills were utilized, sometimes to the disadvantage of other shop floor groups. They refused to passively accept a new order which, in their view, undermined the equity of the wage–effort bargain. Thus, albeit in a more unanticipated manner, a new order was established whereby shop floor workers retained their 'choice' about when and how they would work flexibly.

Further examples of the workforce improvising around HR initiatives are cited by Mallon, who suggests that despite the significant drawbacks associated with portfolio work (e.g. lack of financial security, lack of respectability, social isolation) many of the individuals in her study were trying to make the best of their situation, often finding material success and/or enjoyment of their relative freedoms; and by Beattie and McDougall, who found that, in peer mentoring relationships, mutual learning was more likely to occur where no formal structure existed. In other words, where such relationships are 'forced' on employees (i.e. chosen for them) and where there is a boss–subordinate element, effective and supportive peer mentoring relationships may not develop. In these circumstances it is difficult to develop the communication, mutual support and collaboration essential for effective learning to take place.

There are even some stories told here which appear to meet the stringent demands of *stakeholder* theory, whereby not only are the benefits distributed, but this happens in a consultative manner such that there are no outright winners and losers *and* the long-term interests of the organization are furthered. For instance, Iles, Wilson and Hicks-Clarke argue that there may be benefits to both the organization and the individual by successfully creating 'climates for diversity'. Reviewing the emerging though still limited evidence from the US, they conclude that those organizations which make better use of their total talent perform better than those who do not. They go on to contend, with reference to gender diversity in organizations, that where women's under-representation in management positions is maintained, firm performance may suffer unless certain barriers are removed, in particular those preventing the development of gender-free organizational cultures.

In Chapter 2, Legge notes that 'the ethics of stakeholder analysis, while looking persuasive at first sight, contain potential escape clauses that can render them little more than well-meaning rhetoric in practice.' The case reported by Martin, Beaumont and Staines, like many other accounts in this volume, appears to bear this out. Focus groups held with participants from the Housing Department they researched revealed 'inconsistencies between espoused theory' concerning the attempted culture change and 'the theory in use'. These included the counter-productive effect of increased workloads and the lack of consultation over business planning and target setting, poignantly contrasted with references to supervisors planning their own careers rather than concentrating on managing their own teams and an announcement that the Director of Housing post was to be increased in salary by a third!

So what conclusions can be drawn from this exploration of the inside story of HRM? We would suggest that a number of issues and insights have emerged, some of which serve to consolidate previous research, and some of which offer helpful signposts for the future. First, and undeniably, much *is* happening in the name of HRM. The chapters in this book report on a range of HR initiatives, some of which are 'hard' like new employee agreements and pay systems, some of which are 'soft' like attempts to shift attitudes, socialize and cultivate learning, and some of which combine aspects of both under the banner of, for instance, quality management. Further, we would venture to suggest that many of these instances of HRM are more than hard-pressed managers desperately clutching at seemingly potent panaceas. There is evidence of thoughtful and concerted attempts both to link the HR intervention to the current business imperatives of the organization, and to co-ordinate a number of *different* HR policies in order to achieve these strategic objectives. Less plentiful are examples where these attempts at vertical and horizontal integration, the so-called hallmarks of strategic HRM, have been achieved in practice. Too often, specific and otherwise well-diagnosed HR initiatives are seen to founder because on the one hand they fail to mutually reinforce each other, and on the other hand they underestimate the depth of feeling or miscalculate the intentions and interests at shop floor level.

Second, this relatively modest outcome is not surprising considering the high expectations often loaded upon HRM, and the deep-seated structural, political and cultural contradictions in workplaces it is addressing. What this volume successfully highlights is something of the complexity and variety of these different responses. Far from being passive recipients in the HR process, those on the receiving end have been shown to be co-creating, improvising, resisting and recasting particular HR interventions and in this way playing an active part in their implementation and impact. Thus we have individuals and groups adopting informal working practices despite, rather than because of, certain HR policies; reading their own meaning into HR programmes where the institutional 'signals' are ambiguous and/or unpalatable; and using the HR window of opportunity to renegotiate their relationship with management at shop floor levels.

Third, for these reasons we need some fresh measures for assessing the value of HRM. In the Introduction, a case was made for developing criteria which authentically tap the strength of feeling, the sense of justice or injustice, the perceptions of gain and loss as articulated by those in the lower reaches of organizations. Here in the Conclusion, we have made some limited attempt to see how the various accounts in the book stand up to the scrutiny of the ethical frameworks proposed by Legge in Chapter 2. While business ethics is a subject in its own right, the application of moral criteria to the field of HRM is relatively unusual, and we suggest that such an approach has definite promise for progressing our understanding of the plurality of interests inherent in all HR interventions. Without such a lens, we remain at the mercy of either moribund academic debate; or of interesting but idiosyncratic, uncritical 'success stories'; or of the pseudo-scientific rigour of quantitative analyses which too often oversimplify and neglect the richness and meanings at the heart of HRM.

Fourth, this leads us to the need for more receiving-end research to build our understanding of the purposes and meanings that people attach to the HR events, experiences and activities with which they are involved. Given its inside story focus, it is no accident that the majority of chapters in this collection are based on qualitative case study research. Methodologies which rely on inflexible research instruments leave little room for pursuing the unexpected and can take only limited account of context. Qualitative methods pay greater attention to interdependencies, settings and complexities (Patton,

1990) and focus on '*naturally occurring, ordinary events in natural settings,* so that we have a strong handle on what "real life" is like' (Miles and Huberman, 1994: 10, italics in original). Of course, actors within an HR initiative may not be readily able or willing to reveal their true reactions, emotions and evaluations, perhaps because they are unaware of the ways that their own personal agendas and frames of reference are shaping their interpretation of events.

Necessarily, then, research methods need to be longer term and more interactive. This may be achieved by building a relationship of trust and shared experience over a period as a non-participant observer (e.g. Chapter 6); or via multiple case study research which allows the researcher to identify both themes which are common and those which differ across the group and from this to draw insights to assist the reader in making sense of what is happening (e.g. Chapter 3); or by focusing on a single case organization where the value is depth of understanding rather than replicability and generalizability (e.g. Chapter 7). Our view is that the field of strategic HRM was launched in both the US and the UK from a managerial perspective and was based on a largely untested set of theoretical premises. Given the relative immaturity of the field, what is needed is further cumulative research to be conducted on receiving-end HRM using qualitative techniques, in order to build theoretical frameworks that are rooted in reality rather than conjecture.

Finally, and importantly, by focusing on the individual this volume begins to forge a link between the nature of the new work-based identities, which HR initiatives are seeking to produce, and extra-organizational values. With their promotion and pursuit of such icons as 'excellence', 'flexibility', 'quality focus', and 'customer focus', we regard the organizations featured here as not untypical in seeking to align 'the technologies of work and the technologies of subjectivity' (Miller and Rose, 1990: 27) so that the goals and behaviours of individual employees are coterminous with those of organizational advancement. Viewed in this way, we begin to appreciate that HR initiatives, and their predecessors, in part provide a language and technology which reconstruct work-based identities in accordance with the demands of the prevailing socioeconomic and cultural context. In other words, by seeking to integrate the character and identity of the organization and its members they demonstrate an affinity with extra-organizational values. Sometimes this is done explicitly (as in the accounts which reference 'rising customer demands', 'competitive pressure' or the need for a more 'unified culture', as the justification for a new HR initiative), and in other cases it is more tacit. In this sense the popularity and impact of particular HR initiatives are related less to an assessment of their internal impact, and more to their ability to frame their analyses of contemporary management problems and solutions in such a way that they resonate with and capture the *Zeitgeist* or 'spirit of the times'. This is one further benefit of telling the inside story of HRM: by elevating the individual and the way in which his or her work-based identity is being reconstructed, it rightly situates any analysis of different HR initiatives within a wider socioeconomic and cultural context.

References

Beaumont, P.B. (1994) *Human Resource Management*, London: Sage.

Miles, M.B. and Huberman, A.M. (1994) *Qualitative Data Analysis* (2nd edn). Thousand Oaks, CA: Sage.

Miller, P. and Rose, N. (1990) 'Governing economic life', *Economy and Society*, 19: 1–31.

Patton, M.Q. (1990) *Qualitative Evaluation and Research Methods*. Newbury Park, CA: Sage.

Index

Abernathy, W. 35
Abrahamson, E. 76
academic research in HRM
    analysis of findings 18–20
    managerial focus 4–6, 14–15
accommodation stage, socialization 207,
    213–15
Ackers, P. 57
adjustment burden 8, 10
affective behaviours, peer mentoring
    221, 222, 223
affirmative action 188, 190
    see also positive action
Ahlstrand, B.W. 77
Alimo-Metcalfe, B. 196
Alvesson, M. 3, 75, 76
ambiguity, cultural paradigms 91
Anderson, G.C. 220
Anthony, P.D. 9, 75, 89, 131, 141
anticipatory stage, socialization 207,
    210–1
appeals system, performance-related
    pay 116, 120, 126
Armstrong, M. 114, 116
Armstrong, P. 150
Arnold, J. 205
Arthur, M.B. 172, 174
Ashforth, B.E. 169
Ashton, D. 218
Atkinson, J. 171
attitude surveys *see* employee surveys
attitudinal change 77, 78, 132
    business network case study 136–41
    local government case study 83–7
    organizational socialization 206
attitudinal commitment 75
Austin, S. 8

Australia, culture change case study
    129–43

B&Q plc 15
Bailyn, L. 170, 173, 176
Baldamus, W. 108
bandwagon diffusion processes 76–7, 90
banking, quality management case
    study 42
Barley, S.R. 177
Bate, P. 73, 78, 81, 88, 89, 91, 92, 131
Bauer, T.N. 207
Beattie, R. 220, 221, 224, 227, 229, 230,
    232
Beauchamp, T.L. 24
Beaumont, P.B. 4, 152, 163, 239
Becker, G. 99
Beer, M. 77, 82, 115, 116, 119
behavioural change 77, 78, 131–2, 142,
    206
behavioural commitment 75, 99
    see also compliance
Bem, S.L. 195
benchmarking 132
benefits for employees, of quality
    management 44–6, 56–8, 61–3
Berger, P.L. 68, 173
Berlinger, L.R. 174
'best practice' model of HRM 18, 25
'best practice' programmes 132, 134,
    135–43
Bevan, S. 219
'beyond contract' 99, 109
Bird, A. 175
blame culture 66–7
    see also management through blame
Bogenhold, D. 171

Booth, C. 189
boundaryless careers 174, 175
Bowie, N.E. 24
Boxall, P. 192
BPR *see* business process re-engineering
Bramble, T. 133, 142
Brewster, C. 159, 219
Bridges, W. 169, 170, 173, 174, 175
Briley, S. 219
British Gas 27
broad banding 102
Broadfoot and Ashkanasy instrument 136, 143
Brockner, J. 176
Burawoy, M. 101, 110
bureaucratic careers 172–4
Burrell, G. 2
Burrows, R. 171
business ethics, key concepts 21
business planning, local authority case study 80, 87
business policy decisions, impact of industrial relations considerations 158–9, 164
business process re-engineering 1, 3

Caillods, F. 101
capitalism, business ethics 21
Cappelli, P. 97
career achievement, in climates of diversity 198, 199, 200
career forms 172–5
  see also portfolio workers
Casey, C. 74, 76
casualization of work 170–1
cellular manufacturing 40, 61, 62
Chakiris, B.J. 174
challenging behaviours, peer mentoring 222, 223
Champy, J. 2, 3
change
  attitudinal 77, 78, 83–7, 132, 136–41, 206
  behavioural 77, 78, 131–2, 142, 206
  cultural *see* culture change
  organizational 1, 2–3, 7, 8, 9, 219, 225–6, 231
chemical industry, training case study 102–10
Chia, R. 82

Clark, T. 3, 5, 79
Claydon, T. 220
Clegg, S.R. 2
Cockburn, C. 100
Coe, T. 170, 219
cognitive behaviours, peer mentoring 221, 222, 223
Collard, R. 55
collective bargaining, and culture change 133, 142
collectivism 37, 100, 101, 102, 165–6
Collinson, M. 38
commitment 7–8, 19
  attitudinal commitment 75
  behavioural commitment 75, 99
  'beyond contract' 99, 100
  culture change and 75, 84, 131, 141, 142
  diversity climates and 200
  quality management and 35, 37, 70
  role of training 99, 100
commonality, change programmes 89, 131
communication
  culture change case studies 84, 137, 140
  diversity case study 195
  quality management case studies 39, 41, 42, 44, 67
communicative behaviours, peer mentoring 221, 222, 223
company history *see* organization history
competitive advantage
  and diversity 191–3, 201
  and HRM 4
compliance 19
  culture change 75
  quality management 35
  resigned behavioural compliance 19, 57, 64
compulsory competitive tendering 79
contingency models, quality management 36–8
continuous improvement 33, 35, 41, 46
continuous learning 97, 175
continuous ongoing improvement 40
contracts of employment 175, 181, 182, 183
control 240

culture change and 133
flexibility and 105–8, 240
PRP and 115
quality management and 33–4, 38–9,
    48, 49, 50–1, 240
value engineering 9–10, 76
Conway, C. 220
Cooper, C. 90
Coopey, J. 89
Coote, A. 69
Copeland, L. 189, 190
Corbin, J. 59, 68
Corcoran-Nantes, Y. 55
core competences 191
core/periphery staff 171
    ethics 24, 27, 28
corporate culture *see* culture change;
    organizational culture
corporate planning, local authority case
    study 80
corporate strategies 157–8
    see also strategic integration
Coulson-Thomas, C.J. 219
Covey, S.R. 2
Cox, T. 202
Coyle, A. 100
Crowe, D. 115
Cruise O'Brien, R. 35
culture change 8, 9–10, 19, 73–94,
    129–43
    business network case study 132–43
    criticisms of programmes 73–4, 75–8,
        88, 131–2, 133
    effectiveness criteria 81–2, 89
    evaluation of success 81–3, 88, 136–7
    features of programmes 73
    local government case study 78–91
    motivation for 76–7, 78–9, 90, 135
    operating assumptions 77–8, 131–2
    performance-related pay and 114–15,
        123–4, 125, 126
    and quality management 37, 38, 55,
        57, 58
    retail case study 207–8, 211–12, 216
Cunnington, B. 129, 130
Curran, J. 171
customer focus 9
    ethics 16, 26, 28
    quality management strategies 42, 43,
        50

task-based teamwork 35

Davies, L. 64, 70
Davies, M.S. 12
Deal, T. 130, 131, 141
Deane, J.W. 81
Defillippi, R.J. 174, 175
delayering 1, 9, 19
    local authority case study 80
    peer mentoring case studies 219,
        225–6
Delbridge, R. 26, 35, 67
Deming, W. 54, 55
deontological theories 21, 23
    and HRM 23–5, 27–8
'designer' cultures 76
deskilling 35, 97
Despres, C.J.-N. 82
developmental humanism
    approaches to TQM 56, 68, 69, 71
    models of HRM 20
devolved HRM responsibilities 219
differentiation
    perspectives on culture 74, 75, 88, 91
    Rawlsian ethics 27
direct task participation 39
discipline, quality management
    strategies 47, 67
discrimination 188, 191, 201
distributive justice 22, 28, 202
diversity *see* managing diversity
Donaldson, L. 75
downshifting 180
downsizing 8, 19, 25
    see also redundancies
Driver, M.J. 172
Du Gay, P. 73, 75, 99
durability, change programmes 89
duty, moral law 21
Dwyer, J. 114

Eccles, T. 77
Edwards, P.K. 20, 50
electronics industry, quality
    management 36
Elger, T. 35
employability 169, 175
employee involvement 19
    Ford Motor Company 16
    introduction of PRP 115, 119

employee involvement – *cont.*
  and quality management 33, 38,40,
    56, 57, 60, 62, 63, 70
employee participation
  ethics 26
  and job satisfaction 142
  and quality management 33, 35, 38,
    56, 58, 70
employee perceptions
  of graduate training programmes
    207–16
  organizational culture as 131, 132
  of PRP 119–27
  of quality management 43–8, 61–71
employee perspective on HRM 7–10
employee surveys 82–3, 88, 136–7
empowerment 19
  culture change strategies 81, 89, 132–3
  ethics 25
  quality management strategies 33, 34,
    39–40, 42, 43, 49, 56
  training programmes 105
engineering industry
  culture change case study 133–43
  TQM case study 58–61, 64–8
entrepreneurial career forms 171–2, 174
entry stage, socialization 207, 211–12
equal opportunities 8, 188, 190, 191, 201
  see also managing diversity
equity 102, 115–16, 120, 126–7
ethics
  culture change programmes 76
  HRM 23–8, 240–1, 242
  normative theories 21–3
ethnic groups, Ford Motor Company
  16–18
  see also managing diversity
ethnographic studies 1–2
European Union countries, diversity
  issues 188–9
evaluation of culture change
  programmes 81–3, 88
Evenden, R. 220
Evetts, J. 173–4
excellence 1, 73
expectancy theory 114, 126
expectations and 'realities'
  culture change 82, 84–5, 89
  graduate training 208, 210–16
  TQM 57, 58, 63, 64, 67, 68–70

exploitation
  ethics 21, 25
  quality management models 35–6, 48,
    56
expressiveness, change programmes 89
Ezzamel, M. 7

facilitation, culture change 135, 136, 142
Fagenson, E.A. 212
fairness *see* equity
false consciousness 15, 36, 57
Farnham, D. 79, 89, 91
feedback 115–16, 122, 125–6
  to portfolio workers 182, 183
Fell, A. 159
Felstead, A. 218
Festinger, L. 1
Filella, J. 116
financial incentives, greenfield start-ups
  154
financial services industry, quality
  management case study 42
Finegold, D. 97
Fink, A. 82
Fisher, C.D. 207
flat organizations 9, 101–2, 115, 132
flexibility 19, 171
  case studies 40, 41, 63, 103–8
  role of training 97, 98
flexible specialization 35, 130
Fombrun, C.J. 4
food products industry, PRP case study
  116–27
Ford Motor Company 16–18
foreign-owned firms
  formal strategy development 157–8
  greenfield locations 154–6
  impact of industrial relations on
    policy 158, 159
  levels of strategic integration 162, 163
  role of personnel/IR function 159, 160
Fox, A. 55, 71, 73
fragmentation, cultural paradigms 74, 91
frontier of control 105–8
Frost, P. 74, 91, 92
functional flexibility 19, 35, 98
  case studies 40, 41, 103–8

gap analysis process, perceptions of
  TQM 69

Garavan, T. 218, 219
Garrahan, P. 63
Geary, J.F. 37, 39, 49, 102, 114, 116
gender differences
    attitude change 85
    effects of TQM 62–3
gender diversity 191, 192, 193
gendered cultures 193–7
Germain, C.A. 220
German-owned companies,
greenfield locations 155
Germany 101, 189
Gilbert, P. 228
Goodman, P.S. 81
Gowler, D. 173
graduate recruitment 210–1
graduate training programmes 148–9,
    205–16
    accommodation stage 213–15
    anticipatory stage 210–1
    case study 207–16
    entry stage 211–2
    management support 211–12, 213,
        214–15, 216
    mentoring 212
    socialization theory 206–7
Granger, B. 171, 172, 178, 180
Green, F. 99
Green, S.G. 207
Greenberg, J. 115
greenfield companies 18, 147, 150–66
    definition 150–1
    formal strategy development 157–8
    impact of industrial relations on
        policy 158–9
    location decisions 152, 153, 154–7
    role of personnel/IR function 159–61
    variations in strategic integration
        161–6
Grey, C. 77
Grundy, L.K. 216
Guest, D. 7, 18, 20, 24, 70, 99, 133, 142,
    150, 161, 173
Guimaraes, T. 57
Gunnigle, P. 116, 162, 163
Gunz, H. 172

Hakim, C. 171
Hall, D.T. 174, 175, 176, 181
Hammer, M. 2, 3

Hamner, W. 115
Hampson, I. 133, 142
Handy, C. 129, 169, 170, 178, 182, 183
'hard' model HRM 20, 55, 113
    ethics 25, 28
    and TQM 69
'hard' quality management 37–8, 55, 58
    case studies 40, 41, 45
Harris, D. 37
Hartley, J. 89
Hayday, S. 219
Heath, C.E. 220
'Heathrow management theory' 2
Hegewisch, A. 116, 159, 219
Hendry, C. 6, 55
Hendry, J. 76, 77, 90
Herman, B. 130
Herriot, P. 169, 173, 175
Herzberg, F. 114
high-commitment management 14, 18,
    28, 132–3
high-performance work practices 18,
    28
Hill, S. 35, 37, 55, 56, 57, 62, 67
Hissey, I. 135
historical circumstances
    and culture patterns 78, 82
    and perceptions of TQM 61, 65, 68,
        69
Holbeche, L. 220
holistic peer mentors 222, 223, 229
Hope, V. 76, 77, 90
Hopfl, H. 88
Horton, S. 79, 89, 91
hospitality industry, quality
    management case study 42–3
HRM *see* human resource management
Huber, G. 78
Huberman, A.M. 243
Huczynski, A. 77, 90, 219
human capital advantage 192
human process advantage 192
human resource development 218–20
    case study organizations 226, 231
    see also training and development
human resource management
    academic research 4–6, 14–15, 18–20
    distinguished from personnel
        management 4, 189
    ethics 23–8, 240–1, 242

human resource management – *cont.*
  fulfilment of goals 237–8
  'hard' model 20, 25, 28, 55, 69, 113
  and human resource development
    218–20
  individualism and collectivism 100
  internal contradictions 7–8, 16, 19–20,
    25
  managerialist orientation 1–2, 4–6,
    243
  parallel with managing diversity 189
  perspective of the individual 7–10
  'soft' model 16, 20, 23–5, 55, 56,
    69–70, 113
  strategic integration 4–5, 191–2,
    238–40, 242
Hunger, J.D. 161
Huselid, M. 18
Hutton, W. 171
Hyman, J. 98
Hyman, R. 49, 50, 170

identities, work-based 9, 76, 243
Iles, P.A. 129, 142, 189, 192, 198, 201,
  219, 232
In Search of Excellence (Peters and
  Waterman) 2
individual visibility 77
individualism 37, 100, 101, 102, 162,
  163, 165–6
industrial relations
  collectivism and individualism 100,
    101, 102, 162, 163, 165–6
  impact on policy decisions 158–9
  role of specialist function 159–61, 164
  strategic integration in 150–66
  strategies 157–8
  and TQM 55
industrial sectors, levels of strategic
  integration 163, 165
Inkson, K. 170, 172
Institute of Personnel and Development
  6
integrative cultural paradigms 74, 75,
  88, 91
inter-section variation, culture change
  87, 88
internal labour markets 100–2
  case study 103–4, 105
internalization of values 9–10, 76

Investors in People 218
Ireland
  company strategy development
    157–8
  greenfield site case study 150–66
  industrial relations and business
    policy 158–9
  labour costs 154–6
  labour skills 154
  PRP case study 116–27
  role of personnel/IR function 159–61
Isabella, L. 220, 221
Ishikawa, K. 55

Japan 101, 189
Japanese companies
  role of personnel/IR function 159
  strategy development 157–8
Jelinek, M. 193
JIT *see* just-in-time production
job enlargement 19, 35, 36
  case study 103, 104–5
job evaluation 37
job knowledge 100, 101, 102, 105–6
job redesign 59, 61, 62, 63, 70
job satisfaction 46, 84, 140, 142, 200
job security and insecurity 20, 57–8, 61,
  70, 173
Juran, J. 55
just-in-time production 26, 35, 156–7
  as source of stress 63
justice 21, 22–3

kaizen 41
Kamoche, K. 191, 192
Kanter, R.M. 169, 170, 172, 173, 174,
  175, 220
Kantian ethics 21, 22, 24, 25, 26, 28
Katzenbach, J.R. 193
Keenoy, T. 9, 99, 100
Keep, E. 97, 98, 99, 218, 219
Kennedy, A. 130, 131, 141
Kessler, I. 102, 113, 114, 115, 116, 126
Knights, D. 50
Korabik, K. 179
Kossek, E.E. 197, 199
Kotter, J. 78
Kovach, K.A. 114, 123
Kozlowski, S. 212
Kram, K. 220–1

labour costs, Irish greenfield sites 154–6
labour intensification 15, 20
  culture change programmes 133, 142
  ethics 25, 26
  quality management 35, 36, 40, 46,
    63, 67
labour mobility
  managers 170
  and skills strategies 101
Leach, J.L. 174
lean production 1, 133
learning 218–19, 226, 229–30
learning behaviours, peer mentoring
  222, 223
learning organizations 1, 219
Legge, K. 4, 18, 20, 25, 37, 73, 74, 75,
  78, 100, 113, 131, 133, 170, 173, 219
Limerick, D. 129, 130
local government
  culture change case study 78–91
  diversity case study 196–7
location of greenfield sites 152, 153, 154–7
Louis, M.R. 208
Lovering, J. 101
loyalty 44
Luckman, T. 68, 173
Lukes, S. 26

Mabey, C. 73, 93, 114, 116, 130, 135,
  207, 208, 218, 219, 231, 232
McArdle, L. 36, 64
McCalman, J. 219
McCarthy, W. 2
McDougall, M. 219, 220, 221, 224, 227,
  229, 230, 232
McGoldrick, J. 218
macho management styles 194, 197
McKinlay, A. 16
Maddock, S. 197
Maiden, R.P. 54
management by stress 19, 35, 36
management 'gurus' 2–3, 34, 56, 77, 79
management literature 2–3
management styles
  change 141
  gendered cultures 193–7
  and TQM 57, 61–2, 66, 70
management theories, popular appeal of
  3
management through blame 19, 35

  see also blame culture
management through compliance 19, 35
managerial control *see* control
managerial prerogative 5, 15, 19
managerialism 3, 5
managerialist orientation of HRM 1–2,
  4–6, 243
managers
  career patterns 169–75
  commitment to diversity 198, 199
  mobility 170
  'right to manage' 5–6
  role as defined in literature 3
  role in development 219, 228–9, 232
  support for graduate trainees 211–12,
    213, 214–15, 216
  women managers 191, 193–7, 198,
    199–200, 201, 219
managing diversity 148, 187–202
  business benefits 189–93, 201
  emergence of diversity paradigm 188–9
  gendered cultures 193–7
  indicators and outcomes of climates
    of diversity 197–200
  parallel with HRM 189
Manwaring, T. 100
Marchington, M. 19, 54, 56, 59, 70, 218
Marginson, P. 14, 20
Marglin, S. 100
Marsden, D. 114, 118, 126
Marshall, J. 193
Martin, J. 73, 74, 91, 92
Marxist critiques, organizational ethics
  21, 26
maternity rights 194
Meager, N. 171
Meek, V.L. 74
mentoring, graduate training 212
  see also peer mentoring
Metcalf, D. 20
Meyerson, D. 73, 74, 91, 92
'middle range' theories 33, 36
Miles, M.B. 243
Miller, P. 4, 243
Millward, N. 14
Mirvis, P.H. 174, 175, 176, 181
mission statements
  as indicators of strategy development
    157–8
  local authority case study 79, 80, 84

Mitev, N. 77
modernist critiques, organizational
    culture 74–8
monitoring of employees 35, 36, 40, 47,
    48
moral law 21, 23
morality *see* ethics
Morgan, G. 75, 92
motivation
    performance-related pay and 114,
        122–3, 126
    role of training 99
motor industry
    Ford Motors 16–18
    quality management case studies
        40–1, 58–64
Mueller, F. 192
Mullins, L. 57
multi-skilling 19, 35, 63, 109–10
Mumford, A. 219, 220, 221
Murlis, H. 114
mutuality in HRM 23–4, 27–8

National Health Service
    changes in culture 197
    diversity case studies 195–6, 198–200
networks *see* strategic alliances
Newton, T. 8
Nicholson, N. 172, 209
Nolan, P. 20, 102

objectives, performance measures
    121–2, 126
O'Connell, Davidson, J. 77, 99
Ogbonna, E. 8, 19, 38, 57, 64, 70, 82,
    132
Oliver, N. 38
on-the-job training 101, 102, 105
Opportunity 2000 196
optimistic models, quality management
    34–5
organization history
    and culture patterns 78, 82
    and perceptions of TQM 61, 65, 68,
        69
organizational change 1, 2–3, 7, 8, 9
    peer mentoring case studies 219,
        225–6, 231
    see also culture change
organizational culture

definition and concepts 75–6, 91,
    130–2, 141
distinguished from corporate culture
    131, 141
and diversity 190, 201–2
gendered aspects 193–7
survey instruments 136, 143
see also culture change
organizational ethics, key concepts 21
organizational justice 199, 202
organizational socialization 148, 205–16
    case study 207–16
    methodological issues 207
    nature and theory of 206–7
    stage models 207, 209
Ostroff, C. 212
ownership of firms
    and greenfield locations 154–6
    and impact of industrial relations on
        policy 158–9
    and levels of strategic integration 162,
        163, 165
    and role of personnel/IR function
        159, 160
    and strategy development 157–8

Pahl, R. 173, 183
Palmer, C. 170
Palmer, G. 2
'panopticon' concept 36
Parker, W.S. 131
Parkin, D. 197
Paton, R.A. 219
pay *see* pay differentials; performance-
    related pay; reward strategies
pay differentials, case study 103–4,
    105–6, 107
Payne, R.L. 131, 141
Peccei, R. 56, 66
peer mentoring 149, 220–33
    benefits 230, 231, 233
    case studies 223–33
    definition 221
    degree of formality 227–8, 232
    factors influencing 232, 233
    problems 230–1
    typology 221–3
peer pressure 35, 48, 64, 68
Pemberton, C. 169, 173, 175
penetration, change programmes 89

performance
  appraisal 37, 60
  measurement 116, 121, 125–6
  outcomes from training 98–102,
    109–10
performance-related pay 37, 102, 113–27
  case study 116–27
  extent of take-up 116
  literature 113–14
  as motivator 114, 122–3, 126
  reasons for introduction 114–15,
    118–19, 125
  success factors 115–16, 126–7
personnel function, role in greenfield
  companies 159–61, 164
personnel management, distinguished
  from HRM 4, 189
personnel strategies 157–8
Peters, T. 2–3, 130
Pettigrew, A. 6, 8, 55, 78, 90
Pfeffer, N. 69
Philpott, L. 116
Piore, M. 35, 97, 130, 133
Pollert, A. 35, 171
Porter, B.L. 131
portfolio working 147–8, 169–84, 241
  benefits to individuals 180
  drawbacks for individuals 180–1
  drivers to 178–80
  problems of definition 170
  research study 176–84
  transactional and relational
    relationships 175, 181–3
  trends in managerial careers 170–2
positive action 8, 188
  see also affirmative action
positivism 4–5
post-Fordism 9, 34–5
postmodern critiques, organizational
  culture 92
Preston, D. 206
problem-solving teamwork 45, 61, 62, 67
  see also quality circles
procedural justice 202
Procter, S. 115, 126
product market position, and strategic
  integration 156–7, 158–9, 160
professional career forms 174
promotion, women managers 196
PRP *see* performance-related pay

psychological contracts 175, 179, 184
public sector organizations *see* local
  government; National Health
  Service
Purcell, J. 5, 18, 24, 25, 100, 102, 109,
  115, 150, 156

quality circles 1, 37, 40, 41, 42, 43
quality management 33–51
  assessment of success 50
  case studies 39–48
  contingency models 36–8, 56
  employee perceptions 43–8
  exploitation models 35–6, 56, 57
  optimistic models 34–5, 56
  'paradox' and contradictions in 48–51
  quality–quantity dilemma 36
  reorganization of control models
    38–9, 56
  research literature 34–9
  see also total quality management

Rainbird, H. 180, 218
Rawlsian ethics 22–3, 27, 28
reason, nature of 21
redundancies
  as drivers to portfolio work 179
  TQM programmes 58, 61, 66, 67
  see also downsizing
reengineering *see* business process
  re-engineering
Reengineering the Corporation (Hammer
  and Champy) 2
Rees, C. 33, 50, 56
relational employment contracts 175,
  181–2
reorganization of control 38–9, 48, 49,
  50, 240
requisite variety theory 192, 201
'resigned behavioural compliance' 19,
  57, 64
resource-based theory 191–2, 201
response rates, employee surveys 82, 83
retail industry
  B&Q 15
  socialization case study 207–16
reward strategies 113
  individualization 101, 102
  and quality management 37
  see also performance-related pay

Index

Richardson, R. 114, 118, 126
Richmond Fellowship Scotland 224–31
'right to manage' 5–6
Roberts, K. 55
Robertson, P. 198, 201
Roche, W.K. 152, 157, 163
Rodrigues, S.B. 74, 76
Rogovsky, N. 97
Rose, N. 243
Rosener, J.B. 190, 193
Rosenkopf, L. 76
Rosin, H.M. 179
Rousseau, D.M. 175, 216
Roy, D. 1

Sabel, C. 35, 97, 130, 133
Saks, A.M. 169
Salaman, G. 3, 73, 79, 99, 114, 116, 130, 135, 218, 231
Savage, M. 171
Scandura, T.A. 212
Schein, E. 130, 131, 172, 194, 206, 207
school leavers 24
Schuler, R. 37
Scragg, T. 228
Seddon, J. 37
self-employment 171–2, 178–9
self-regulation 132, 142
Semple, J. 55
seniority 101
Seven Habits of Highly Effective People (Covey) 2
Sewell, G. 36, 56, 64
Shapiro, G. 8
shareholders 22, 24, 26, 27
Sheppard, L. 116
Shivanath, G. 159
short-term objectives 121
Sisson, K. 20, 36, 99, 100, 116, 134, 218
size of company, and strategic integration 159, 161
skills
  deskilling 35, 97
  location of greenfield sites 154
  multi-skilling 19, 35, 63, 109–10
  social and political processes 99–102, 109
Smircich, L. 131
Smith, B. 220
Smith, I. 113

socialization *see* organizational socialization
'soft' model HRM 16, 20, 55, 113
  and ethics 23–5, 28
  and TQM 56, 61, 63, 69–70
'soft' quality management 37, 40, 42, 45, 55, 58
Soskice, D. 97, 101
Staber, U. 171
Stacey, R. 81, 91, 92
stakeholder theory
  and diversity 192, 201
  ethics 22, 23, 26–7, 28, 241
Stanworth, C. 171
Starkey, K. 16
statistical process control 35, 40, 58
Stepping Stones in Scotland 224–31
Stewart, J. 218
Stewart, P. 63
Stewart, V. 194
Stokes, S.L. 220
Storey, J. 7, 14, 15, 16, 36, 55, 99, 100, 113, 116, 133, 150, 218, 219
strategic alliances
  culture change case study 133–42
  definition and nature of 129–30
strategic integration
  and HRM 4–5, 191–2, 238–40, 242
  and industrial relations 150–66
strategy development, level of 157–8, 164
Strauss, A. 59, 68
Streeck, W. 97, 98
Street Corner Society (Whyte) 1
stress, and quality management 47–8, 63–4
stress management workshops 8
structural change, driving behavioural change 77, 89
surveillance of employees 35, 36, 40, 47, 68

task-based teamworking 35, 44–5
task enlargement *see* job enlargement
task participation 39
team briefing 60, 81
teamwork 19
  and compliance 35, 47–8
  culture change programmes 81, 208, 211–12

employee attitudes to 44–5, 62, 84
pay strategies 37, 116, 123
technological complexity, and strategic
    integration in industrial relations
    161, 163
technology, as cause of stress 48
theory Y 90
theory Z 1
Thompson, P. 77, 99
Tolliday, S. 35
total quality control 35
total quality management 1, 8, 54–71
    analysis of individual perceptions
        68–71
    benefits for employees 56–8, 61–3, 66
    case studies 58–68
    'hard' TQM 37, 55, 58
    history and principles 54–6
    negative perceptions of 66–8
    perceived pressure on employees 63–4
    'soft' TQM 37, 55, 58, 70
Townley, B. 152
TQM *see* total quality management
trade unions
    and high-commitment management
        133, 134, 142
    and PRP 115, 118, 125
    and TQM 57, 64
training and development 97–110
    case study 102–8
    culture change 81, 84, 86, 135–6, 142
    diversity initiatives 190, 192
    performance outcomes 98–102,
        109–10
    portfolio workers 182
    see also graduate training
        programmes; human resource
        development
transaction costs 101
transactional contracts 175, 181–3
tripod of subjugation 19
tripod of success 19
trust 21, 44, 89
    peer mentoring 223, 227, 228, 229,
        232
    quality strategies 44, 57, 58, 64, 65,
        66, 67, 70
Turnbull, P. 26, 35, 63
Turner, T. 152, 157, 163
Tyson, S. 159

unitarism
    culture change 74, 75, 88, 131, 141
    TQM models 55, 57, 64, 71
United States
    development of HRM 189
    diversity initiatives 190
    diversity paradigm 188–9
US-owned companies
    greenfield locations 154, 155, 156
    impact of industrial relations on
        policy 158, 159
    levels of strategic integration 162, 163,
        165
    role of personnel/IR function 159, 160
    strategy development 157
utilitarian peer mentors 222, 223, 229
utilitarianism 21–2, 23
    and HRM 20, 25–6, 28, 240

valence, expectancy theory 114, 126
values
    culture change 19, 38, 78, 90–1,
        131–2, 141, 142
    Ford Motors 16–18
    internalization 9–10, 76
    local authority case study 79, 80
Van de Ven, A. 78
Van Maanen, J. 74, 217
Vecchio, R. 130
'veil of ignorance' 22, 27
Vielba, C.A. 19
Vince, R. 189
voluntary sector organizations, peer
        mentoring 224–31
Vroom, V. 114, 126

Walsh, J. 102
Walton, R.E. 23, 24, 99
Wanous, J.P. 206
Warr, P.B. 69
Waterman, R. 2, 130, 175
Watson, T.J. 84, 88
Weick, K.E. 174
Weirsema, M.F. 191
West, M.A. 172
Wheelen, T.L. 161
When Prophecy Fails (Festinger) 1
Whipp, R. 8
Whitaker, A. 154, 163

White, B. 90
Whitston, C. 20
Whittington, R. 91
Whyte, W.F. 1
Wickens, P. 15
Wierner, Y. 131, 141
Wilkins, A.L. 38
Wilkinson, A. 36, 37, 38, 49, 54, 55, 56,
    57, 62, 66, 67, 70, 218
Wilkinson, B. 8, 19, 36, 38, 56, 57, 64,
    70
Williamson, O.E. 101, 102, 110
Willmott, H. 8, 9, 54, 56, 62, 67, 73, 74,
    75, 76, 90, 99, 131
WIRS *see* Workplace Industrial
    Relations Survey
Witcher, B. 36, 57, 66, 70
women employees
    attitude change 85
    perceptions of TQM 62–3
women managers 191, 193–7, 198,
    199–200, 201, 219

Wood, S. 9, 14, 18, 56, 66, 100, 132, 133
work-based identities 9, 76, 243
work intensification *see* labour
    intensification
work pressure 47–8, 50, 86–7
    see also labour intensification; stress
working relationships, and TQM 57, 62,
    65, 66, 69
workplace culture, distinguished from
    corporate culture 131, 141
Workplace Industrial Relations Survey
    14
Wright, M. 64, 70

Xerox Corporation 190

Yin, R.K. 223
Yuen, E.C. 161, 163

Zeitlin, J. 35
zero defects 41
Zonia, S.C. 197, 199